WFA Scale

Showing the allowance in lbs which a 3yo v

	5 furlongs	6 furlongs
March and April 1st–15th	13	15
April 16th–30th	12	14
May 1st–15th	11	13
May 16th–31st	10	12
June 1st–15th	9	11
June 16th–30th	8	10
July 1st–15th	7	9
July 16th–31st	6	8
August 1st–15th	5	7
August 16th–31st	4	6
September 1st–15th	3	5
September 16th–30th	2	4
October 1st–15th	1	3
October 16th–31st	0	2
November	0	1

Thus, the weight-for-age allowance that a 3yo would receive from an older horse over 5 furlongs on June 10th would be 9 lbs whereas over the same distance on September 17th the allowance would be 2 lbs.

Similarly, a 3yo competing against an older horse over 6 furlongs on, say, April 18th would receive 14 lbs but on July 2nd only 9 lbs.

Note that from October 16th onwards the weight-for-age allowance over 5 furlongs is nil.

Sprint Handicapping Explained

Jim Adams

Foreword by Lord Oaksey

J. A. Allen
London

British Library Cataloguing in Publication Data

Adams, Jim
Sprint Handicapping Explained
1. Gambling – Great Britain
2. Horse-racing – Great Britain
I. Title

798.4'3 SF333.G7

ISBN 0–85131–407–4

Published in Great Britain in 1985 by
J. A. Allen & Company Limited,
1, Lower Grosvenor Place, Buckingham Palace Road,
London, SW1W 0EL.

Book production Bill Ireson

Filmset by Fakenham Photosetting Limited, Fakenham, Norfolk
Printed and bound by St. Edmundsbury Press, Bury St. Edmunds, Suffolk

Contents

Foreword

As a lifelong losing punter and notoriously unsuccessful "tipster" I can only say that if I had read this book twenty-five years ago my bookmaker would be poorer and my bank manager a lot happier.

Mind you, Jim Adams does not for a moment pretend to be giving anyone a license to print money. What he does, quite rightly, claim is to fill a gap in the literature of racing – by explaining how handicaps are made, how they and the form they are based on should be interpreted and how, by combining these skills, anyone prepared to devote a little time and application can hugely increase the pleasure and interest they get from racing.

They may also, quite possibly, make some money – or at any rate lose less. But even if you never have another bet this would still be a fascinating book, worth many times its price.

Jim Adams' years of experience enable him to explain in clear and entertaining English facets of the game about which a vast majority of the so-called "racing world" live their whole lives in blissful and expensive ignorance. I certainly have.'

Anyone sensible and industrious enough to follow Jim's advice will acquire genuine opinions of their own, not 100 per cent right of course (who ever was in racing?) but at least, as the author says "real information, the sort that springs from first hand knowledge – not what the milkman has heard from his brother who knows a friend of the blacksmith!"

When Paul Mellon's father told him scornfully that "any damned fool knows one horse runs faster than another" Mr. Mellon sensibly refused to be put off. To anyone who agrees with him and wants to make informed guesses about which horse runs faster in any given race, I wholeheartedly recommend this book as an invaluable aid.

JOHN OAKSEY

Introduction

For many years now the author has sought in vain for a book which could be called a practicable and, in particular, an in-depth approach to the study of form and an explanation of the art of handicapping.

It seemed to the author that, if such a book was ever going to be on the market, then he would have to write it himself. The book you are now holding is the result.

Within these pages is an analysis of every 5 and 6 furlong handicap, with the exception of selling races, that was run under Jockey Club rules during 1982. Using these 277 races the author has compiled a race-by-race explanation of the methods to be used to establish accurate form assessments for every horse placed in the first six in such races.

A serious study of this book will bring the "inexact science" of handicapping within the understanding of all who are prepared to devote a little of their spare time to a task which, however, is one of the most fascinating and satisfying in the world of horse-racing.

Good luck!

JIM ADAMS

Acknowledgements

The author and publisher would like to thank the editor and proprietors of *Raceform-Up-To-Date* for permission to use their race numbers in this book.

SECTION ONE

METHOD

Chapter 1

The methods used in the handicapping of the thoroughbred racehorse can truly be called the "art of the impossible" and the difficulties involved make the entire enterprise extremely daunting.

To take say, a dozen racehorses, all of widely differing racing ability, set them to carry different weights ranging from 10 st to 7 st 7 lbs over 5 furlongs and expect them to finish more or less together calls for optimism of a high order.

Yet a body of experts is employed by the Jockey Club to do just that – not only over 5 furlongs but at all distances up to 2½ miles. And it is generally acknowledged that these Jockey Club official handicappers, as they are called, are among the finest judges of "form" in the world and certainly the system seems to work.

Let us see how!

If one were to saddle up two racehorses of known equal racing merit, put an 8 st jockey on each and run them over their correct racing distance, the chances are that they would pass the winning post together. But replace one jockey with another weighing 7 st, run the race again and this time it would be "no race" such would be the effect of the difference in weight carried by each animal. Theorists will argue that "horses cannot go faster than they can", but it is undeniable that extra weight will slow a racehorse down and that, basically, is what handicapping is all about.

The vast majority of racehorses start their careers in races confined to 2yo's (two-year-olds) and where they are all set to carry the same weight, apart from a "sex" allowance which lays down that fillies and geldings shall receive 3 lbs from colts. Other systems of penalties for winning races come into play so that during the season the 2yo's sort themselves out into a very rough order of merit. When the racing merit of these animals is fairly well exposed, the Jockey Club handicapper is in the position to allot them all weights according to racing ability and so the "Nursery" season begins. "Nurseries" are handicaps confined to 2yo's only and in passing it can be pointed out that they are extremely tricky events for the punter and on balance probably best left alone as a betting medium.

However, at the end of the flat racing season, the handicapper responsible allots a weight to all 2yo's which have done enough to be given an assessment and publishes a list which forms the Free Handicap for 3yo's which is run over 7 furlongs at Newmarket the following season.

So it can be seen how horses start their racing lives on more or less equal terms, sort themselves out into very approximate order during the season and are then finally assessed by the official handicapper.

The "Free Handicap" ratings will, of course, include the best of the 2yo's – horses who will be aimed at the next year's classic races and whose owners and trainers have no intention of running them in the Free Handicap. It is not, however, unknown for a horse to win or be placed in the Free Handicap and go on to do well in the 2000 Guineas or the Derby but they are the exception rather than the rule. Nevertheless this particular race is always good form and can usually be relied upon as a guide to the future.

But we go on too far! And why are we talking about handicaps at all? Many racing experts will tell you not to bet in handicaps under any circumstances and to involve oneself only in what are known as "weight-for-age" races in which no attempt has been made to bring the horses together, apart, of course, from the laid down scale of penalties which a horse picks up by winning a race of a certain value or certain class.

Now readers may well be of a similar frame of mind and have already decided that handicaps are not for them and the author would not wish to influence them unduly but the fact that you are reading these lines at least demonstrates a passing interest in one of the most interesting and fascinating aspects of horse-racing. Let me respectfully suggest that you give the matter further thought!

Weight-for-age races can, in point of fact, be extremely difficult and nowhere near as easy to solve as opponents of handicap betting would have one believe. Certainly, form in such races can be very misleading, whilst, from a betting point of view, if one horse – a near classic type – towers above his or her rivals then it will be well nigh unbackable as far as the average punter is concerned.

Form in these races is often unexposed – horses with high reputations for running fast past trees at home, or purchased for an unseemly amount of American dollars – all these and similar types unproven on a racecourse run in these races and all too often prove the flops of the century. Readers will undoubtedly remember quite a few of these alleged equine wonders that subsequently proved themselves unable to go fast enough to catch a cold! Excuses galore are made for these unfortunate animals who have previously been hailed as the wonder horse of the year, the only wonder being that the bemused punter still believes it all and loses hard earned cash on animals which have yet to prove that they can win a race.

This brings us to a racing truism which, unfortunately, is often ignored: *a horse should only be backed to do what it has done before*. By this is meant that one should never back a horse to win a race until one has concrete racecourse evidence that it has the ability to do so. This also means that one should turn a deaf ear to tales about unraced 2yo's that "can catch pigeons" at home. Possibly they can but bookmakers pay out on horses that pass the post first in front of other racehorses.

It is true that one can thereby "miss the price" and those "in-the-know" folk who helped themselves in 1982 to 6–1 about a 2yo called Horage to win the Hillhouse Stakes at Ayr in the first outing of his career will probably never forget it in view of that brilliant animal's record; but the Horages of this world are few and far between and the chances of the average punter knowing about such a delightful animal before its first outing are very small. Far better to wait until the horse has actually shown what it can do on a racecourse. Note too that even Horage could have been backed at 6–1 again to win the Garter Stakes at Ascot later in the April of that same year and by that time he had already won two races! True, he was taking on Brondesbury who had also won two races and looked a very useful animal but he was no value at 11–8 on, a clear case of punters being influenced by matters other than what happened on the track.

Who does the reader think would have been favourite if Horage had been trained by Henry Cecil?

So, mark the lesson well and *never* back a horse until it has shown merit of some sort on a racecourse.

Chapter 2

In the previous chapter we have discussed some of the dangers involved in non-handicap races where horses of unknown merit run against horses of similar status. The "form book" is often quite useless in such races.

Handicaps, on the other hand, are full of horses with sufficiently exposed form to be assessed by the official handicappers and simple reasoning will show that, unless these horses ran fairly true to form, the entire system of handicapping would become a farce. The essence of handicapping is that the horses concerned must run to their official "rating" often enough for the handicapper to be confident that he has each animal's measure.

Perhaps an explanation of how weights are allotted is not out of place at this juncture. For flat racing purposes four handicappers are appointed by the Jockey Club and each of these officials is responsible for a particular distance group. At the start of the season, a combined list of those horses qualified for handicaps is published in the *Racing Calendar* showing the official rating for each horse expressed in pounds weight but rounded down to the nearest 5 lbs. This means that a horse which is officially assessed as 49 is listed as 45 and a horse assessed as 33 will be shown as 30 and so on. This is a little misleading from the layman's point of view since it means that horses with a 4 lbs difference in their rating, and therefore in ability, will each be listed on the same mark if they happen to come within the same 5 lbs group. Fortunately there is a way to "decode" a handicap so as to reveal the exact official "rating" for each horse and we will go into that at a later stage.

However, to resume. The individual lists of each official's ratings are fed into a computer to be stored and used to indicate the weight to be carried by each horse in future handicaps. It must be explained that, although each future handicap's weights are allotted from the computer's "memory", the exact ratings have been programmed according to the considered opinion of the individual experts.

During the season they will also make adjustments to any horse showing evidence of improvement or deterioration and these supplementary ratings are fed into the computer so that these horses can be weighted in line with the latest opinion of its merit. One can see therefore that the entries for each race are weighted in accordance with these published amendments and it is fairly easy to see if any particular horse has been upgraded or downgraded by the official concerned.

One must, however, bear in mind that a horse uprated to the next 5 lbs group above may in fact have been raised by only 1 lb. If, for example, a horse rated at 49 (listed at 45) is regraded at 50, it will then be included in the 50's group. Only a separate analysis of the races for which it is entered will show the extent of any re-assessment for any particular animal. As a matter of fact, things would be somewhat easier for the amateur handicapper if the *Racing Calendar* were to show the exact rating against the top weight in every handicap. It would then be easy to calculate the precise rating for each horse by simple deduction with, of course, due allowance for weight-for-age.

Readers will doubtless be aware that handicaps are advertised as being open to horses rated at say, 0–45, which means that only those animals rated from 49 (official rating 45) to 0 can be entered.

And, since all horses rated at 14 or less are shown with a grading figure of 10, one can see that a quick glance at the official list published in the *Racing Calendar* is not enough to give an exact indication of the esteem, or otherwise, in which each particular horse is held by the handicapping official concerned. Do not make the mistake of assuming that a horse carrying top weight of 10 st in a race open to horses rated 0–45 is necessarily a "45". As we have seen it can easily be a "49" and there is also the possibility that no "45's" have been entered in which case the top weight may be a "40". This however, is unlikely. But it would certainly make life easier if the *Racing Calendar* were to implement the suggestion to give the exact rating by the side of the top weight – but making things easier is not perhaps the function of the Jockey Club.

Chapter 3

Readers will by now be wondering when this book is going to get down to the business of backing winners but let me sound a word of caution. Compiling one's own handicap, in other words pitting your wits against the official handicappers and matching your opinion of a horse's merit against theirs, is an exercise which should be done mainly for the sheer interest and certainly not with the intention of making a quick fortune. Horse-racing is a fascinating sport and thousands of people get enormous pleasure from it without, if the truth be known, knowing too much about its technical side.

The idea of this book is to put you in the position of knowing exactly why a horse is carrying your money without being dependent on other people's opinion. For the truth is that your opinion is just as valid as anyone else's and better than most if it is backed by the sort of know-how which this book hopes to give anyone with sufficient enthusiasm to put a bit of work into the game and devote just a few hours of study per week as a change from watching the television.

With these thoughts in mind let us begin.

Before selecting any horse to win any race one really needs to know only two things! A simplistic statement indeed, but readers will soon become aware that the answers to even these two questions require a considerable degree of analysis and understanding.

Let us first ask the two questions:

1. *How good is the horse?*
2. *Is it good enough to win today's race?*

Asking questions is usually a lot easier than giving the answers and such is indeed the case here. Let us now deal with the first question.

How good is the horse?

Remembering that we are concerning ourselves only with handicaps, we are fortunate in that we are greatly assisted in getting an accurate answer to this particular question by the official handicapper. His job is to weight each horse in accordance with the animal's performance on a racecourse. He is an expert and is therefore unlikely to be too far out with his estimate. However, he is only human and can place the wrong, or perhaps we should say "different", interpretation on the same set of facts that would lead another person to a somewhat different conclusion. Let us also remember the case of that brilliant filly Soba, one of the best sprinters of 1982, whose astonishing improvement of upwards of 4 st outstripped the continual re-assessment by the handicapper. Heartwarming though her performance was in winning the 1982 Stewards Cup in a canter, this smashing filly must have been the bane of official handicapper Major Dangar's life! Imagine the difficulty in re-assessing an animal who kept on carrying penalty after penalty and giving weight to older horses in race after race! A horse to remember!

But, such rarities apart, handicappers are extremely experienced and shrewd men and one can assume that the weight allotted in a race is usually a very close estimate of that horse's merit. But, you will say, the same horse will be set to carry say, 8.7 in a race at Pontefract and yet only 7.10 in a Sandown event. How do we then arrive at the animal's actual merit as estimated by the handicapper? Happily for our sanity it is really a very straightforward procedure which will be explained later but even that is not enough to answer our original question *how good is the horse?*

For it is an undeniable fact that practically every handicap result proves the handicapper "wrong". If he was right all the time the runners would all dead-heat, bookmakers would take themselves off to the Bahamas and we punters would have to find something else to bet on. So, be thankful for the sake of our sport that the handicapper's estimate of a horse's ability is not strictly accurate. To be fair to the officials concerned it must be remembered that their difficulties arise because weights have to be allotted a considerable time before the races are due to be run and many things can happen during that time. Horses start to improve or deteriorate with the consequence that races are run with horses carrying weights based on form shown at least 12 days before. The only weapon the official has in this, to him, somewhat unfair state of affairs is the system of penalties which lays down that winners of races after the publication of the weights shall carry a stated extra amount of weight. There is a strong possibility however, that the present time-lag will be reduced by bringing the closing date nearer to the actual date of the race. This will enable the official handicappers to use more recent form when framing the weights.

The penalty clause only applies to winners of races (and in the case of apprentice handicaps not even then) and any horse showing improved form without actually winning does not earn any penalty. And these are the horses we must learn to look out for!

So the answer to our question is not necessarily that given by the handicapper's estimate and we may well be able to make a better guess because we are lucky enough to have more information than did the handicapper when he compiled the weights. Methods which will be shown in complete detail later on will therefore be the means of giving a reasonably accurate answer to our question.

Which brings us logically to the next question.

Is it good enough to win today's race?

This, quite obviously, is the key question. One does not have to be a racing expert to see that to know with absolute certainty the true racing merit of a horse does not make it a betting proposition if it is running against horses better than itself on unfavourable terms. But only by knowing the actual racing merit of each horse and comparing our rating with those allotted in the race can we truly be in the position of saying that such and such a horse has a good chance at the weights.

All this preamble may sound rather complicated and perhaps a long way from what you may have thought the study of "form" was all about but do not despair! All will be made clear in the next two chapters. In order to do so it is my intention to show the reader the exact working methods that were used for the 1982 flat-racing season. Readers will see that the only races dealt with are 5 and 6 furlong sprint handicaps. The main reason is that, apart from the time which would be involved in trying to deal with all handicaps over many different distances, it is my opinion that it is better to specialise in a relatively clear cut division of the total racehorse population. Horses which run in handicaps over these two distances seldom tackle anything else and one is consequently always studying the same animals time after time and getting an intimate knowledge of each particular animal, their likes and dislikes and so on. One cannot know too much about the idiosyncracies of each horse and specialisation is the best way to gain this knowledge. In addition, form in these races is usually very reliable. Sprint handicaps are invariably run at a cracking pace from start to finish, being contested by animals that know only one way to race – get up and *go*!

Chapter 4

We have touched upon problems involved in arriving at the actual racing merit of each horse from a study of the handicaps as published in the *Racing Calendar*. At this point it is perhaps pertinent to say that this official organ of the Jockey Club, whilst not particularly cheap at £1.10 per week, is the best publication from which to work as it contains information in advance of that obtainable elsewhere. But for anyone with a real interest in such an absorbing hobby then the cost of a packet of cigarettes per week is cheap at the price. The *Racing Calendar* can be obtained from Messrs. Weatherby's, Sanders Road, Wellingborough, Northants, NN8 4BX.

It is, of course, perfectly feasible to work out another system of working by using say, the *Raceform Handicap Book* but only the *Racing Calendar* publishes the official Rating List, working from which enables us to have a direct link between our ratings and those of the official handicappers.

With the *Racing Calendar* in our hands we first mark off all the 5 and 6 furlong handicaps and it is suggested that a circle is drawn round the race number at the top of each list of entries. If this is done in red ink it is easier to pin-point the races due for analysis.

Our next task is to calculate the exact *official* rating for each horse engaged in these selected races but at this stage it is necessary to establish the rating for only one horse. The rest can then be worked out by simple arithmetic. If, for example, we determine that an animal set to carry 8.5 has an official rating of 34, then another horse set to carry 7.11 or 8 lbs less, will have a rating of 26 (34–8).

To arrive at the *official* rating for what we will call our "link" horse we consult the Rating List which is supplied with the *Racing Calendar* before the start of the flat racing season and at intervals thereafter.

Using the Rating List we can pencil in the official grading by the side of about ten or twelve horses near the top of the handicap. This will give us a number of horses graded at say, 55, then a group at 50, followed by a few at 45 and so on. It will be easier to understand if we show the actual workings from the Batthany Handicap, run at Doncaster in March 1982.

3.05 Doncaster. Batthany Handicap 5 furlongs. March 25th 1982

				(Pencil in)
Captain Henry	R. W. Armstrong	3	8 12	55
Diamond Cutter	R. J. R. Williams	3	8 11	50
Blue Emmanuelle	N. A. Callaghan	3	8 10	50
Windmills	....	3	8 5	45
Worlingworth	M. J. Ryan	3	8 3	45
Pleasant Dream	H. Thomson Jones	3	8 1	40
Hello Sunshine	L. J. Holt	3	8 1	40
Thunderbridge	S. G. Norton	3	8 0	40
Feather Sound	R. W. Armstrong	3	7 13	40
Preparation	R. V. Smyth	3	7 12	40
Roman Quest	T. Fairhurst	3	7 11	40
Godstruth	H. Thomson Jones	3	7 11	40
The Cairnwell	H. Thomson Jones	3	7 7	35

Now we do not know the exact rating for any of the above animals but a little thought and trial and error will soon give us the answer.

The trick is to discover the "break" point, that is to say, where the 40's become 45's and so on. In the Batthany Handicap you will notice that Pleasant Dream, set to carry 8.1 is rated at 40. Since we know that it can have an actual rating of anything between 40 to 44 we begin by assuming that it is perhaps a "40". But this cannot be so because in that case, Captain Henry, weighted 11 lbs above, would be a "51" and we know that the Captain is at least 55. To give Captain Henry a minimum figure of 55 Pleasant Dream must be 44. (It cannot be 43 because then Captain Henry would have a figure of 54 (43+11) and so that must be wrong.) A few minutes experimentation will show that Pleasant Dream must be a "44".

Although all this sounds very complicated, in practice it takes only a few minutes to find the true rating of one horse and, as we have seen, simple addition or subtraction will give us the rest. So our first race will now look like this.

			Groupings	*"Actual rating"*
Captain Henry	3	8 12	55	55
Diamond Cutter	3	8 11	50	54
Blue Emmanuelle	3	8 10	50	53
Windmills	3	8 5	45	48
Worlingworth	3	8 3	45	46
Pleasant Dream	3	8 1	40	44
Hello Sunshine	3	8 1	40	44
Thunderbridge	3	8 0	40	43

				Groupings	"Actual rating"
Feather Sound	3	7	13	40	42
Preparation	3	7	12	40	41
Roman Quest	3	7	11	40	40
Godstruth	3	7	11	40	40
The Cairnwell	3	7	7	35	36

All fairly straightforward really.

In passing it can be pointed out that, very occasionally, there is a short cut towards establishing actual ratings.

This occurs when two horses who are separated by only one pound in the handicap weights are nevertheless in two different 5 lbs groups. It can be seen from the details for the Batthany Handicap that Captain Henry (set to carry 8.12) is in the 55 group, whilst Diamond Cutter (8.11) is in the 50 group. A few moments thought will show that, in such a case, the lower weighted horse must be officially rated only one pound behind the other and Diamond Cutter *must* be a 54.

It is, therefore, often worth a quick check on the official ratings of horses weighted at only a pound difference to see if their respective ratings are in different 5 lbs groups. It can be a time-saver.

We have now made very good progress since we now have a firm and accurate rating for all the Batthany Handicap entries. It remains to "tie" this race in with the other selected races during the week.

This is done quite simply by finding a horse entered in the Batthany who is also entered in another race. It so happens that in 1982 we were lucky in that Preparation, with 7.12 in the Batthany, was entered in the next race on the list, the Bronte Handicap due to be run at Doncaster on the same day. In this race, however, Preparation is set to carry 8.8 (or 10 lbs more) but this does not matter. As far as we are concerned Preparation is a "41" and we pencil this figure in alongside its name. Used as a "link" horse in this way, Preparation's actual rating will therefore give us the exact rating for all the horses in the Bronte Handicap.

The 10 lbs difference in weight does, however, show that the Batthany Handicap is a 10 lbs "better" race than the Bronte and this information may be of use to us at another time.

The question arises as to what do we do if we cannot find a "link" horse to bring two races together? Well, it can happen at the start of the season when flat-racing gets off to its usual slow start, but in such a case it would only be necessary to carry out the preliminary analysis as before – write in the official gradings and calculate the exact ratings and the task is done. Let me reassure readers, however, that once the season is under way, there is seldom any problem since so many horses are entered in two, three or even more races in one particular week. A diligent search will always produce "link" horses to connect all the races in which we are interested. One such animal in 1982 was Feather Sound, who seemed to be entered in everything bar the Boat Race and must have cost his owner a small fortune in entry fees! But he was a friend to us and acted as a "link" horse on many occasions.

Our initial preparation is now complete. Races are clearly identified and exact ratings have been calculated for every horse in every race coming within our orbit. As far as the first week of the 1982 season was concerned, it was established that in the Batthany Handicap Preparation at 7.12 was a "41" and the fact that he was set to carry 8.8 in the Bronte Handicap makes no difference to our conception. As far as we are concerned Preparation is still a "41" and will remain so until the handicapper sees fit to amend the rating up or down.

The second week of the season was easy. As no horse could have run before the second *Racing Calendar* was published it followed that the ratings could not have altered. All that was necessary was to use one horse entered in the first week (our old friend Feather Sound) who was also entered in one of the races in the second week. We know that Feather Sound was rated at 42 (see Batthany Handicap figures) and it was necessary only to pencil that figure by its name in every race in which it was entered. This procedure gave us the basis to link up all the 5 and 6 furlong races during the period.

But at this juncture we must explain the effect of the official WFA (weight-for-age) Scale upon our workings. This scale, drawn up many years ago by Admiral Rous, has stood the test of time with only a few minor changes. The object of the scale is to act as a guide to handicappers and others. It lays down the amount of weight that an older horse shall be required to concede to a younger horse, depending upon the distance over which the race is run and the time of year. It is essential to ones understanding of the WFA Scale to appreciate that, in a match between a 3yo and a 4yo of approximately equal racing merit, the 4yo will be required to concede such amount of weight as is laid down in the scale.

If the reader will refer to the WFA Scale (printed on the first page of this book) it will be seen that, in March, a 4yo will be expected to concede 13 lbs to a 3yo over 5 furlongs, whereas it would be required to concede only 3 lbs over that distance in the first half of September. The general theory is that the younger horse will need a smaller allowance from its elders as it gets older and stronger.

Much confusion arises concerning the application of the WFA Scale and it is vital to understand that the scale takes into account only physical progression and not actual racing ability.

If a 3yo and an older horse of equal racing merit meet in an all-aged handicap the older horse will be required to concede the appropriate weight-for-age difference simply because of superior physical strength. Published handicaps based on the official ratings automatically make this adjustment and here a reference to the Aldington Handicap below will perhaps assist the reader towards an understanding.

In this race the 4yo Bracadale is officially rated some 2 lbs in *racing ability* above the 3yo Feather Sound but, because of the age difference between the two horses, Bracadale has to concede 15 lbs, made up of 2 lbs racing superiority and 13 lbs weight-for-age. If these two horses maintained the same relative difference in *racing ability* throughout the season Bracadale would be asked to concede only 5 lbs in early September simply because his capacity to concede weight lessens as the 3yo progresses physically. It must be clearly understood that the difference in weights brought about by the WFA Scale has nothing to do with actual racing merit. To take an extreme case, a poor 4yo selling plater would still be asked to concede the appropriate weight-for-age difference to a 3yo Derby winner if the two horses met in a weight-for-age race. If, by some remote chance, the two were to meet in a handicap then they would be weighted according to ability after the weight-for-age difference had been calculated.

Thus, if the handicapper considered that the Derby winner was say, 5 st in front of the selling plater and the WFA difference should be a stone, then the younger horse would be required to concede 4 st, i.e., 5 st in racing ability, less 14 lbs for the weight-for-age difference.

As the WFA difference is compensated for in published handicaps it is necessary to understand that any amendment to the animal's rating is solely in accordance with its individual improvement or deterioration and that no special adjustment is made for weight-for-age. (Note, however, that the equation which we put at the top of all-aged races is amended throughout the year in accordance with the WFA Scale in order to preserve the differential between the age groups.)

The WFA Scale and its application can be very puzzling to the layman and readers are urged to make the effort to grasp the essentials to avoid error. Let us repeat, for it cannot be stressed too often, that, *if the official handicapper considers a 3yo and a 4yo to be of equal racing merit, the 4yo will be set to concede weight to the younger animal.*

To make the matter clear let us go back to our efforts to "link" the ratings for the first week of the season with those of the second week. The only two sprint handicaps during the first week, the Batthany and Bronte Handicaps, were confined to 3yo's only and our "link" horses can only therefore be a 3yo. We obviously need an all-aged handicap in the second week to establish our link. Such a race is the Aldington Handicap to be run at Folkestone on March 29th, a race for 3yo's and upwards and among the 3yo's entered we find our old friend Feather Sound who has been allotted 8.13. The top part of this handicap is shown below.

Folkestone Aldington Handicap	*5 furlongs*			*March 29th 1982*
				Rating
Bracadale	4	10	0	44
New Embassy	5	9	8	38
Vorvados	5	9	7	37
Windmills	3	9	5	48
Pettistree	4	9	4	34
Swinging Rhythm	4	9	2	32
Piencourt	4	9	2	32
Charles Street	5	8	13	29
Feather Sound	3	8	13	42 (from the Batthany)
Fast Lad	3	8	12	41
Northern Eclipse	5	8	12	28
Covergirls Choice	5	8	9	25
Humble Blue	4	8	7	23
El Presidente	4	8	6	22
Mercy Cure	6	8	4	20

Now, we know from the Batthany Handicap that Feather Sound's actual official rating is 42. To calculate the rest of the 3yo's is simple arithmetic, but to work out the corresponding ratings for the older horses we proceed as follows.

Reference to the WFA Scale shows us that, at this time of the year and over 5 furlongs, an older horse must concede 13 lbs to a 3yo. If you look at the entries you will note that the 5yo Charles Street is set to carry the same weight as the 3yo Feather Sound. Now, since a 5yo is expected to be 13 lbs better than a 3yo at this time it follows that if the handicapper allots them both the same weight then the 5yo is actually 13 lbs inferior in racing ability to the 3yo.

The reader is urged to consider this last statement. It is vital to a complete understanding of the WFA Scale.

If, therefore, the 5yo Charles Street is 13 lbs inferior to the 3yo Feather Sound, its rating must be the rating of Feather Sound *less* 13, that is to say, 29 (42−13).

Having established the rating for any older horse the rest of his colleagues can easily be worked out. (This has been done for you in the second column of figures alongside the entries for the Aldington Handicap.) Study the calculations well and all will become crystal clear.

Inter-connecting races in this way, using either a 3yo or an older horse is really a quite straightforward procedure. There is no mystery. No degree in mathematics is required. Reasonable care and the correct application of the WFA Scale is all that is needed.

The procedures for ensuing weeks is precisely the same. One establishes the "official" ratings for one race and, by using "link" horses, inter-connect each race. It should be mentioned here that whilst the official rating list is published in full only every few weeks, any amendments are printed on the back page or the inside back page of the *Racing Calendar* every week. It is important that all such amendments should be taken into consideration when entering up ratings by the side of the entries.

It is also a good idea to select one or two horses who are entered in two successive weeks and check that their ratings are the same. For this purpose care is needed to ensure that one chooses horses that have not run or whose ratings have not been changed. This is really only a precaution and if the "decoding" of the official ratings has been done carefully all should be well. The reader must appreciate however that the tie-up from one week to another must be accurate. It would never do to use as a "link" horse an animal who was a 40 one week and a 46 the next!

This chapter has been a hard, galloping one but careful study will show that we have indeed gone a long way towards getting an answer to the question – *how good is the horse?*

For now we know exactly how good the official handicapper thinks it is. Only the race itself will show us how right, or how far wrong, is his opinion.

Using the *Raceform Handicap Book*

Working from the *Racing Calendar* ties ones own figures in with the official ratings but for all practical purposes it is not strictly necessary to do so and for those readers who for reasons of choice or economy wish to work from the *Handicap Book* we offer the following guidance.

The first thing to remember is that if a horse is officially rated at 44 and another at 34 then the only important factor is the 10 lbs difference between the two. It would make no difference if the ratings were 144 and 134 respectively for the relative difference is exactly the same. In other words the actual figures used are not important.

To further illustrate this point let us return to the Batthany Handicap referred to earlier. Now, in the *Handicap Book* this will be listed along with other Doncaster races for the following week. At the top of the Batthany will be shown the race is for horses rated from 0–60. We will also note that the top weight, Path to Glory, is set to carry 9.7. This does not necessarily mean that Path to Glory is actually rated at 60. As readers will know by now its official rating could be anything from 60 to 64 but as far as we are concerned it would do no great harm to assume that it is indeed 60 and rate all the rest accordingly. This may or may not be exactly right but it will not be more than 4 lbs out at the worst and that will make no difference to us if it is intended to work from the *Handicap Book* all the season.

Let us, therefore, make the assumption that we have put Path to Glory in at 60. Now, since Preparation, our link horse is weighted 23 lbs below the top weight we must therefore call Preparation 37 (60−23) and use that rating when tying in with other races. Feather Sound, weighted a pound above Preparation in the Batthany would become a 38 and would use that figure in moving on to the Aldington Handicap and rate all the others in line with that.

As long as the relative difference between the horses is maintained this method of working need cause no difficulties. One could also argue that, not only is the *Handicap Book* cheaper than the *Racing Calendar* but it is also a bit more readable!

One does need to be careful, however, in going from one week to the next. The selection of link horses takes a little thought. One must obviously avoid using a horse as a link if it is likely to be re-rated by the official handicapper and for this reason it is often best to use a horse that has not run for some time. Its rating is not likely to change and one is usually safe in using such an animal. Also, horses that have run third or fourth in their recent outings are quite often left as they are and whilst this is not absolutely certain they can be used for checking against a link horse.

Once one has picked a particular horse as a link then by far the wisest policy is to make a few random checks with other likely horses.

Say, for example, that one has used Feather Sound at 38 in a race the following week then have a quick look through the other entries and try to find a few horses that were entered the previous week in sprint handicaps coming under our notice. If their figures are the same as before, by using Feather Sound's rating then you can be reasonably sure that you are on safe ground.

Chapter 5

So now, at long last, we come to the first day of the Doncaster meeting held on March 25th 1982 – the day when the first two of our races are being run, namely the Batthany and the Bronte handicaps.

The first thing we notice, however, is that, in the Batthany, the horses are all carrying different weights from those published in the *Racing Calendar*!

Do not panic! All that has happened is that defections among the top weights have caused the weights to be raised 8 lbs. In our original analysis we calculated that the weight carried by Preparation (7.12) equalled a rating of 41 so we must now amend that equation in view of the rise in weights. It is essential to understand that the actual rating of 41 does not change. All that alters is the poundage equivalent, thus, instead of 7.12 equals 41, it should now be amended to 8.6 equals 41. In other words, Feather Sound, favourite for the Batthany, is still a "42" despite the fact that it is now carrying 8.7 instead of the original 7.13. This procedure can easily be understood once one understands the principle involved.

It is far too early in the season for us to have any financial interest in the race so we watch, listen in the betting shop or perhaps just wait for the next morning's paper. The result is what we really want and this must be tabulated in our records book. (The author uses the kind of book which can be purchased from any stationers – foolscap size with ruled horizontal lines, no vertical columns and a stiff cover.)

From the *Racing Calendar* we should have marked up the first page so that it looks like that shown below. Note that, by the time the first day of Doncaster had dawned, we would have the races for the second week of the season. We will also have worked out our poundage equivalents for each race.

Race 32 *3.05 Doncaster* *5 furlongs* *March 25th* (8.6=41)

Race 35 *4.35 Doncaster* *6 furlongs* *March 25th* (8.9=42)

Race 41 *4.35 Doncaster* *5 furlongs* *March 26th* (9.0=45)

Race 56 *3.15 Folkestone* *5 furlongs* *March 29th* (9.0=23)

The result of the 3.05 at Doncaster (The Batthany Handicap) is now to hand and so we enter it under the appropriate heading. It is not usually possible to obtain placings beyond the first six but that is quite enough for us. Placings beyond that mean very little from our point of view. The first stage is to enter the bare result together with our ratings thus.

	Age & Weight	*Rating*	*Distances*	*New Rating*	*S.P.*
Worlingworth	3 8 11	46	–	?	7–1
Feather Sound	3 8 7	42	2	?	6–4
Blakesware Saint	3 7 9	30	1½	?	12–1
Dragunn	3 7 11	32	½	?	11–2
Roman Quest	3 8 5	40	1½	?	13–2
My Fancy	3 7 9	30	Short-head	?	16–1

Apprentice allowances are not taken into account. Expert opinion holds that the apprentice allowance is designed to compensate for the relative inexperience of the young rider and the author would hesitate to disagree with this. It is obvious that a 7lbs "claimer" cannot compare in ability with a first-class senior jockey but nevertheless one should not underestimate the value of the weight concession to a top-class apprentice. An exceptional lad is well worth the 5lbs that he claims and a well handicapped horse ridden by a good boy might well be in the nature of a good thing. However, on balance it seems best to ignore any apprentice allowance and list only the weight allotted by the handicapper.

Overweight, however, is an entirely different affair and *must* be taken into consideration. A horse allotted 7.9 and actually carrying 7.11 must be shown at that weight *and the rating must be amended accordingly*. After all, if an animal set to carry 7.9 and rated at 30, is in reality carrying 7.11 then it is running to a rating of 32 and must be assessed on that figure.

As a real point of interest the overweight situation is quite a puzzling one. Readers will know that the minimum weight to be carried in any handicap is 7.7 and a horse assessed in a long handicap at 7.1 would of necessity have to carry 6lbs more than its original impost. The amount of overweight can, in some cases, be quite considerable and it is not unknown for a horse to carry up to a stone more than its original assessment. Since the horses concerned must be assessed on the actual weight carried one can get a situation where such a horse runs a good race despite the overweight, with the consequence that it appears to have improved by that amount. In the author's experience, however, an apparently improved performance by any horse carrying much more than that allotted by the handicapper should be taken with a very large pinch of salt!

Illogical though it may seem do not accept such a performance at its face value. Of course, we have to be consistent in our analysis and take the overweight into account but heed the warning! Do not rely implicitly on the revised rating. It does no great harm to leave a final decision until the horse runs again when perhaps the situation may be clearer.

It is, of course, quite possible that the handicapper has badly underestimated the horse or that it has improved; but always have a very healthy doubt in such circumstances.

The author can certainly point to instances where a horse has run well carrying considerably more than originally set and yet failed to run up to its new figure on any later occasion. Parabems and Pat Pong, respectively second and third in Race 35, both ran well carrying 6 lbs extra but failed to run up to their revised rating. On the other hand, Miss Poinciana carried 8 lbs overweight in Race 41 and subsequently confirmed its improvement by easy wins at Edinburgh (Race 100) and at Newcastle (Race 174). But the lesson is clear. Wait until the apparent improvement is confirmed before taking ones figures as being beyond doubt.

Readers will see that we are also taking note of the S.P. (starting price) of the first six to finish. Too much importance must not, however, be attached to the S.P. The horse doesn't know what price it is and, hopefully, will run out its race just the same! There are occasions, however, when the price of a horse will give a good indication as to whether or not the horse is fancied by its connections and an animal which shows improved form when backed to do so is probably a better candidate for "promotion" than a "flukey" run by a 33–1 chance. Nevertheless, our figures must always reflect the actual running of the horses concerned. Use the S.P. as a guide – no more than that!

But we must get back to our desk! We have entered all the factual details of the Batthany but as yet made no attempt to fill in anything under the heading "New Rating". And this is where the interesting part starts!

Chapter 6

We have reached the stage where we can enter the bare result of the Batthany Handicap in our records book but without making any attempt to analyse the race to see whether the ratings should be amended in the light of the result. Since there was just over 5½ lengths between the winner Worlingworth and the sixth horse it is clear that, purely academically, the handicapper was "wrong". His effort to get these six horses to finish in a line has failed. Our job is to estimate where he was "wrong" and by how much.

All sorts of questions are raised by this result. Has the winner improved? Did the placed horses run below form? Did the going have any effect on the result? And so on. Only experience and constant application will enable one to make anything more than an intelligent guess but we must always make the attempt.

To try to assist the reader into making a reasonably accurate assessment of each race result, we later propose to list the result of every 5 and 6 furlong handicap run during 1982. After each race we will give a full analysis explaining the reasoning behind the view taken about each race. The author claims no infallibility for opinions expressed – they were often wrong – but it is hoped that the many examples will give a fascinating insight to an absorbing hobby. The pleasure obtained, quite apart from any possible financial gain, in getting ones figures borne out by the result is ample reward for any time taken up by the comparatively small amount of clerical work involved.

Backing ones opinion is a somewhat different question and one upon which the author has definite views. Suffice to say that, as has been stated before, the entire exercise should be entered upon as an interesting hobby with no real thought of retiring on the proceeds.

Handicapping is one of the most intriguing aspects of horse-racing and each race brings with it new problems to solve with the myriad of complexities and interpretations which are possible. Be prepared to be proved wrong – often! Horses are not machines and do not appreciate that they ought to win according to our ratings!

Such imponderables as luck in running, changes in the going, unsuitability to the course and more can affect the result of the race. Sprint handicaps are often won or lost at the start, for a slow beginning in a 5 furlong race at

Epsom, Brighton or Goodwood can be the kiss of death as far as the chances of that unfortunate animal are concerned.

In going through the results for an entire season, the reader will notice the tentative and tenuous estimates made in the beginning of the flat season and perhaps will be fascinated by the way the results begin to "make sense" as the season progresses.

The reader is urged to go through the races with an inquiring mind and if the end product is an understanding and, dare we say, an approval of the methods used by the author then the object of this book will have been achieved.

A word about allowances to make, in calculating amendments to ratings.

In making allowances for distances beaten it is customary to allow 3 lbs for each length, 2 lbs for ½ length and 1 lb for a neck or less. It is obvious, however, that one cannot in every case allow 12 lbs to a horse beaten 4 lengths. Horses are eased when obviously beaten and the handicapper would certainly not dream of adjusting ratings on this scale.

It takes quite a few bad races for a horse to drop any appreciable amount otherwise an astute trainer could easily get all his charges down to a mouth-watering level! In cases of extended distances one should hesitate before reducing any horse's rating by more than 7 lbs and even then to put a bracket round the figure to remind one that nothing in racing is certain. One has to use judgment in every case but one can learn by experience and develop an instinct for the sort of allowances to make with the expectation of not being too far out.

The real art of course is to work out which horse or horses have run to their true rating.

For the form student's guidance we append below the scale of approximate allowances for distances on firm and soft going.

	Firm	*Soft*
Short-head or head	1	1 or 0
Neck	1	1
½ length	2	1
¾ length	2	1
1 length	3	2 maximum
1½ lengths	4	2
2 lengths	5	3
2½ lengths	6	3
3 lengths	7	3–4
4 lengths	8	4
5 lengths	10	5
6 lengths	11	5–6

A good consistent type who always gives of its best in running is worth its weight in gold and you will soon learn to spot these types and bless their consistency. If you find that two or three of the first six horses appear to have run to their previous rating then one must stand by the figures and rate the others accordingly.

It is a truly fascinating endeavour and only those who have tried know the satisfaction derived from "getting it right".

Use your own judgement here. An easy 4 lengths win with the third horse a further 4 or 5 lengths away is not at all the same thing as when the second and third are fighting it out for the second spot, especially in a good-class race. In the first example the second is not having to be "pushed", whereas in the other example a grim struggle for second place means giving the winner full value for the win.

So, *now to work*!

SECTION TWO

RESULTS

This section of the book analyses the result of every 5 and 6 furlong handicap race – with the exception of selling handicaps – run under Jockey Club rules during the 1982 flat racing season.

In order to save space in the typographical layout the details relating to each race are:

At the top of each race is given a number which corresponds to its entry in *Raceform 1982*, followed by the time of the race, location, distance, going, date and weight equation. Below the line the following details are shown reading from left to right.

1st column	Horse's name* (Where preceded by figures these indicate the horse's previous race entry but figures which are bracketed refer to races in which the horse has run but which are not analysed in this book)
2nd column	Age of horse
3rd column	Weight allotted (Apprentice allowances are ignored)
4th column	Official handicap rating
5th column	Distances between placed horses
6th column	Our rating
7th column	Starting price

* Plus figures shown immediately after the horse's name show the amount of lbs extra carried due to a penalty for winning a previous race or because the rider could not make the weight.

Race 32	*3.05 Doncaster*	*5 furlongs*	*Good*	*March 25th*		(8.6=41)		
	Worlingworth	3	8 11	46	–	52	7–1	
	Feather Sound	3	8 7	42	2	42	6–4	
	Blakesware Saint	3	7 9	30	1½	26	12–1	
	Dragunn	3	7 11	32	½	26	11–2	
	Roman Quest	3	8 5	40	1½	(33+)	13–2	
	My Fancy	3	7 9	30	Short-head	(23)	16–1	

Analysis: Feather Sound, well backed favourite for this race, had already had two runs in France and it seemed safe to assume that he was fit and had run up to his rating of 42, so it remains unchanged. The winner had won well and to advance his rating by 6 lbs for the 2 length beating he had given the second seemed reasonable at the time. The remaining adjustments were made strictly in accordance with the scale but note that Roman Quest is given a (+) sign signifying that he is probably better than that. The reason for this was that he had been outpaced all the way but finished best of all, suggesting that 6 furlongs would suit him best. We do not attempt any adjustment to the rating to compensate for apparent bad luck in running – the figures must try to reflect the result.

Whilst we could not know this at the time, the second, third, fourth and fifth all went on to win a race within the next four weeks, which confirmed the impression that Worlingworth had put up a smart performance and was well worth the 6 lbs rise in his rating. Fortunately for our sanity, however, we also did not know that he was never to run to this rating in any subsequent race and did not win again until he triumphed in a 7 furlong event at Lingfield on September 21st. By that time the official handicapper had him rated some 7 lbs lower than his rating for the Batthany. The only reasonable explanation is that Worlingworth was fit to run for his life at Doncaster and looked very good against horses that, apart from Feather Sound, probably needed the race.

A fascinating race upon which to look back and wonder!

Race 35	*4.35 Doncaster*	*6 furlongs*	*Good*	*March 25th*		(8.9=42)		
	Sonseri	3	8 9	42	–	46	9–2	
	Parabems (+6)*	3	7 7	26	¾	28	11–1	
	Pat Pong (+6)	3	7 7	26	¾	26	50–1	
	Gimita	3	7 10	29	3	(22)	25–1	
	Broadway Lodge	3	8 3	36	3	(29)	16–1	
	Channing Girl	3	7 13	32	3	(25)	9–1	

* denotes overweight carried

Analysis: With only 1½ lengths separating the first three one can assume that they had probably all run more or less to their rating. The second and third both carried 6 lbs overweight, a factor which tends to complicate matters. However, it was decided that Pat Pong had run to its "amended" rating of 26 (remember that the handicapper considered it to be a "20") and so the winner and third were adjusted accordingly. With no less than 9 lengths between the sixth horse and Pat Pong one can only deduct a tentative 7 lbs from the ratings of the fourth, fifth and sixth and put a bracket round the figure to denote our lack of certainty.

In retrospect, it seemed surprising that Sonseri, receiving only 4 lbs was able to beat Worlingworth out of sight over 6 furlongs at Kempton Park on April 10th. But more of that when we come to Race 166.

Race 41 *4.35 Doncaster* *5 furlongs* *Good* *March 26th* (9.0=45)

New Embassy	5	8	7	38	–	44	9–2
Miss Poinciana (+8)	5	7	7	24	2	24?	15–2
Piencourt (+1)	4	8	2	33	¾	31+	18–1
Susarma	6	10	0	59	½	55	8–1
Friendly Fun (+1)	7	8	6	37	4	(30)	14–1
Andy Lou (+12)	4	7	9	26	3	(19)	33–1

Analysis: Piencourt was rather slowly away and running on well at the finish so maybe he had run a little below his best – hence the + sign to remind us. In the circumstances, to assume that the second horse carrying 8 lbs overweight had improved that much and had run to its new rating did not seem too unreasonable, despite the reservations about accepting its rating as correct. So Miss Poinciana is given a somewhat tentative rating of 24, which makes New Embassy 44 and Piencourt 31+. Susarma, ½ length behind Piencourt gets a 55 whilst Friendly Fun and Andy Lou were too far back for any reliable estimates so they both get 7 lbs off their ratings with brackets as before.

Race 56	*3.15 Folkestone*	*5 furlongs*	*Good–Soft*	*March 29th* (9.0=23)				
Balatina	4	7	10	5	–	8	20–1
Humble Blue	4	9	0	23	1	23	9–2
Charles Street	5	9	6	29	2	25	6–1
Lord Scrap	6	8	6	15	4	(8)	6–1
Covergirls Choice	5	9	2	25	3	(18)	4–1
Byroc Boy	5	8	2	11	Neck	(4)	20–1

Analysis: Government Warning!! Softish going. We cannot make the same allowances for extended distances as we do when the going is firm. With just over 10 lengths between the winner and the sixth horse in a race run in March on softish going we can have no real confidence in our revised ratings. However, Humble Blue is a fairly consistent horse and was well backed, so we take his running to be equal to its rating. Balatina had run on strongly to win this and seemed worth a rise of 3 in his rating.

We allow Charles Street 4 lbs for a 2 lengths beating by Humble Blue giving him a new figure of 25. The rest we reduce by the usual bracketed 7 lbs.

Race 62	*3.0 Ayr*	*6 furlongs*	*Good–Soft*	*March 29th*	(10.0=44)			
Dawns Delight	4	9	3	33	–	35	9–2
Kathred	4	10	0	44	2	42	9–2
Pettistree	4	9	4	34	2½	(27)	4–1
Longlands Lady	4	7	10	12	3	(5)	10–1
Bretton Park	4	9	6	36	4	(29)	5–2
The Huyton Girls	4	8	3	19	Neck	(12)	12–1

Analysis: With the finishers strung out like fairy lights we cannot take too much notice of the actual distances. In consequence we split an allowance of 4 lbs for the 2 lengths by which the winner beat the second. We do this by adding 2 lbs to Dawns Delight and deduct the same amount from Kathred, making them 35 and 42 respectively. The rest we demote by a notional 7 lbs. Only time will show how right or wrong we are.

Race 71	*4.30 Ayr*	*5 furlongs*	*Good–Soft*	*March 30th*				(9.7=41)
	Mrs Love It	3	8	3	23	–	26	6–1
	Fast Lad	3	9	7	41	Head	43	5–2
	She's my Girl	3	8	5	25	3	21+	5–2
	Blue Sapphire (+1)	3	7	11	17	$\frac{3}{4}$	12	12–1
	Cool Wind	3	8	0	20	$1\frac{1}{2}$	13	10–1
	Central Carpets	3	8	2	22	1	15	8–1

Analysis: She's my Girl was well backed to win this but missed the break so any note that we make for the future ought to be tempered by that circumstance. The going was on the soft side so we allow a maximum of 6 lbs for the 3 lengths, giving 2 lbs to Fast Lad and deducting 4 lbs from She's my Girl but with a "plus". To Mrs Love It we must give the 2 lbs we have given Fast Lad plus 1 lb for the head win. Blue Sapphire finished $\frac{3}{4}$ length behind She's my Girl and as we have lowered the latter's rating by 4 lbs we must do the same to Blue Sapphire plus 1 lb for the $\frac{3}{4}$ length. Cool Wind, not then the horse he was to become, "loses" 7 lbs as does Central Carpets.

Race 83	*4.45 Leicester*	*5 furlongs*	*Good–Soft*	*March 30th*				(8.0=25)
	Countach	3	7	13	24	–	29	12–1
35	Parabems	3	7	9	20	Head	24	5–2
	Spanish Point	3	8	0	25	4	21	8–1
	Etoile D'or (+4)	3	7	7	18	4	(11)	25–1
	Flavell's Record (+3)	3	7	7	18	6	(11)	25–1
	Manchesterskytrain	3	8	13	38	$\frac{1}{2}$	(31)	6–1

Analysis: For the first time we have a horse to deal with who has had a previous race, namely Parabems who was second in race 35 carrying 6 lbs more than its original assessment. Our decision there had been to give Parabems a rating of 28 which meant of course that, set here to do only 20, she had only to run to her previous figure to be a good thing. But the going was much softer than at Doncaster and she did not run up to her earlier figure although well backed to do so. It is still early in the season and we do not throw all the books out of the window! We are still guessing and it was decided to split the 8 lbs difference between her rating here and her earlier run and call her a 24. In other words we do not now accept the apparent 8 lbs improvement, that is the difference between her original "official" rating of 20 and her performance in race 35 carrying 6 lbs overweight. We have therefore credited her with half that amount and upgraded her by 4 lbs to make her 24. Countach has to go up that 4 lbs plus 1 lb for the head beating but the others are rated very tentatively. We proved to be wrong with Parabems (as we shall see later) and this illustrates very well the doubts that one must have about any horse's performance when carrying considerable overweight.

Race 86	*3.15 Catterick*	*6 furlongs*			*Good–Firm*	*March 31st*	**(10.0=45)**	
	Winter Wind	8	10	0	45	–	52+	7–2
	Dhuard	5	8	5	22	3	22	5–1
	Relative Ease	11	7	9	12	1	10	14–1
	Danzig (+)	5	7	9	12	2	(5)	25–1
	Jeckel	4	7	11	14	½	(7)	4–1
	Lindy Bay	5	8	2	19	1½	(12)	9–1

Analysis: Winter Wind was very fit, well backed and won comfortably. It was a good performance with 10.0 and it seemed reasonable to uprate him by 7 lbs with a plus. He may be better than that but we must not be too reckless! We also make the assumption, admittedly with no real evidence, that Dhuard has run to his figure and leave him at 22. We take 2 lbs from the rating of Relative Ease for the length beating. It could be 3 lbs but with the winner "home and dry" there was no real need for Relative Ease's jockey to do more than coast into third place and so we call it 2 lbs. In retrospect, we were not far out with Winter Wind (see races 187 and 1386) but we would not take too much credit for what was no more than a good guess.

Race 100	*2.40 Edinburgh*	*5 furlongs*			*Good*	*April 3rd*	**(10.0=34)**	
41	Miss Poinciana	5	8	10	16	–	24	8–11
	Miss Import	4	9	10	30	1½	34	6–1
	Marton Boy	4	8	2	8	1	9	14–1
	Bri Eden	8	10	0	34	¾	33	6–1
	Kings Offering	7	8	13	19	1½	15	6–1
	String of Stars	4	7	8	0	6	0	14–1

Analysis: If our figure of 24 for Miss Poinciana in race 41 was correct then, with only a rating of 16 to run up to, the mare was a certainty. In the hands of E. Hide she won easily and our estimate looked reasonably accurate.

Accordingly we kept her at the Race 41 mark. To be logical we must, therefore, upgrade the second and third horses who have finished fairly close up to what appears to be an improved horse. The winner goes up 8 lbs (16 to 24) so Miss Import goes up the same 8 lbs *less* 4 lbs for the 1½ lengths beating, a net increase of 4 lbs. Marton Boy finished a length behind Miss Import so goes up Miss Import's 4 lbs *less* 3 lbs for the length, i.e., an increase of 1 lb. Bri Eden's rating is calculated in the same way and gets Marton Boy's 1 lb increase *less* 2 lbs for the ¾ length, a net decrease of 1 lb. In the case of Kings Offering we allow only 3 lbs for the 1½ lengths behind Bri Eden because we reckon that to be full value for that distance at the finish of a race. We were adrift with Miss Import's figure (see Races 174, 329 and 684) and the truth was that Miss Poinciana had improved more than appeared and made her opponents look better than they were at that time. Ah well, one cannot win them all!

Race 107	*2.30 Salisbury*		*6 furlongs*		*Good–Soft*	*April 3rd*		(9.1=37)
	Vorvados	5	9	1	37	–	39	8–1
	Rollin Hand	4	8	11	33	Neck	34	11–2
62	Dawns Delight (+7)	4	9	4	40	3	35	5–1
	In Rhythm	5	8	1	23	2	(16)	20–1
	Banbury Cross	4	7	9	17	1	(10)	10–1
	Davenport Boy	6	9	4	40	1½	(33)	16–1

Analysis: Here we have Dawns Delight, a good winner of Race 62 coming out again within a few days. Our form figure of 35 from that race did not speak too highly of his chances here with a 7 lbs penalty, setting him to win on a 40 rating. Despite this the punters made him favourite but although he ran a fair race he had no chance with the first two. We could assume however, that he had run to his race 62 figure and leave him at 35. On softish going we allow 6 lbs for the 3 lengths between Rollin Hand and Dawns Delight but note that, as we have already dropped the latter by 5 lbs we must only raise Rollin Hand by 1 lb. As that horse goes up 1 lb then Vorvados also goes up that lb plus another 1 lb for the neck beating. The others we reduce by 7 lbs with a bracket for doubt. The reader is urged to study these figures carefully to ensure that the method is completely understood.

Race 109	4.0 Salisbury	5 furlongs			Good–Soft	April 3rd		(9.0=38)
	Leekmore	3	7	12	22	–	30+	20–1
	Milk Heart	3	9	1	39	3	40	10–1
83	Spanish Point	3	8	1	25	1½	23	11–2
	Harpers Bazaar	3	9	7	45	Head	42	10–1
	Saint Crespin Bay	3	8	4	28	¾	24	14–1
	Gentle Star	3	8	7	31	Short-head	26	12–1

Analysis: One or two horses are beginning to come out again and the fascinating business of fitting the jigsaw pieces together begins. Spanish Point, third here, had run off the 25 mark in Race 83 and we had downrated him by 4 lbs to 21. Unless he had improved with a run under his belt we couldn't expect too much from him here. To assess this result we follow the same procedure as in Race 83 in that we split the difference between the "official" rating and our form figure. In Spanish Point's case this means that we split his official 25 and our form figure of 21 and call him 23. Using this figure as our base we assess the second, fourth, fifth and sixth horses in line with the distances involved since they had finished pretty well grouped apart from the winner. Thus, having reduced Spanish Point by 2 lbs we deduct 3 lbs from Harpers Bazaar, 4 lbs from Saint Crespin Bay and 5 lbs from Gentle Star. To assess the winner correctly however, we have to consider that he had won easily and as we have raised Milk Heart by 1 lb (see above) we must therefore credit Leekmore with that lb plus a conservative 7 lbs for the 3 lengths beating, i.e., a total increase of 8 lbs. It could be more so we give the figure a plus.

Race 114	3.45 Chepstow	5 furlongs			Soft	April 5th		(10.0=65)
	Lightning Label	6	9	13	64	–	69	9–4
41	Piencourt	4	7	9	32	½	36	7–1
62	Pettistree	4	7	11	34	6	(27)	12–1
41	New Embassy (+5)	5	8	6	43	¾	(36)	9–4
	Sparkling Boy	5	9	11	62	¾	(55)	10–1
	Touch Boy	6	9	3	54	6	(44)	8–1

Analysis: Things were now beginning to hang together and here we had three horses who had previous form figures. New Embassy looked to have a good chance with a rating of 43 (including a 5 lb penalty) since he had achieved a form figure of 44 in race 41. The going was much softer here than at Doncaster and New Embassy could not reproduce his figure. This was a difficult race to assess. Lightning Label and Piencourt had left the remainder of the field 6 lengths behind and the form looked a bit suspect with no less than 14 lengths between the winner and the sixth horse. We must give some credit to the front two for the 6 lengths and we took the view that Piencourt had improved 5 lbs on his initial run and called him a 36. As this is an increase of 4 lbs on his "official" rating Lightning Label must also go up that 4 lbs plus 1 lb (on soft going) for the ½ length he beat Piencourt. The rest go down 7 lbs except Touch Boy who "lost" 10 lbs.

Race 117	*2.0 Nottingham*	*6 furlongs*			*Good–Firm*	*April 5th*	(8.12=33)	
	Broons Secret	8	8	5	26	–	27	10–3
	Welsh Noble	4	7	9	16	2	11	16–1
56	Balatina (+9)	4	7	7	14	Head	8	10–3
	Cumulus	4	8	12	33	4	(26)	9–1
	Miss Twiggy	4	7	7	14	1	(7)	20–1
	Brentex	4	8	2	23	1½	(16)	11–1

Analysis: Carrying 9 lbs over its original assessment, Balatina, winner of race 56 and with a form figure of 8 had more to do here and although favourite and running a good race had no chance with the comfortable winner, eventually finishing third. We would hesitate to believe from the evidence of one race that the 8yo Broons Secret had improved dramatically so we take Balatina's form figure of 8 to be about right, which meant that, with an allowance of 7 lbs for the 2 lengths and a head between winner and third, the winner goes up just 1 lb. As it happened Broons Secret went on to win two more races (332 and 398) and as a result was punished heavily by the handicapper. It took at least one more race before we caught up with the amazing improvement. The remainder go down 7 lbs being too far away to rate accurately.

Race 128	*4.0 Nottingham*	*5 furlongs*			*Soft*	*April 6th*		(9.7=43)
32	Blakesware Saint	3	8	8	30	–	32	8–1
71	Fast Lad	3	9	5	41	½	40	11–8
32	Dragunn	3	8	10	32	2	30	7–1
83	Parabems	3	7	12	20	2	(13)	10–3
*(35)	El Pato (+2)	3	7	7	15	6	(5)	25–1
71	She's my Girl	3	8	3	25	6	(15)	6–1

* Note. El Pato's race reference refers to a race not among our group and therefore not analysed in this book.

Analysis: For the first time we have a race where most of the runners have been out before this season and we therefore have a form figure for practically all the field. As an example of how we assess the respective chances we now show the horses concerned with their official rating, our form figures and whether they are plus or minus

	Weight	*Rating*	*Form Figure*	*+ or –*
Fast Lad	9.5	41	43	–
Dragunn	8.10	32	26	+6
Blakesware Saint	8.8	30	26	+4
She's my Girl	8.3	25	21+	+4
Parabems	7.12	20	24	−4

In prospective "chance" order the horses are rated as follows:

Parabems	−4	(4th)
Fast Lad	−2	(2nd)
Blakesware Saint	+4	(Won)
She's my Girl	+4	(6th)
Dragunn	+6	(3rd)

To explain further, what we are really saying is that Parabems is carrying 4 lbs less than we think he should have, Fast Lad has 2 lbs less but Blakesware Saint and She's my Girl are set to carry 4 lbs more than their form warrants. In view of the actual result we obviously need to do better than this if we are going to spend a month on the Isle of Capri but it is still early days, horses are "finding a bit" following an initial outing and the going is very soft.

Now that the race has been decided we have to assess the result and make the revised ratings make some sort of sense without cheating! On the same terms, Blakesware Saint has finished 2½ lengths in front of Dragunn compared with the ½ length at Doncaster so perhaps he has improved a bit. Fast Lad does not appear to have run to his figure of race 71 and we were already beginning to have grave doubts about Parabems in Race 35. (That overweight again.)

The 2½ lengths between the first and third would not be worth more than about 4 lbs on soft going so we split that amount between them, that is to say, that we raise the winner by 2 lbs, lower the third 2 lbs and drop the second by 1 lb. Parabems we demote by 7 lbs and El Pato and She's my Girl "lose" 10 lbs for finishing in the next county!

As we have said before, we are still trying to make educated guesses and readers should not get disheartened with similar "disasters" in their own efforts after only a few races. Believe me, official handicappers have the same problem.

Race 134	*4.0 Folkestone*		*6 furlongs*		*Good*	*April 6th*		(9.13=29)
	Ta Morgan	4	10	0	30	–	35	6–1
(54)	Derring Prince	4	7	13	1	2	1	25–1
56	Charles Street	5	9	13	29	1½	25	5–1
(54)	Heathen Prince	4	8	7	9	¾	4	5–1
	Ratamataz	8	8	4	6	½	0	25–1
56	Byroc Boy	5	8	9	11	1	4	20–1

Analysis: This was not a good race and we had only two horses with a form figure. Charles Street had finished third at Folkestone one week earlier with a form figure of 25. He was beaten 2½ lengths here and the chances were that he had probably run up to that figure. So we call him 25 and leave Derring Prince on his official, if lowly, rating. Ta Morgan, the comfortable winner is put up 5 lbs for the 2 lengths win whilst we lower Heathen Prince by 5 lbs. (That is the 4 lbs we have taken from Charles Street plus 1 lb for the ¾ length.) Ratamataz goes off the scale and Byroc Boy loses 7 lbs.

Race 139	*3.45 Hamilton Park*		*6 furlongs*		*Soft*	*April 6th*		(4.9.0=22)* (3.9.0=37)*
	Island Walk	4	8	4	12	–	13	5–1
62	The Huyton Girls	4	8	11	19	Neck	19	10–1
	Saga's Humour	3	7	12	21	1½	19	14–1
(66)	Mott the Hoople	4	9	0	22	1½	18	6–1
	Winner Takes All	5	7	12	6	4	0	8–1
(69)	Bracken Gill	4	8	5	13	1	6	33–1

* (Note that in our equation we have given two figures. The WFA Scale decrees that a 4yo shall be asked to give a 3yo 15 lbs over this distance in April. Hence the level of 9.0 is equivalent to 22 for the older horse and 37 for the 3yo.)

Analysis: This was a fairly well contested affair with just over 3 lengths covering the first four to finish. Again the going was soft and we would not want to allow more than 5 lbs for this, so, if we take the view that The Huyton Girls has run to her official rating, we can share the 5 lbs out in proportion. Look at the amended ratings to see how this has been done. Note that the ratings are calculated round the figure for the second horse.

Race 144	*3.15 Hamilton Park*	*5 furlongs*			*Heavy*	*April 7th*		(9.7=41)
71	Cool Wind	3	8	0	20	–	24	10–1
	Bonne Baiser	3	9	7	41	3	41	2–1
	Swinging Baby	3	8	5	25	Neck	24	13–2
71	Mrs Love It (+7)	3	8	10	30	1	27	3–1
	Rhy Van Tudor	3	8	0	20	Short-head	17	16–1
	Aqua Verde	3	7	11	17	4	(10)	6–1

Analysis: Mrs Love It, winner of Race 71 at Ayr has a 7 lbs penalty and seems likely to have too much to do as she has to "find" a further 4 or 5 lbs to win this. Cool Wind was nearly 5½ lengths behind Mrs Love It in the same race and is 7 lbs better off today. On the face of it he did not have to improve much to have a chance. At 10–1 he was a good each way bet. To assess this race we took the view that the second and third had more or less run to their offical rating and that made Mrs Love It's figure about right compared to her existing form figure of 26. Cool Wind had almost certainly improved a bit so we put him up 4 lbs for the 3 lengths in heavy going. One cannot be too precise in such cases and we are still a bit in the dark at this stage.

Race 153	*4.45 Haydock Park*	*6 furlongs*			*Soft*	*April 7th*		(9.0=43)
32	Roman Quest	3	8	11	40	–	41	11–2
(78)	Video King	3	7	13	28	Short-head	28	6–4
	Hazim	3	8	11	40	1	38	7–2
	Thijssen	3	7	10	25	4	(18)	10–1
(43)	Ultrasonic	3	7	9	24	2½	(17)	14–1
	Nagalia	3	9	0	43	6	(36)	10–1

Analysis: Roman Quest had finished well over 5 furlongs at Doncaster in Race 32 and gained a plus sign from us. In addition, Blakesware Saint, third in that race had won nicely the day before so the form of Race 32 was looking reasonable. Video King, hot favourite for this event had no figure from us having run in a non-handicap over 7 furlongs at Leicester. In the race Roman Quest was again outpaced but finished like the proverbial train to snatch the race on the line. We were on this one and 11–2 was a good price. With the second obviously fit and fancied we assessed him as having run to his rating of 28 and amended the winner and third in line with that. The others were well beaten and get 7 lbs knocked off as a result.

Race 166	4.0 Kempton Park				6 furlongs	Good–Soft	April 10th	(8.11=49)
35	Sonseri (+7)	3	8	11	49	–	54	4–1
	Skyboot	3	7	9	33	Neck	37	33–1
83	Countach (+7)	3	7	7	31	10	(24)	10–1
	Diamond King	3	8	4	42	1	(35)	20–1
35	Broadway Lodge	3	7	12	36	Neck	(29)	14–1
	Mubhedj	3	8	12	50	2	(43)	16–1

Analysis: In this race Worlingworth, hero of Race 32, had 9.1 to carry, equivalent to a rating of 53 including a 7 lbs penalty. Now, since we estimated he had run to a form figure of 52, well supported by the evidence supplied by Blakesware Saint and Roman Quest, he did not seem to have too much to do to win this and he was, in fact, backed down from 6–1 to 7–2. Unfortunately, in the soft conditions and with another furlong to go he failed to reproduce his running. On the other hand, Sonseri, who was assessed as +3 (see how), revelled in the going and got home by a head from Skyboot. They finished 10 lengths in front of the rest of the field which destroyed the race from the point of view of accurate assessment. The placings from the third horse back are impossible to calculate and so we reduce them all by 7 lbs with a big query! But what to do with the first two? They must be given some credit for the 10 lengths and it was decided to raise Sonseri by 5 lbs, Skyboot by 4 lbs and wait for subsequent confirmation.

Race 174	2.15 Newcastle				5 furlongs	Good	April 10th	(10.0=46)
100	Miss Poinciana (+7)	5	8	5	23	–	28	6–5
41	Friendly Fun	7	9	4	36	2	35	11–1
	Tom Dowdeswell	6	8	1	19	1½	14	14–1
100	Miss Import	4	8	12	30	Short-head	25	11–2
	Sammy Bear	4	9	3	35	1½	29	14–1
	Mary Maguire	5	7	10	14	1½	7	25–1

Analysis: Miss Poinciana again. Strictly on their running in Race 100 she had it all to do to beat Miss Import at a difference of only 7 lbs against the 14 lbs she had been getting previously. The mare was on the crest of the wave however and neither Miss Import nor any of the others was any real danger. After this race it seemed clear that we had over-rated Miss Import in Race 100 and that Miss Poinciana must have had a lot in hand.

To assess this race we took the view that the winner had run 5 lbs better than its present official rating and gave her a new figure of 28. Friendly Fun, beaten 2 lengths on good going, gets Miss Poinciana's 5 lbs *less* the 6 lbs by which he was beaten, a net decrease of 1 lb whilst the reader is invited to calculate the ratings which have been made for the others.

Race 187	*3.15 Nottingham*	*6 furlongs*			*Soft*	*April 12th*	(4.8.7=32)* (3.8.7=47)*	
86	Winter Wind (+7)	6	9	13	52	–	53	9–4
(113)	Swinging Rhythm	4	8	7	32	½	32	8–1
(134)	Scottish Agent	6	7	7	18	1½	16	20–1
114	Pettistree	4	8	9	34	2½	28	8–1
(86)	Renovate	5	8	9	34	3	(27)	10–1
	Avonmore Wind	3	8	4	44	Head	(37)	12–1

* See note following Race 139 concerning the WFA Scale.

Analysis: Even with a 7 lbs penalty Winter Wind had only to run to the Race 86 rating to win this. So it proved and at 9–4 a very good price. We have no concrete evidence of any further improvement and we give the winner a nominal 1 lb increase and revise the ratings down to the fourth horse according to the distances involved on soft going. After the fourth horse we fall back on the 7 lbs yardstick. Readers may like to take note that Pettistree has run to a form figure of 27 or 28 on three separate occasions and we are entitled to think that the handicapper has this horse about 7 lbs too high in the handicap.

Race 195	*4.15 Warwick*	*5 furlongs*			*Good–Soft*	*April 12th*	(10.0=40)	
117	Brentex	4	8	11	23	–	25+	6–1
	Over the Rainbow	5	9	13	39	1½	39	12–1
	Eagles Quest	4	8	4	16	Neck	15	12–1
(107)	Royal Diplomat	5	8	7	19	1	16	7–2
(134)	Sitex (+1)	4	8	1	13	Neck	9	25–1
(107)	Northern Eclipse	5	9	2	28	Neck	23	10–1

Analysis: The value of a previous race was again demonstrated here when Brentex showed at least 9 lbs improvement on his running in Race 117. Over the Rainbow and Eagles Quest finished well to fight out the second and third places and we can safely assume that they have run to their ratings. The going was yielding and we can only allow 2 lbs for the 1½ lengths win.

This was a well contested race and we can have some confidence in our revised ratings.

Race 221	*3.0 Newmarket*		*6 furlongs*		*Good–Firm*		*April 15th*	(9.0=48)
	Music Lover	3	9	5	53	–	58	4–1
109	Harpers Bazaar	3	8	11	45	2	45	7–2
	Sussex Queen	3	8	9	43	¾	41	10–1
	Illicit	3	8	11	45	¾	41	7–1
	Strapless	3	8	9	43	Head	38	6–1
	Master Cawston	3	9	7	55	Dead-heat	50	7–1

Analysis: With a previous race under his belt we can safely assume that Harpers Bazaar has improved upon his Race 109 form assessment of 42 and that he has run to his official mark of 45.

With less than 4 lengths covering the first six the form looks reliable and the winner worth an increase of 5 lbs for the 2 lengths win. Sussex Queen goes down 2 lbs for the ¾ length behind Harpers Bazaar whilst Illicit is reduced by that 2 lbs plus a further 2 lbs for the same distance behind the third horse. Strapless and Master Cawston fit into place with their reductions of 5 lbs each.

Race 234	*3.45 Pontefract*		*6 furlongs*		*Good–Firm*		*April 15th*	(9.7=48)
(127)	Boatrocker	3	8	6	33	–	38	11–10
(28)	Divine Madness	3	8	7	34	1	36	4–1
139	Saga's Humour	3	7	8	21	¾	21	10–1
(35)	Knight Security	3	8	9	36	3	29	9–2
	Royal Revenge	3	9	7	48	2	(41)	12–1
153	Nagalia	3	9	2	43	3	(36)	14–1

Analysis: There was not too much to go on here, the only small clue being that Saga's Humour has probably run to her rating after her pipe opener in Race 139. Taking her as our measuring stick meant that Boatrocker would have to go up 5 lbs for the 1¾ lengths he had beaten the filly. The colt had run a fine race in a good-class stakes event at Nottingham nine days before and had almost certainly improved. (The handicapper took an even more exalted view of this performance following his Nottingham race and in Race 600 the colt was rated on the 41 mark.) It is interesting to note that Nagalia has twice running been "awarded" the rating of (36) and she came down to an official mark of 34 when running second to Town Flier in Race 871 towards the end of May. At least that showed that we were thinking along the same lines as the official handicapper!

Race 240 *3.0 Newbury* *5 furlongs* *Good* *April 16th* (9.7=59)

(166)	Street Market	3	9 7	59	–	63+	10–3
	To the Point	3	9 7	59	4	53	9–2
	Miss Trilli	3	9 1	53	½	45	7–1
	Ritual Dance	3	8 10	48	½	38	3–1
(35)	Preparation	3	8 3	41	2½	(31)	7–2
	Welwyn	3	8 6	44	½	(34)	15–2

Analysis: When a horse wins a competitive handicap at a Group One track by 4 lengths one is liable to assume that it has probably improved at least 7 lbs but things are not as straightforward as that! Apart from Preparation none of the other runners had had Street Market's advantage of a previous outing and so it would be optimistic to upgrade the winner by more than, say, 4 lbs. On the other hand Street Market had certainly handed out a 10 lbs beating to the second horse. We therefore decided to split this amount between the front two, raising the winner by 4 lbs and lowering To the Point by 6 lbs. Miss Trilli and Ritual Dance are revised in proportion to the distances they are beaten. The fifth and sixth horses seem to have run at least 10 lbs below their ratings but we bracket the figures to ensure that we remember the enormous discrepancy. As a matter of interest we point out that Miss Trilli, third here, was officially rated in the 50's at the start of the flat racing season but by August had been demoted to the 20's when she finally won a poor race at Redcar (Race 2136).

Race 261 *3.05 Thirsk* *5 furlongs* *Firm* *April 17th* (8.0=32)

128	Dragunn	3	8 0	32	–	35	7–2
32	My Fancy	3	7 11	29	1	29	12–1
109	Leekmore (+7)	3	7 7	25	1½	23	9–4
144	Mrs Love It	3	7 8	26	1	22	15–2
32	Worlingworth (+7)	3	9 7	53	½	48	4–1
	Here's Sue	3	8 6	38	½	31	8–1

Analysis: Was it the change in going or did Leekmore just run a poor race? On our form figure in Race 109 he was a good thing to win this with a rating of −5 even with a 7 lbs penalty. Dragunn, My Fancy and Worlingworth had all run in Race 32 and on our figures in that race Worlingworth looked best. It should be noted however that Dragunn had already improved upon that run in Race 128 and only needed to show some slight further improvement to go close here. This was a rather confusing result however and we were not at all sure what to make of it. With 4 lengths covering the first five it was decided to split an allowance of 8 lbs between them.

We therefore upgraded the winner by 3 lbs, demoted the fifth horse by 5 lbs and adjusted those between according to distance. It was however, unsatisfactory that, as a result of these amendments, Leekmore, Mrs Love It and Worlingworth all seemed to have run 7, 5 and 4 lbs respectively below their best figures which had not however been set up on a course as sharp as Thirsk, or on going as firm as they found on the Yorkshire track. All in all a puzzling affair!

Race 292	*3.0 Wolverhampton*	*5 furlongs*			*Good–Firm*	*April 19th*	**(8.9=31)**	
144	Cool Wind (+7)	3	8	4	26	–	32+	5–2
	Luan Casca	3	8	5	27	1½	29	12–1
71	Blue Sapphire	3	7	7	15	1	14	6–1
166	Countach	3	8	9	31	Short-head	29	5–4
(61)	Superb Singer (+1)	3	7	7	15	Head	12	16–1
(35)	High Authority	3	8	11	33	3	(26)	10–1

Analysis: Countach's performance in Race 83 had not been enhanced by its run in Race 166 and with a rating of 31 to live up to did not look a 5–4 chance. Cool Wind, on the other hand had to "do a 26" to win this and we knew that he was at least 24 on the evidence of Race 144. We leave it to the reader to decide which was the "value" bet! In assessing the result we took the view that Countach had run to his Race 83 figure and fitted the others in accordingly. It meant putting Cool Wind up another 6 lbs but he was beginning to look worth it!

Race 301	*4.30 Wolverhampton*	*5 furlongs*			*Good–Firm*		*April 20th*	(9.0=21)
117	Balatina	4	8	2	9	–	10	5–1
195	Brentex (+7)	4	9	9	30	1	28	11–2
*(195)	Curzon House	5	7	7	0	1	0	33–1
	Crowebronze	4	7	12	5	½	0	25–1
100	Bri Eden	8	9	13	34	1	28	10–3
	Solar Grass	7	8	2	9	1	1	20–1

* Curzon House ran in Race 195 but was not in the first six.

This race raises the question as to what one should expect of any method of private handicapping. It would, of course, be very gratifying if the top-rated horse won most of the time but common sense tells one that this is an impossible dream only encouraged by purveyors of handicapping "systems" based on illogical methods which do not stand up to objective analysis. A method such as we are using undertakes only to show which horses have a chance at today's weights based on a sensible assessment of their previous running.

To backtrack a little we now say that we hope to have the answers to the two questions which were first posed. We think we know *how good the horse is* and able to estimate *is it good enough to win today*.

In Race 301 our previous form figures showed that Balatina, Bri Eden, Eagles Quest and Humble Blue all had a rating with us of +1, or, to put it another way, that they all had shown public form only a pound below that which they were set to do today.

In the event Balatina won, Bri Eden was fifth, Eagles Quest was close up seventh and Humble Blue's saddle slipped giving the rider no chance. We would suggest that to get the winner from the top four is all one can ask. Unfortunately, it is possible to get such a result in, say, 7 races out of 10 and still lose money by picking the wrong one!

One can only use ones judgment in such cases. In certain races one might consider backing more than one horse or indulging in a few dual forecasts – it is all a matter for the individual. In the case of Balatina the use of a good boy like Paul Eddery claiming 5 lbs was a good extra pointer to its chance and could have been the encouragement needed for a bet.

Analysis: This was not a very good race and we split 3 lbs between the first two as shown with Curzon House and Crowebronze getting a zero rating which might be good for VAT purposes but says very little for their racing ability. Bri Eden finished 3½ lengths behind the winner and "loses" 6 lbs for that.

Race 323	*3.35 Epsom*	*6 furlongs*			*Good–Firm*		*April 21st*		(4.9.0=36)
107	Davenport Boy	6	9	4	40	–	43	4–1	
	Lord Wimpy	4	8	1	23	1	23	10–1	
(107)	Old Dominion	5	10	0	50	Neck	49	6–1	
(169)	Barnet Heir	4	9	1	37	3	(30)	7–2	
(62)	Kassak	6	8	8	30	1½	(23)	16–1	
(107)	Denmore	6	9	9	45	½	(38)	11–4	

Analysis: Davenport Boy had apparently needed the race when sixth to Vorvados in Race 107 but had been well beaten to get a (33) from us. With so many of the runners having no rateable form we were clearly not taking more than a recording angel's point of view. Despite his poor showing when 16–1 in Race 107 Davenport Boy was well backed to win here so, with there being little between the front three, we leave Lord Wimpy at 23, deduct 1 lb from Old Dominion for the neck he was behind the second and give Davenport Boy the full 3 lbs for his win on fast going. The rest cannot be given a firm figure.

Race 329	*3.35 Epsom*	*5 furlongs*			*Firm*	*April 22nd*			(4.9.8=53) (3.9.8=65)
	Pontin Lad	4	9	8	53	–	56	11–2	
	Mumruffin	3	9	2	59	½	61	7–1	
	Steel Charger	5	8	3	34	1	33	5–1	
(195)	Go Total	6	8	9	40	Head	38	12–1	
174	Miss Import	4	7	13	30	1½	24	11–2	
(114)	Star of Enzo	4	8	8	39	1	32	14–1	

Analysis: A good race home for the first four so we share out 5 lbs for the 1½ lengths and a neck by giving 3 lbs to the winner and working backwards from there. Note here that Mumruffin, being a 3yo should receive 12 lbs from an older horse over 5 furlongs at this time of the year and to come second here with 9.2 was a good performance. In her next race (511) she was a good bet against her own age group and duly obliged being backed from 6–4 to 11–10.

Here we see Miss Import running to almost the identical rating as in Race 174 confirming yet again that we had overrated her in Race 100. Such is the inherent uncertainty of the racing game however that this young lady subsequently "came good" again, winning Races 752, 1491, 1755 and 2065 – in the latter race running to a rating of 44!

These things happen!

Race 332	*2.45 Ripon*	*6 furlongs*			*Firm*	*April 21st*		(9.1=33)
117	Broons Secret (+7)	8	9	1	33	–	36	9–4
107	In Rhythm	5	8	5	23	1	23	9–2
174	Mary Maguire	5	7	10	14	1½	10	11–1
*86 (174)	Relative Ease	11	7	8	12	¾	6	12–1
	Russian Winter	7	8	11	29	2½	(22)	12–1
	April Lucky	9	8	3	21	1	(14)	16–1

* Relative Ease ran out of the first six in race 174 but is last rated in Race 86

Analysis: (See comments below Race 117.) Broon's Secret goes from strength to strength. Here he shoulders a 7 lbs penalty with the minimum of fuss. In Rhythm had obviously improved since Race 107 and we take its rating to be about right here. Broon's Secret goes up 3 lbs for the 1 length win, Mary Maguire goes down 4 lbs for the 1½ lengths behind In Rhythm whilst Relative Ease is demoted 6 lbs.

Race 339	*3.0 Beverley*	*5 furlongs*			*Firm*	*April 23rd*		(10.0=46)
	Ferriby Hall	5	10	0	46	–	47	20–1
174	Miss Poinciana (+7)	5	8	12	30	Short-head	30	2–1
(117)	El Presidente	4	8	1	19	1½	15	12–1
332	Relative Ease	11	7	8	12	½	7	6–1
41 (187)	Andy Lou	4	7	10	14	¾	8	20–1
	Silent Tears	5	7	7	11	1	4	20–1

Analysis: In Race 174 we had put Miss Poinciana on the 28 mark and here she was set to do a 30 (with a 7 lbs penalty) and fails by the shortest of short heads after being hampered soon after the start. So we were not too far out. We can assume that she had run to her new level, call her 30 and assess the others all round her rating. Relative Ease comes out about right compared to his figure in Race 332 only two days before and we can be reasonably confident that we have the winner correctly assessed at 47.

Race 350	*4.0 Beverley*	*5 furlongs*		*Firm*		*April 24th*		*(9.0=31)*
	Transonic	3	8 2	19	–	22	14–1	
144 (237)	Swinging Baby (+7)	3	9 1	32	¾	33	7–2	
292	Cool Wind (+7)	3	9 0	31	Head	31	3–1	
292	Blue Sapphire	3	7 12	15	4	(8)	10–1	
261	Mrs Love It	3	8 11	28	1½	(18)	9–1	
	Witch's Point	3	9 7	38	¾	(28)	10–1	

Analysis: After Race 144, where she was assessed at 24, Swinging Baby went on to win a maiden race at Pontefract, thus picking up a penalty for this event. Cool Wind seemed to have a good chance rated at 31, including the penalty, for in Race 292 we had given him a figure of 32+. However, in a well contested finish Transonic, with no previous outing in 1982, held on to beat Swinging Baby by ¾ length with Cool Wind a head away. We may have been a little too enthusiastic about Cool Wind's win in Race 292 but if we take it that he has run to his present rating including the penalty we still won't be too far out. The first two are adjusted from Cool Wind's figure but the fourth, fifth and sixth are a bit too far behind for accurate assessment. Swinging Baby appears to have improved since Race 144 but we must watch that penalty which artificially inflates the rating.

Race 352	*2.30 Sandown Park*	*5 furlongs*		*Good–Firm*		*April 23rd*	*(9.7=59)*
(43)	Ellerene	3	8 12	50	–	54	10–1
	Town Flier	3	8 4	42	2	43	6–1
	Sylvan Barbarosa	3	8 13	51	2	50	11–2
	Ibtihaj	3	9 7	59	¾	56	14–1
	Pilot Flyer	3	7 13	37	2	(30)	20–1
261	Worlingworth	3	9 1	53	1½	(43)	10–1

Analysis: Worlingworth seems to be getting worse and worse! Here he runs a good 9 lbs below his figure of Race 32. We do not have much to go on in the way of solid lines of form and have to cast our thoughts around for guidance. Ritual Dance, a runner here but out of the first six, had been rated at 38 in Race 240 and being set to carry 8.10, or 48 on our scale, naturally made no show.

Worlingworth is obviously no good to us as a yardstick and we are left to our own devices. In such cases it is usually best to take a rough poundage equivalent for the distances between the first three or four horses and share it between them. With the leaders spread out a bit we decided to allow 7 lbs, giving 4 lbs to the winner and deducting 3 lbs from the fourth horse with appropriate amendments for the second and third. We begin to despair of Worlingworth and mark him down to (43).

Race 375 *4.15 Brighton* *6 furlongs* *Firm* *April 26th* (9.0=37)

32	Feather Sound	3	9	6	43	–	44	5–1
	Sound of the Sea	3	8	3	26	Head	26	11–2
(295)	Typecast	3	8	3	26	1½	22	16–1
(319)	Stylish Mover (+2)	3	7	13	22	½	16	15–8
144	Bonne Baiser	3	9	4	41	1	34	9–2
(166)	Kash In	3	9	6	43	Neck	36	12–1

Analysis: By now we knew that Race 32 was working out really well – apart from Worlingworth! – and Feather Sound with a form figure of 42 from that race and set to do 43 here had an excellent chance. Bonne Baiser too, with a figure of 41 and set to do the same could also be fancied. It could be argued that, whereas Race 32 had already proved to be a prolific source of winners, Race 144, run in very heavy going, was not the best of form guides at the time. With Feather Sound scrambling home all out from Sound of the Sea we can safely assume that both had run to their official rating except that we put the winner up by 1 lb for the short head win. Typecast gets a 4 lb drop for 1½ lengths and Stylish Mover goes down Typecast's 4 lbs plus 2 lbs for ½ length.

We are sure that by now readers are getting used to things and well able to anticipate our decisions and even perhaps to disagree!

Race 398 *3.0 Nottingham* *6 furlongs* *Firm* *April 27th* (9.7=37)

332	Broon's Secret (7+)	8	9	1	31	–	38+	13–8
	Courageous Buzby	6	8	5	21	4	21	14–1
301	Crowebronze (+4)	4	7	7	9	Short-head	8	10–1
	General Wade	7	9	7	37	1	33	8–1
	Blessed Silence	4	7	7	9	1	2	25–1
	Hillsdown Lad	4	8	1	17	1½	(10)	20–1

Analysis: A one horse race! Broon's Secret with a form figure of 36 from Race 332 is here set to do a 31!! With the competent apprentice T. Jarvis once more on his back and claiming 7 lbs and backed from 5–2 to 13–8 he was the bet of the season so far. Seeing that Courageous Buzby had been hustled along by Crowebronze we took the view that the second had run to his rating and left him at 21. The easy 4 lengths win makes us give Broon's Secret a further 7 lbs to put him on the 38+ mark. The remainder we adjust in keeping with the distances involved.

Race 404	*3.15 Thirsk*	*6 furlongs*			*Firm*	*April 27th*		*(10.0=53)*
117	Cumulus	4	8	8	33	–	32	5–4
332	Mary Maguire (+4)	5	7	7	18	1	14	5–1
	Zoilo	4	7	12	23	2	16	11–2
	Tree Fella (+1)	5	7	8	19	½	12	33–1
	Rambling River	5	8	1	26	2½	(16)	20–1
(187)	Primula Boy	7	10	0	53	1½	(43)	10–1

Analysis: In making Cumulus a 5–4 favourite to win this race bookmakers and punters alike were doubtless reasoning that Broon's Secret and Balatine had not done any discredit to the form shown in Race 117 and they were not mistaken!

To assess this event we reasoned as follows: Mary Maguire, set to do 18 here, had run to a rating of 10 in Race 332. If we split the difference and assess her at 14 we may not be far out, especially as her original official rating before the 4 lbs overweight which she carried was in fact 14! After all, we can allow the handicapper to be right sometimes! Using Mary Maguire as the yardstick gives us the assessments for the others.

Rough and ready, you say? Well, it is all educated guesswork and we are not computing a rocket's flight path to the moon.

Race 419	*4.15 Catterick Bdge*	*6 furlongs*			*Firm*	*April 28th*		*(10.0=39)*
195	Over the Rainbow	5	10	0	39	–	40	Evens
117	Welsh Noble	4	8	5	16	Short-head	16	7–2
174 (339)	Tom Dowdeswell	6	8	8	19	1½	15	7–1
(332)	Little Atom	5	8	9	20	¾	15	10–1
(195)	Miss Twiggy	4	7	10	7	Head	1	14–1
	Blochairn Skolar (+2)	4	7	7	4	¾	0	33–1

Analysis: With the form of Race 117 working out so well Welsh Noble looked to have a good chance here but unfortunately he was set to do 16 against his form rating of 11. He could be expected to show some improvement from his first outing however. But Over the Rainbow's figure of 39 from Race 195 meant he had to do no better than that to score here. He did – but only just! Welsh Noble just failed to get up and went down by a short head. The straight forecast of just over 9–2 was good value.

Things tie up nicely with previous form figures if we assume that Welsh Noble has run to his rating. Over the Rainbow goes up to 40 and Tom Dowdeswell fits in almost exactly right at 15. The form looks reliable.

Race 424	*3.40 Newmarket*	*6 furlongs*			*Good*	*April 29th*	*(8.13=44)*	
	Camisite	4	8	7	38	–	42	7–1
62 (187)	Kathred	4	8	13	44	1	45	15–2
114	Piencourt	4	8	4	35	Short-head	35	11–2
323	Old Dominion	5	9	5	50	1½	46	4–1
(175)	Murillo	6	9	11	56	Short-head	52	10–3
	Dungeon Ghyl	4	8	4	35	5	(28)	10–1

Analysis: This had all the makings of a good race. Our pre-race ratings had it very close between Kathred, Piencourt and Old Dominion but they were all beaten by Camisite on his first outing of 1982 – something that is of course always a possibility. But with a reasonably close finish and tight ratings we could be well satisfied with our assessments for this race. Piencourt had run a "blinder" and just missed second place by a short-head so we took him as the "key" horse.

By taking his rating as being correct – it was only 1 lb different from its Race 114 form rating – and adjusting the others round him made the whole race tie up nicely with previous figures.

Race 428	*2.30 Newmarket*	*6 furlongs*			*Good*	*April 30th*	*(9.0=55)*	
(199)	Four For Music	3	7	13	40	–	47+	5–1
(210)	Anstruther	3	9	7	62	5	62	15–2
(180)	Strath of Orchy	3	9	0	55	Head	54	11–2
221	Master Cawston	3	9	0	55	2	48	10–1
261	Dragunn (+7)	3	7	12	39	¾	31	12–1
221	Sussex Queen (+2)	3	8	4	45	1½	35	4–1

Analysis: Four for Music had been a well backed favourite for Race 109 won by Leekmore but, from an official rating of 41 and ridden by Lester Piggott, he was unable to get a clear run and was eased in the last furlong to finish out of the first ten. He subsequently appeared not to stay the trip when runner up to Lavender Gray over 7 furlongs at Warwick.

Brought back to 6 furlongs and in the hands of Willie Carson the colt made no mistake, coming home 5 lengths clear of the field. Easy wins like this are difficult to assess correctly. However, by taking Anstruther's form figure to be equivalent to its rating we calculated the others accordingly. This indicated that Master Cawston, Dragunn and Sussex Queen had all run a few pounds below their previous best figures, not usually the best confirmatory evidence. But if we uprate the form figures too much this would mean that Four for Music would have to go up to an unrealistic figure and we were not inclined to do that!

So Anstruther had to be the touchstone, right or wrong. There was also of course, the possibility that our form figures for the fourth, fifth and sixth horses were over-estimated. A depressing thought but one that must be borne in mind.

Race 442	*3.15 Carlisle*		*6 furlongs*		*Firm*	*April 30th*		(9.0=35)
(278)	Bloemfontein	3	7	13	20	–	22	4–1
	In Slips	3	8	7	28	1½	26	3–1
	No Clown	3	9	1	36	3	29	8–1
(146)	Adjusted	3	8	7	28	1	(21)	16–1
(256)	Autumn Daze	3	8	4	25	2½	(18)	12–1
	L'Angelo di Carlo	3	7	9	16	¾	(9)	20–1

Analysis: Most form experts will constantly caution against using non-handicap form when weighing up a handicap race and certainly one is well advised to exercise care in such cases. It was to be noted here however, that Bloemfontein had worked out about 12 lbs inferior to Blakesware Saint in a stakes event at Edinburgh some 11 days earlier. Now, from Race 128, we know that the latter is a "32" with us, so with Bloemfontein handicapped at 20 here we appeared to be in the same parish. The race itself told us very little so this little snippet of information was useful in evaluating the level of the form.

With this to guide us we split 4 lbs for the 1½ lengths between first and second, adjusted the others with a fair degree of uncertainty and hoped for the best. Happily, there was some confirmation when In Slips came out just over two weeks later (Race 679) and ran to its rating.

We have all of us experienced the inherent cussedness of inanimate objects – fortunately our friend the racehorse is not often the same. Life is not all disappointments!

Race 450	*4.15 Ripon*	*6 furlongs*	*Firm*			*May 1st*		(4.9.0=42) (3.9.0=55)	
(188)	Cyril's Choice	3	8	7	48	–		52	16–1
332	April Lucky	9	7	7	21	1½		21	20–1
404	Zoilo	4	7	9	23	Short-head		22	11–1
419	Welsh Noble (+5)	4	7	7	21	1½		16	13–2
	Cree Song	6	9	0	42	¾		35	16–1
398	Broon's Secret (+5)	8	8	8	36	½		28	11–10

Analysis: After our philosophical discourse following Race 442 we now have that stalwart campaigner Broon's Secret running a "stinker". Handicapped 2 lbs below his form figure of Race 398 he started 11–10 favourite and ran some 10 lbs below form! In two races afterwards (566 and 1159) the gelding ran right up to and slightly beyond our previous best figure and we can only speculate on the reasons for his surprising defeat. In assessing the race we took note that Welsh Noble had run a good race a few days before and we decided to take that form as correct, amended his rating to our form figure of 16 and adjusted the rest in line with that. April Lucky and Zoilo had probably improved after their initial outing and looked about right.

But Broon's Secret's disappointing show took some believing!

Race 458	*4.0 Haydock Park*	*5 furlongs*			*Firm*	*May 1st*	(10.0=43)	
339	Miss Poinciana	5	9	3	32	–	36	6–4
332	Russian Winter	7	9	0	29	1½	29	4–1
301	Balatina (+7)	4	8	7	22	3	15	2–1
404	Rambling River	5	8	11	26	½	19	6–1
62 (339)	Longlands Lady	4	7	10	11	3	(4)	14–1
(301)	Bella Travaille (+7)	4	7	10	11	3	(4)	16–1

Analysis: The handicapper had "gone to town" over Balatina's win at Folkestone (56) and with a 7 lbs penalty for his success at Wolverhampton (301) the gelding was here set to do a "22" with a best form figure of 10. With respect, those punters who backed Balatina at 2–1 to win this race would perhaps benefit from a reading of this book! Miss Poinciana, on the other hand, with steadily improving form figures of 24, 24, 28 and 30, was handicapped at 32 here and to improve the necessary couple of pounds to win this race was well within the bounds of possibility. With Russian Winter and Rambling River needing to find at least 7–10 pounds on previous running there was really only one bet. To assess this race we acknowledge Russian Winter's probable improvement and credit him with the same form figure as his official rating and rate the others in line with that.

Strictly on the figures Balatina did, in fact, improve 5 lbs on previous running to attain a new rating of 15 and this was subsequently confirmed in Race 1074. Note that Rambling River improved about 3 lbs on his running in Race 404 but he took a long time to get up to his autumn official rating of 32.

Race 467	*2.30 Kempton Park*	*6 furlongs*		*Good*	*May 1st*	(10.0=62)	
323	Barnet Heir	4	8 2	36	–	41+	4–1
(202)	Amorous	4	7 10	30	7	25	7–2
	Ponchielli	4	9 11	59	1½	51	11–2
114	Sparkling Boy	5	10 0	62	1½	(52)	9–2
	Case History (+13)	4	7 7	27	2	(17)?	16–1
(107)	Manilow	5	8 5	39	¾	(29)	12–1

Analysis: After his run at Epsom in Race 323 we were not prepared for Barnet Heir's 7 lengths win here. At the time of his earlier defeat the experts pointed out that the chestnut had never won beyond 5 furlongs. Here he was presumably confounding the same experts by winning over six!

This was a puzzle however and after due reflection we concluded that the 7 lengths was probably worth about 10 lbs and so we split that amount equally between the first two, took 8 lbs away from Ponchielli and 10 lbs from the remainder. It was some comfort to learn later that the handicapper took precisely the same view and put Barnet Heir on the 41 mark in Race 775 where, however, he ran unplaced.

Barnet Heir never ran to that figure again so perhaps we were all wrong. Note the query mark for Case History – 13 lbs overweight!

Race 475	4.0 Kempton Park	6 furlongs			Good	May 3rd		(9.0=47)
(295)	Purnima	3	7	8	27	–	29	2–1
109 (361)	Spanish Point	3	7	7	26	2	24	15–2
352	Town Flier	3	8	9	42	3	(35)	5–1
(106)	Senorita Querida	3	8	12	45	½	(38)	16–1
109 (315)	Milk Heart (+7)	3	9	4	51	½	(44)	11–4
187	Avonmore Wind	3	8	11	44	2½	(37)	12–1

Analysis: Assessed on 5 furlong form only Town Flier was "best in" here with −1, with Spanish Point second best at +3. This was over 6 furlongs however, albeit a relatively easy trip. With 8½ lengths between the winner and the sixth horse it was not easy to "rationalise" the result. We eventually split 4 lbs equally between the first and second and deducted the "doubtful seven" from the rest.

The handicapper took a slightly harsher view of Purnima's performance and put the colt up to 31 under which he won at Nottingham in July (Race 1482) so he may have been right.

Race 481	4.15 Doncaster	5 furlongs			Good–Firm	May 3rd		(4.10.0=59) (3.10.0=70)
329	Steel Charger	5	8	3	34	–	42	11–4
(287)	Never Talk	3	9	11	67	2	69	8–1
240	Street Market (+5)	3	9	8	64	¾	64	11–2
329	Pontin Lad (+5)	4	9	13	58	Neck	57	11–2
339	Ferriby Hall (+5)	5	9	8	53	2	48	7–1
339	Relative Ease (+12)	11	7	7	24	1½	16	20–1

Our pre-race ratings were as follows:

Steel Charger	+1	Won
Street Market	+1	3rd
Pontin Lad	+2	4th
Ferriby Hall	+6	5th
New Embassy	+7	10th
Touch Boy	+9	7th
Relative Ease	+14	6th

Analysis: As pretty a picture as could be seen and it was a pity about Never Talk for whom we had no figure! We took Street Market as the key horse here. He had run well at Newbury (240) and had been ridden out for third place a neck in front of Pontin Lad who had won well at Epsom (329). It was easy to fit the rest in and Steel Charger goes up 8 lbs for a comfortable win. We could be well satisfied with this result which was almost an action replay of our ratings.

Race 483 *2.15 Warwick* *5 furlongs* *Good* *May 3rd* (4.10.0=20) (3.10.0=31)

134 (329)	Byroc Boy	5	9 3	9	–	14	12–1
	Colonial Line	4	9 4	10	1½	11	7–2
(339)	Mercy Cure	6	10 0	20	Head	20	8–1
(398)	Boldly Go	4	9 1	7	1	4	16–1
(361)	Boodlebird	3	9 3	20	Short-head	16	7–1
(105)	Pete Rocket	3	9 12	29	Neck	24	8–1

Analysis: An apprentice race and the weights had been raised 23 lbs so these were not the best sprinters in the country. Byroc Boy appeared to need to improve at least 5 lbs on our figures to win this but he had, in fact, ran quite well when 7th behind Pontin Lad in a good race at Epsom (Race 329). There he had finished ½ length behind Star of Enzo who was conceding Byroc Boy 15 lbs but even so the run was probably worth a form figure of about 20 which made Byroc Boy a certainty for this! Unfortunately, one tends to appreciate these things after the result and what is more, an apprentice handicap at Warwick is hardly the sort of race to inspire confidence.

Moral: Overlook nothing in the never ending quest for winners!

To assess this race we took Mercy Cure as the key horse. The mare had led till close home and had probably given her best. Colonial Line goes up 1 lb and the winner is promoted that 1 lb plus a further 4 lbs for the 1½ lengths win. The rest was straightforward calculation.

Race 497 *3.30 Redcar* *5 furlongs* *Firm* *May 4th* (8.8=41)

261	Leekmore	3	7 12	31	–	32	6–1
(261)	Errol's Boy	3	8 8	41	Head	41	12–1
153	Hazim	3	8 7	40	1	37	11–8
428	Dragunn (+7)	3	8 6	39	1	33	9–2
350	Cool Wind (+7)	3	7 12	31	Head	24?	9–2
350	Witch's Point	3	8 5	38	1½	(30)	6–1

Analysis: Cool Wind (−1) and Leekmore (+1) appeared to be the best handicapped horses in this race and Hazim (+2) did not seem to be a genuine 11–8 chance. Mysterious indeed are the ways of punters.

In the race Cool Wind seemed unlucky. He failed to get a clear run in the final furlong and finished fifth, little more than two lengths behind the winner. Leekmore, set to do only 1 lb better than our Race 109 figure seemed generously priced at 6–1.

It seemed reasonable to take the runner-up as the key here and the others were rated round Errol's Boy. The final figures looked approximately right apart from that of Cool Wind, about whom we already had a reasonable explanation for his apparent loss of form.

Race 511	*4.15 Chester*	*5 furlongs*			*Good–Firm*	*May 4th*		(9.7=59)
329	Mumruffin	3	9	7	59	–	66	11–10
375	Kash-In	3	8	5	43	4	42	12–1
261	My Fancy (+2)	3	7	9	33	Short-head	31	13–2
292	Luan Casca (+4)	3	7	7	31	2	26	14–1
(300)	Athersmith (+11)	3	7	7	31	½	(24)?	33–1
352	Ibtihaj	3	9	7	59	Head	(52)	12–1

Analysis: Mumruffin's form figure of 61 from Race 329 looked very solid here as it had been well confirmed by Race 481 the previous day, when Steel Charger and Pontin Lad had run up to and beyond their previous figures. Luan Casca had a "squeak" on her second to Cool Wind in Race 292 but had moved up in class. She managed to stay with the front running Mumruffin for 3 furlongs but neither she nor anything else had any chance with the winner, who coasted home by 4 lengths. We had to enlist the aid of the official handicapper to rate this race. My Fancy had run to a form figure of 29 in Race 261 according to us but it should be noted that she had been uprated to 31 since then. (She carried 2 lbs overweight here.) So, acting on the general principle that the official probably knew better than us we put My Fancy in at 31 and adjusted the others round it.

What to do with Mumruffin? The 4 lengths win looked worth a good 8 lbs so with Kash-In demoted 1 lb the winner goes up 7 lbs to a figure of 66. The rest fit in reasonably enough but we take note of the 11 lbs overweight carried by Athersmith. The calculated form figure of (24) "looks wrong" being 4 lbs better than its official rating of 20 and we resolve not to place too much credence on it.

Race 523	4.15 Chester	5 furlongs			Good	May 6th		(10.0=59)
41 (151)	Susarma	6	10	0	59	–	61	10–1
329	Go Total	6	8	9	40	Head	41	15–2
(94)	Arch Melody	4	8	8	39	½	38	13–2
56 (301)	Humble Blue (+1)	4	7	8	25	Short-head	23	4–1
404	Tree Fella (+7)	5	7	8	25	Head	22?	16–1
139	The Huyton Girls (+4)	4	7	7	24	Neck	20	8–1

Analysis: After his saddle slipping episode in Race 301, Humble Blue was made favourite to win this and was unlucky not to do so. On his form figure from Race 56 Humble Blue had a good chance here whilst Bri-Eden (who finished seventh) had only to run to its figure in Race 100 to be in the shake-up. Readers will remember, however, that we were already wondering if we had over-rated that race, perhaps misled by the field's comparatively close proximity to Miss Poinciana.

Susarma was (+4) with us from Race 41 but had since run prominently in a top-class stakes event at Haydock, a race which did not come under our scrutiny in any real analytical context. This "dodging" about between handicaps (which we rate) and stakes events (which we do not) is most inconsiderate!

Chester form is not always the best guide to the future but we cannot be too carping here. Seven horses flashed past the post in a packed finish and rating the race was easy. No more than 7 lbs would cover the first six, of which we gave the winner 2 lbs, deducted 4 lbs from The Huyton Girls to tie in with her Race 139 figure, with the rest being fitted in. We also note Tree Fella's 7 lbs overweight, giving him a form figure 10 lbs better than that of Race 404 and give him a question mark. It is worth noting here that Tree Fella came out at Chester later in the year (Race 1595) and won at 13–2 from an official mark of 22! The figure he was "awarded" in Race 523 had, in the meantime, been confirmed in Race 997. We must always be prepared to "believe" our figures when they are duly substantiated.

Race 526	2.30 Salisbury	6 furlongs			Good–Firm	May 5th		(8.3=26)
(109)	Shiny Hour	3	8	7	30	–	34	12–1
(158)	Geomancer	3	7	13	22	3	21	10–1
(377)	Bud's Gift	3	7	10	19	1½	14	20–1
128	Parabems	3	8	3	26	Neck	20	9–1
(231)	Tai Lee	3	8	0	23	1½	(16)	10–1
(158)	Webb's Jewel	3	7	12	21	½	(14)	8–1

Analysis: Parabems was suffering from her performance in Race 35 where we rated her at 28. Here the handicapper set her to do 26 but it was clear that the filly had gone backwards since her first run with decreasing form figures of 28, 24 and 13. There was no way she could win this but she ran a good race beaten only a neck for third place.

We had no idea which, if any, of the first three had run to form. Geomancer, second here, had occupied the same position in a maiden seller at Haydock in April so the level of the form was not very high. The 4½ lengths between the first three we took to be worth about 9 lbs and we shared that out by giving the winner 4 lbs, putting Geomancer down 1 lb and the third horse down 4 lbs. This put Parabems back on the 20 mark but she was on firm going for the first time this year so perhaps it was not far out. Time would tell.

Race 541 *2.30 Lingfield Park* *6 furlongs* *Good–Firm* *May 7th* (8.10=51)

240	Welwyn (+1)	3	8	1	42	–	44	20–1
352	Sylvan Barbarosa	3	8	10	51	Neck	52	6–1
(170)	Silojoka	3	8	9	50	Short-head	50	20–1
(315)	Nawab	3	8	8	49	2	45	20–1
475	Purnima (+5)	3	7	7	34	Head	29	7–4
(319)	Rhinestone Cowboy (+5)	3	7	12	39	6	(29)	33–1

Analysis: Sylvan Barbarosa (+1), Purnima (+5) and Welwyn (+8) were the only horses with a form figure and they finished second, fifth and first in that order. Welwyn, the 20–1 winner had run well below her official mark in Race 240 and had obviously improved, whilst the sixth furlong probably suited her better. In a close finish of a neck and a short head we take Silojoka's running to be about right and leave his figure unchanged at 50. Note that the form figure for Purnima is exactly in line with the form of Race 475, a clear case of a penalty having an effect upon a horse's running.

Race 553 *5.0 Lingfield Park* *5 furlongs* *Good–Firm* *May 8th* (10.0=48)

424	Piencourt	4	9	1	35	–	36	10–3
(398)	Pusey Street	5	8	11	31	2½	27	9–2
467	Manilow	5	9	5	39	½	33	10–3
	Ferryman	6	10	0	48	1	(41)	3–1
	Queens Bidder	5	7	8	14	1½	(6)	25–1
483	Mercy Cure	6	8	0	20	½	(10)	6–1

Analysis: Piencourt and Mercy Cure were both set to do their best form figures here, the former from Race 114 and the latter from Race 483. It should be noted however, that there was a considerable difference in class between the two races concerned. Race 114 had been open to horses rated 30–75 and worth £7180 to the winner, whereas Race 483 was an apprentice handicap for those rated between 0–40 and worth only £1080 to the winner. On the face of it therefore, Piencourt's form was superior to that of Mercy Cure and the colt was in fact set to concede Mercy Cure 15 lbs.

This he did comfortably and we calculated that he had run to his best figure of Race 114 adjusting the rest to that. This meant putting Mercy Cure down 10 lbs but the alternative was to raise Piencourt inordinately and there was no real evidence for that. The rest of the field gave no clues apart from Manilow who came out 4 lbs better than his first run in Race 467, which looked possible.

Race 556	*2.45 Bath*	*5 furlongs & 167 yards*			*Firm*		*May 8th*	*(9.0=57)*
(287)	On Return	3	8	12	55	–	58	2–1
(300)	Carreg Cennen (+7)	3	7	9	38	Head	40	20–1
	Curve the Wind	3	7	10	39	2	37	2–1
(221)	Wicked Wave	3	8	1	44	6	(34)	13–2
(221)	B A Poundstretcher	3	7	10	39	2	(29)	10–1
240	Preparation	3	7	11	40	1½	(30)	6–1

Analysis: Only Preparation had a figure in this race but rated at +9 had little chance. To assess the race for the future was mainly guesswork but, in keeping with our usual practice, we split 5 lbs between the first three to take account of the head and 2 lengths separating them. With the rest of the field 6 lengths further back any ratings must be tentative and not to be relied upon implicitly.

Race 566	*4.30 Thirsk*	*6 furlongs*			*Firm*	*May 8th*		*(9.3=37)*
(263)	Willie Gan	4	7	12	18	–	20	11–2
398	General Wade	7	9	3	37	½	37	7–2
450	Broon's Secret	8	9	8	42	1½	39	11–2
(252)	Spoilt for Choice	4	7	8	14	Head	11	16–1
	Java Tiger	4	8	9	29	1½	23	10–1
	Young Croftie (+5)	5	7	12	18	Neck	11	25–1

Analysis: One hour before this race was run a seemingly moderate filly had won the Millgate Maiden Stakes by 4 lengths at 33–1. Her name was Soba! A crystal ball would have been worth more than all the form books! However, we can be sure that Willie Gan did not realize that he was running in the illustrious hoofprints made by one of the finest sprinters in the country and he had to put his best foot forward to beat General Wade by ½ length.

Russian Winter (−1) and Zoilo (+1) had the best chance on our figures but, although well backed, neither finished in the first six. General Wade had improved a little on his Race 398 figure and we decided he had run to his best and use him as a prop to work out the rest as shown. Some prop! The only race he managed to win the whole of the season was a very moderate claiming handicap in October and that from a rating of 23. But we were not to know that at the time. Even so, using General Wade in this way put our old friend Broon's Secret on a figure of 39, a rating well in line with his performances before his alarming show in Race 450.

Race 567 *2.15 Edinburgh* *5 furlongs* *Good–Firm* *May 10th* (4.10.0=27) (3.10.0=38)

(441)	H R Micro	4	8	8	7	–	9	11–2
195 (339)	Northern Eclipse	5	10	0	27	Neck	28	8–1
458	Rambling River	5	9	13	26	Head	26	4–1
(226)	Royal Question	3	7	12	8	Head	8	25–1
458	Longlands Lady	4	8	12	11	¾	9	10–1
187 (398)	Scottish Agent	6	9	1	14	2	9	10–1

Analysis: The handicapper had made a good job of this and the race resolution needed little thought. With the first four home in a finish of heads one has to assume that they have all run more or less to form. Amendments are minimal.

Race 577 *8.05 Windsor* *6 furlongs* *Good* *May 10th* (9.0=48)

(473)	Premier Lass	3	7	7	27	–	33	11–2
(467)	Lindsey	3	8	13	47	2	48	33–1
511	Kash-In	3	8	9	43	Short head	43	12–1
(321)	Bernard Sunley	3	8	2	36	Neck	35	10–1
475	Senorita Querida	3	8	11	45	½	42	6–1
428	Four for Music (+5)	3	9	0	48	4	(41)	2–1

Analysis: Four for Music's useful win at Newmarket (Race 428), with a form rating of 47+ made him a good favourite here, even with a 5 lbs penalty. Set to do 48 and with Lester Piggott aboard, the colt started at 2–1 but never really got into the race. What is more, judging by his subsequent form he was never again the same horse that had strolled home so majestically ten days before.

On the face of it Kash-In appeared to have run to his figure from Race 511 and we rated the others round him strictly in line with the distances.

Race 581	*3.0 Wolverhampton*		*5 furlongs*		*Good–Firm*	*May 10th*	(8.0=31)	
292	Countach	3	7	11	28	–	32	7–1
(195)	St Crespin Bay	3	7	9	26	4	22	13–2
(300)	Fast Service	3	7	12	29	Short head	25	10–1
(300)	Lochtillum (+5)	3	7	7	24	1	18	14–1
153 (460)	Ultrasonic	3	7	7	24	½	17	50–1
292	High Authority	3	7	8	25	¾	17	20–1

Analysis: Countach had twice run to a figure of 29 in Races 83 and 292, and with a rating here of 28, looked to have a good chance. My Fancy, favourite for the race with a rating of 31 had run to that figure in Race 511 and could also be fancied. But with T. Quinn claiming 7 lbs on Countach the combination looked good value at 7–1 and even better when winning by 4 lengths! The author is second to none in his admiration for our senior jockeys but do not overlook the claims of a horse that has a chance on the book just because it is ridden by a boy. A good motto in such cases is – if he is good enough for the trainer, he is good enough for us.

Race 588	*3.30 York*		*5 furlongs*		*Good–Firm*	*May 11th*	(4.10.0=67) (3.10.0=78)	
523	Susarma (+10)	6	10	2	69	–	71	10–1
467	Ponchielli	4	9	6	59	1½	58	7–1
450	Cree Song	6	8	3	42	Head	40	20–1
481	Never Talk	3	9	2	66	Head	63	4–1
481	Steel Charger (+10)	5	8	5	44	1½	39	6–1
(339)	Dutch Girl	5	7	7	32	¾	26	20–1

Analysis: The result of Race 481 had been strikingly in accord with our pre-race ratings and Never Talk seemed to have a good chance here. Set to do 66 with a form figure of 69, he looked a good favourite and it was a surprise when he was beaten into fourth place. Even more unexpected however, was the performance of Susarma. In a finish of heads he had won at Chester five days before (Race 523) but there had been nothing in the form to make his win worth more than a rating of 61.

Yet here he was, with a 10 lbs penalty, out of the stalls like a flash to lead all the way for a convincing win. Unfortunately, Susarma did not run again and we could not test the value of this performance.

The later form of the other runners was much in line with their ratings here and it is evident that Susarma had made considerable improvement during the early part of the season.

To assess this race we took the line that an allowance of 5 lbs would cover the first four home and amended the ratings as shown.

Race 600	*2.30 York*	*6 furlongs*		*Firm*	*May 13th*			(9.0=43)
(435)	Prevail	3	9	1	44	–	45	7–1
234	Boatrocker	3	8	12	41	Neck	41	4–1
352	Ellerene (+7)	3	10	0	57	3	53	8–1
350	Swinging Baby	3	7	10	25	2	19	6–1
153 (428)	Roman Quest	3	8	13	42	1½	(35)	17–2
221	Strapless	3	9	0	43	Head	(36)	14–1

Analysis: Once again we have a performance by an animal carrying over-weight casting doubt upon the figures! In Race 350 Swinging Baby, with a 7 lbs penalty, had run to a figure of 33 well authenticated by collateral form. Set to do only 25 here she could have been expected to better than finish fourth. However, she was a bit unlucky as the race was run. Well behind in the early stages she failed to get a clear run when making her run from 2 furlongs out. She has not won beyond 5 furlongs and that may be her best trip. Certainly that is the evidence of the figures.

Boatrocker had proved his well-being with a win at Pontefract (Race 234) and had probably run to its improved rating of 41. Taking this official figure as the "bench-mark" and a less than enthusiastic view of the 3 lengths and 2 lengths between the second, third and fourth, made Ellerene's figure very close to its figure from Race 352. Roman Quest has possibly lost his spring momentum and is running below his figure of Race 153 set up on soft going.

Race 610	*3.45 Brighton*	*6 furlongs*		*Firm*		*May 12th*		(8.2=24)
(521)	Hit the Line	3	8	2	24	–	25	7–1
375	Sound of the Sea	3	8	4	26	Neck	26	5–4
(377)	Red Ellette	3	8	3	25	1½	22	7–1
(78)	St Conal	3	7	12	20	4	(13)	33–1
(78)	Moat House	3	8	8	30	½	(23)	14–1
375	Typecast	3	7	13	21	1	(14)	9–4

Analysis: With so few horses with a form figure we can only use what material there is – in this case that provided by Sound of the Sea. At the previous Brighton meeting she had run a good race when second to Feather Sound (Race 375) setting up a form figure of 26. With no more to do here she was firm favourite at 5–4 and should have won. Taking the lead from Hit the Line with 2 furlongs to go Sound of the Sea was all over a winner until Hit the Line fought back under strong driving to win by a neck. We take Sound of the Sea's running to be on a par with Race 375, leave her on the same rating and put the winner up by 1 lb. In finishing third, 1½ lengths behind Sound of the Sea, Red Ellette had only to "coast" home and cannot be downgraded by more than 3 lbs.

Race 622	*4.15 Beverley*	*5 furlongs*		*Firm*		*May 14th*		(4.8.4=7) (3.8.4=18)
	Mel's Choice	4	8	4	7	–	13	2–1
567	H R Micro	4	8	4	7	1½	9	4–1
(339)	Caledonian	6	8	13	16	¾	16	10–1
419	Blochairn Skolar	4	7	12	1	¾	0	12–1
(564)	Cree Bay	3	7	13	13	1	10	14–1
(398)	Sailor's Prayer	4	9	8	25	2	18	7–1

Analysis: A moderate race. Caledonian was "pushed" into third place by the close-up Blochairn Skolar and looks to have run to its official rating. We therefore make our assessments round him and there is confirmation from the resultant figure for H R Micro which is exactly in line with that horse's figure in Race 567. Mel's Choice was heavily backed from 5–1 to 2–1 to win this and has almost certainly improved.

Race 641	4.0 Newbury	6 furlongs			Firm	May 15th		(10.0=54)
	Gabitat	4	9	11	51	–	52	20–1
323	Davenport Boy	6	9	5	45	¾	44	5–1
467	Case History (+5)	4	7	7	19	Head	18?	20–1
424	Kathred	4	9	3	43	3	38	6–1
	Gambler's Dream	5	9	7	47	½	41	33–1
107 (411)	Vorvados	5	9	0	40	4	(33)	4–1

Analysis: This was a very closely knit handicap and pre-race ratings gave chances to several horses with Kathred having the edge on her running in Race 424. With Paul Eddery claiming 5 lbs she looked good value at 6–1 and was given every chance by her young rider.

Very smartly away, she led for a long way but weakened in the final furlongs to finish fourth. There did not appear to be anything particularly amiss with our figures for Race 424 and Piencourt, who had finished close up third in that race duly confirmed his rating with a win in Race 553. Whatever the reason Kathred did not run to her figure.

Her amended rating of 38 was subsequently established in Races 1386 and 2950 and it looks as if she ran above herself in Race 424.

To assess this race however, we took Davenport Boy's form to be about the same as his figure from Race 323 and rated the rest from that.

Case History gets a query – the dreaded overweight!

Race 645	7.20 Newcastle	6 furlongs			Firm	May 14th		(8.7=22)
566	Willie Gan	4	8	3	18	–	23	8–11
450	Welsh Noble	4	8	3	17	5	16	5–2
(566)	Bettabet Geraghty	4	8	3	18	2	13	4–1
	Carpenter's Boy (+8)	4	7	7	8	10	0	33–1

Analysis: Willie Gan was rightly odds-on to win this race which only attracted four runners. Rating this was rather unsatisfactory with extended distances between the horses at the finish. We took the 7 lengths covering the first three to be worth 10 lbs and gave 5 lbs to the winner for an easy win. It so happens that Welsh Noble's adjusted figure is about right if compared to his figures in Races 450 and 419 so we may not be too far adrift.

								(4.10.0=52)
Race 659	*4.30 Newmarket*	*5 furlongs*		*Good–Firm*		*May 14th*		(3.10.0=63)

588	Steel Charger (+7)	5	9	4	42	–	42	7–4
553	Manilow	5	9	1	39	1	36	9–2
	Spectacular Sky	4	10	0	52	5	(45)	14–1
	Hollow Heart	3	9	10	59	Dead heat	(52)	11–2
553	Pusey Street	5	8	6	30	¾	(23)	3–1
114 (481)	New Embassy	5	9	5	43	2½	(36)	9–1

Analysis: New Embassy had not run to its Race 41 figure set up at Doncaster way back in March in two races since then and did not appear to be fancied. Steel Charger, on the other hand, had run to a rating of 42 in Race 481 and only a few pounds below that with a 10 lbs penalty in Race 588. Even with his 7 lbs penalty here he was set to do 42 again and with Pusey Street (+3) and Manilow (+6) having to find a few pounds, Steel Charger looked excellent value at 7–4. Ridden by the Maestro himself, the colt was never in danger of defeat and made all the running to win by a length from Manilow.

The winner's form is well in line with previous running and we leave him at 42. Manilow goes down 3 lbs for the length but note that this is still a slight improvement on Race 553. After a rather disappointing show next time out at Epsom (Race 987) Manilow made amends with an easy win at Yarmouth (Race 1074), from a rating of 37.

The remaining runners are too far behind for accurate assessment and are downgraded 7 lbs to await confirmation in the future.

Race 663	*2.30 Newmarket*	*6 furlongs*		*Good–Firm*		*May 15th*		(9.0=69)

	Admiral's Princess	3	9	2	71	–	74	14–1
	Celestial Dancer	3	7	9	50	Short head	52	12–1
(258)	Welsh Partner	3	8	2	57	1½	56	13–2
(215)	Not for Show	3	9	1	70	Neck	68	6–1
556	On Return (+7)	3	8	7	62	¾	58	8–1
588	Never Talk	3	8	11	66	1½	60	8–1

Analysis: Never Talk gets another opportunity to confirm his form figure of 69 from Race 481, this time over 6 furlongs but again failed to do so. To rate this race we split 5 lbs for the distances between the first four as shown and, as we finish up with On Return on the same figure as in Race 556, there might not be too much wrong with our assessment.

Race 671	*3.45 Pontefract*	*6 furlongs*			*Firm*	*May 17th*		*(8.8=24)*
323 (523)	Lord Wimpy	4	8	8	24	–	26	11–2
566	Spoilt for Choice	4	7	12	14	1	14	12–1
566	Java Tiger	4	8	13	29	Short head	28	11–4
450	April Lucky	9	8	4	20	2	16+	11–2
(226)	Secret Express	6	7	7	9	1	4	33–1
	Waresley	4	8	9	25	¾	18	20–1

Analysis: Lord Wimpy (+1) was one of four horses we could rate with a chance, the more so because Davenport Boy had not let the form of Race 323 down by his performance in Race 641 two days previous to this.

These form confirmations must always be noted as they often give a very good guide to how the form of a particular race is shaping up.

Lord Wimpy won fairly comfortably and we split 3 lbs for the length and short-head between the first and third. April Lucky was given a lot to do in the race and found himself with nowhere to go in the last furlongs and his downgrading to 16 is perhaps a bit open to doubt, so we give it a plus to remind us. He had set a figure of 21 in Race 450 and subsequently won a race at Hamilton (Race 1065) from a rating of 20.

Race 673	*4.45 Pontefract*	*5 furlongs*			*Firm*	*May 17th*		*(9.0=37)*
71 (564)	Central Carpets	3	7	10	19	–	22	5–1
(497)	Magnamala (+1)	3	7	7	16	1	16	12–1
497	Cool Wind	3	8	7	30	1	28	9–4
(567)	Quick off the Mark (+12)	3	7	7	16	3	(9)	25–1
511	Luan Casca	3	8	4	27	2½	(20)	15–8
(442)	Cedrella	3	8	6	29	1	(22)	5–1

Analysis: Central Carpets had been downgraded by the handicapper and was now set to do 19 as against his mark of 22 in Race 71. Cool Wind had run to a figure of 32+ in Race 292 but had run below that figure twice since. It is always a problem to know how far back to go in reviewing a horse's form for, as we have said before and will doubtless say again, what an animal has done before he can always do again – but how long after? This race was almost a month since Cool Wind's best figure and we are certainly entitled to look askance at a horse's prospects of repeating a performance if he or she has twice failed to confirm the figure. In order to assess this race we took the view that, as no less than 3 lengths had separated the placed horses from the rest, we were only interested in obtaining a figure for the first three. This we did by splitting 5 lbs between the first, second and third with a 7 lbs deduction for the rest. This includes the favourite, Luan Casca, who appears to have run a good 9 lbs below its best figure.

Race 679	*8.15 Windsor*	*6 furlongs*			*Good*	*May 17th*		*(8.9=32)*
577	Premier Lass (+10) (Disq. Placed 2nd)	3	8	13	36	–	36	7–1
442	In Slips (Awarded race)	3	8	5	28	1½	26	5–1
483	Pete Rocket	3	8	6	29	¾	25	14–1
(368)	Northorpe	3	8	9	32	3	25	6–1
526	Parabems	3	8	3	26	Neck	19	7–1
(577)	Another Way	3	8	5	28	1	21	50–1

Analysis: Even with a 10 lbs penalty, Premier Lass was not out of this. With a form figure of 33 from Race 577 and a rating of 36 to run up to here, she did not have to show much improvement, especially with Steve Dawson claiming 5 lbs. The danger was In Slips, rated here at 28 with a form figure of 26 from Race 442. The rest were either "unknown" to us or, like Pete Rocket and Parabems, seemed to have too much to do. Premier Lass made all the running and finished first by 1½ lengths from In Slips.

A very good result for the form book but, unfortunately for the backers of Premier Lass, she was subsequently disqualified for "taking the second's ground" and placed second. For rating purposes we take the original result as it stands but use our discretion for the 1½ lengths beating. We assume that Premier Lass had improved slightly since Race 577 and had run to her new figure. We allow In Slips 2 lbs for the controversial 1½ lengths. The rest are in line with the distances involved and we note that Pete Rocket and Parabems look about right.

Race 684	*3.30 Wolverhampton*	*5 furlongs*			*Good–Firm*	*May 17th*		*(10.0=35)*
523	Bri Eden	8	9	9	30	–	31	12–1
483	Colonial Line	4	8	3	10	Neck	10	4–1
329	Miss Import	4	9	6	27	Neck	26	9–1
301	Curzon House	5	7	8	1	1	0	10–1
(398)	Powerscourt	5	8	9	16	2½	(9)	20–1
553	Mercy Cure	4	8	1	20	3	(13)	12–1

Analysis: On our pre-race figures there was little to choose between half-a-dozen horses including Bri Eden who was (+2) on his form in Races 301 and 523 but (−3) if we went back as far as Race 100. As discussed under Race 673 there is often the question of how far back to go for a horse's figure.

Bri Eden had been dropped 4 lbs (34 to 30) by the official handicapper and since our figures showed the same we were at least in good company! One has to accept that a horse can always do an "action replay" but it must be a matter for the individual to judge. Such factors as the going, distance, jockey, type of track and so on can influence ones view of a race. If it was all clear-cut the game would be too easy!

Sufficient to say that Bri Eden won at 12–1 from our actual "best-in" Colonial Line, with Miss Import a neck away third. There did not look much wrong with the form and we take the second to have run to its rating and adjust the rest from him.

Race 692	*4.45 Wolverhampton*	*5 furlongs*			*Firm*	*May 18th*	*(9.0=37)*	
581	Countach (+7)	3	8	12	35	–	35	6–5
375	Bonne Baiser	3	9	1	38	Neck	37	9–2
497	Dragunn	3	9	0	37	1	33	5–1
475	Avonmore Wind	3	9	7	44	1	37	7–1
511 (581)	Athersmith	3	7	11	20	1½	(10)	20–1
581	Fast Service	3	8	6	29	7	(19)	12–1

Analysis: This business of how far to go back for a horse's figure is getting monotonous! Do we take Bonne Baiser's figure of 34 from Race 375 to be its true merit or the 41 from Race 144?

As Race 144 was run on heavy going, Race 375 on firm going and here we are at sunny Wolverhampton once more on firm going, one feels that we ought to take the figure made on similar going to be the one. As if that wasn't enough to worry about, what do we do about Athersmith? Who, dear reader, you will recall set up a figure of 24 in Race 511. But – and it is a big but – in that race she was carrying no less than 11 lbs overweight and we have already voiced our doubts about that. Our advice is – don't believe it until it is confirmed.

If we ignore Athersmith our ratings gave chances to Bonne Baiser, Dragunn and Countach and they finished second, third and first. We give full credit to Countach for the win under a penalty and leave his rating unchanged at 35 and in adjusting the rest, we note that Dragunn is about right compared to the form shown in Race 497. Athersmith goes down to 10 which is almost certainly nearer her true racing ability.

Race 698	4.30 Redcar	5 furlongs			Firm	May 18th		(9.4=37)
497	Erroll's Boy	3	9	4	37	–	41	2–9
	Firespark	3	8	1	20	1½	20	33–1
581	Ultrasonic	3	8	0	19	¾	17	8–1
(506)	Ben Jarrow (+7)	3	9	3	36	1½	30	5–1

Analysis: Erroll's Boy was rightly hot favourite for this and if we accept that he has run to his figure from Race 497, then Ultrasonic comes out at 17, exactly the same as in Race 581.

Race 711	2.0 Goodwood	6 furlongs			Good–Firm	May 20th		(10.0=50)
(424)	Bracadale	4	9	8	44	–	46	8–1
424	Old Dominion	5	10	0	50	¾	50	4–1
553	Piencourt (+4)	4	9	3	39	1½	35	9–2
566	General Wade	7	9	1	37	3	(30)	7–2
(195)	Royal Diplomat	5	7	10	18	2½	(11)	8–1
	Vernham Street	4	8	2	24	1	(17)	8–1

Analysis: General Wade confirmed that he is not the most reliable yardstick on the turf. On his running in Race 566 he had every chance of winning this race from the well treated Old Dominion and Piencourt but, although his loyal supporters made him favourite the "General" joined the lower ranks and finished fourth, just over 5 lengths behind the winner. Bracadale had been seventh of eight behind Camisite in Race 424 but, on the same handicap mark here, albeit reduced 7 lbs by the "claimer" S. Dennison, he was ridden out to beat Old Dominion by ¾ length. We considered that Old Dominion, based on his running in Race 323, had probably run to his official rating of 50 and we handicap round him. By doing so Piencourt seemed correct whilst Bracadale had probably improved a couple of pounds.

Race 732	8.20 Ripon	6 furlongs			Firm	May 19th		(9.0=38)
588	Cree Song	6	9	4	42	–	43	7–2
(450)	Polly's Brother	4	8	12	36	Short head	36	2–1
419 (566)	Little Atom	5	7	7	17	¾	15	13–2
645	Willie Gan (+8)	4	8	2	26	3	(19)	5–2
(566)	Karen's Star	5	8	0	24	3	(17)	20–1
	City's Sister	4	7	8	18	Head	(11)	25–1

Analysis: On our figures, Cree Song (+2), Little Atom (+2) and Willie Gan (+3) had this between them and, apart from the intervention of Polly's Brother who was unrated with us, that is how they finished. Any adjustment is quite straightforward.

We take Polly's Brother, who was probably fitter now than in Race 450, to be the key horse and calculate accordingly. Willie Gan comes out a bit below his 645 figure but we have to accept that.

Race 742 *7.35 Hamilton Park* *5 furlongs* *Good–Firm* *May 21st* (8.2=14)

	Kaimlaw	8	8	13	25	–	29	16–1
404 (671)	Mary Maguire	5	8	2	14	¾	16	7–1
523	Tree Fella	6	8	5	17	1½	16	4–1
523	Go Total	6	10	0	40	½	38	11–8
458 (622)	Russian Winter	7	9	2	28	½	25	8–1
(226)	French Touch	5	7	11	9	¾	5	20–1

Analysis: The result of this race illustrates how easily one can be mis-led by so-called collateral form. Go Total ran second to Susarma at Chester (Race 523) and they had form figures of 61 and 41 respectively. Susarma came out five days later to win with a penalty of 10 lbs to record a new figure of 71, an improvement of 10 lbs. Do we then put Go Total up 10 lbs also? No, we do not!

To assume improved form on the part of one horse because it has run well against an animal which appears to have improved is illogical and can be very costly. Go Total's running in Race 523 was absolutely in line with his performances in Race 329, whereas Susarma's win in Race 588 was well beyond anything he had done before. The two situations were not at all the same and to think about Go Total in terms of a 10 lbs improvement would court financial disaster.

Students of form should judge a horse upon the general level of its form and not come to exaggerated conclusions on the evidence of one race. This applies to winners as well as losers and even in Susarma's case, although the arithmetic compelled us to put him up 10 lbs we would still look for confirmation of the figure. To return to Race 742 we would be reluctant to accept too much improvement from an 8yo and we split 8 lbs for the cumulative distances, putting Kaimlaw up 4 lbs which we are prepared to tolerate.

Race 752	2.15 Thirsk	5 furlongs			Firm	May 21st		(9.0=26)
684	Miss Import	4	9	1	27	–	29	7–1
671	Waresley	4	8	13	25	½	25	4–1
567	Rambling River	5	8	8	20	2½	16	11–2
622	Mel's Choice (+7)	4	8	2	14	2½	7	13–8
458	Bella Travaille (+4)	4	7	7	5	1	0	50–1
622	Caledonian	6	8	4	16	1½	(9)	10–1

Analysis: Rambling River's earlier performances had persuaded the handicapper to lower his rating from 26 to 20 just about the time that he showed a return to form in Race 567, where he ran a fine race to record a form figure of 26, a neck behind Northern Eclipse who was giving him 1 lb. In this race the latter had to concede 5 lbs to Rambling River so had the worst of it. Miss Import, after her initial run where we had overrated her, had since been running to a rating of between 24 and 26 so did not need to improve much to win this.

Mel's Choice, the 13–8 favourite, was set to do a figure only 1 lb better than in Race 622 which he had won in a canter.

In the race Miss Import caught Waresley near the line to win by ½ length with Rambling River plugging on for third place. Mel's Choice had drifted in the market, in stark contrast to his race at Beverley when he was backed to win a small fortune, and was eased when beaten inside the last furlong. Waresley had obviously benefitted from his first outing and we took his figure as being equivalent to his rating and revised the rest in keeping with their performances.

Race 769	4.0 Kempton Park	6 furlongs			Good	May 22nd		(9.0=51)
(497)	Diamond Cutter	3	8	13	50	–	54	16–1
577	Lindsey	3	8	5	42	Neck	45	11–2
(565)	Fidalco	3	7	7	30	1½	30	25–1
450	Cyril's Choice	3	9	2	53	3	48+	10–1
(663)	Blue Emmanuelle	3	7	12	35	½	29	9–1
541	Nawab	3	8	12	49	2	(42)	8–1

Analysis: On his running in Race 577 Lindsey was a really good bet. Set to do a rating of 42 with a form figure of 48 he looked marvellous value at 11–2 but, after making all the running, he was caught close home by Diamond Cutter who had finished seventh of ten behind Leekmore in Race 497. It was difficult to allocate figures that made sense with both Lindsey and Cyril's Choice who appeared to have run below form but we finally decided to split the difference between Lindsey's official rating of 42 and our form figure of 48 and set him at 45, using him as a guide to the rest. We were not happy with this but the handicapper put Lindsey up to 46 subsequently so we were not too far away. We also felt that Cyril's Choice was better than 48 and gave him a plus sign to remind us for the future.

Race 775	*7.0 Kempton Park*	*6 furlongs*			*Good*	*May 24th*	(4.9.5=58) (3.9.5=70)	
641	Gabitat (+7)	4	9	5	58	–	62	9–1
352 (577)	Worlingworth	3	7	13	50	1	51	16–1
641	Davenport Boy	6	8	6	45	½	44	3–1
(241)	Bless the Match	3	9	0	65	2½	58	8–1
641	Gambler's Dream	5	8	8	47	¾	40	14–1
	Hampton Bay	3	9	0	65	½	(58)	25–1

Analysis: In Race 641 Gabitat had given Davenport Boy 6 lbs and beaten him ¾ length. Here he gave the same horse 13 lbs and beat him 1½ lengths! Worlingworth decided to come back from the dead with a run only 1 lb below his best figure and Old Dominion, set to do 49 against a form figure of 50, was backed from 11–1 to 15–2 and finished seventh.

Such are the trials and tribulations of private handicappers!

We noticed that Davenport Boy and Gambler's Dream had reproduced their form in Race 641 and decided to use these two as sheet anchors to solve this puzzle. Old Dominion should have done better and he recovered his form – and his backers' money – to win at Bath (Race 1134) from a rating of 49.

Race 784	*4.0 Bath*	*5 furlongs and 167 yards*			*Firm*	*May 24th*	(10.0=37)	
671	Lord Wimpy (+7)	4	9	8	31	–	32	5–4
483	Byroc Boy (Disq)	5	8	5	14	Short-head	14	7–1
	Dewberry (Placed 2nd)	4	8	9	18	2½	13	14–1
(566)	St Terramar (Placed 3rd)	7	8	12	21	1½	15	11–1
	Musical Minx (Placed 4th)	4	8	11	20	Short-head	14	9–1
(534)	Disco	4	8	11	20	3	(13)	20–1

Analysis: Readers will remember that, in our comment on Race 483, we pointed out – after the race – that Byroc Boy was a good thing at 12–1. He won well that day and Colonial Line had done the form no harm with a close second to Bri Eden in Race 684 for a confirmatory figure of 10. Byroc Boy's form figure of 14 from Race 483 was the same as he was called upon to do here. The favourite, Lord Wimpy, had won a fair sort of race at Pontefract (Race 671) for a form figure of 26 but with a 7 lbs penalty he had to improve at least 5 lbs to win this. It was quite obvious – this time before the race – that, at 7–1 and the boy claiming 7 lbs, Byroc Boy was a marvellous each-way bet. And so he was! With a strong run in the last hundred yards he failed by the shortest of short heads to catch Lord Wimpy who had in fact improved enough to win. But disaster was to strike! In making his run, Byroc Boy came off a straight line and at the subsequent enquiry was disqualified and placed last. There are times when one begins to wonder if it is all worth it! But we must accept these things in a philosophical manner – at least the figures had worked out.

We took Byroc Boy as the key and the rest fell into place.

Race 786	*6.30 Edinburgh*	*5 furlongs*			*Good*	*May 24th*		(4.8.9=13) (3.8.9=23)
(339)	Brians Star	7	8	1	5	–	6	10–1
622	H R Micro (+6)	4	8	9	13	Neck	13?	13–8
567	Longlands Lady	4	7	13	3	2½	0	5–1
645	Carpenters Boy	4	7	10	0	½	0	20–1
567	Royal Question	3	7	8	8	½	0	5–1
	Another Rumbo	4	9	6	24	Short-head	(17)	14–1

Analysis: This was a very poor apprentice handicap but it was certainly not obvious why H R Micro, who had twice run to a figure of 9, was favourite at 13–8 to win it. With a 6 lbs penalty putting it on a rating of 13 she certainly had it all to do. Longlands Lady and Royal Question had made each other's acquaintance in Race 567 and the first named had the best of it today. It was hardly a race to bet on however and it was really no surprise when H R Micro was beaten. With strong reservations about the penalty we left H R Micro on the 13 mark, put Brians Star up 1 lb for the neck and knocked all the others off the scale except Another Rumbo who goes down to a bracketed 17.

Race 797	*4.15 Folkestone*	*6 furlongs*			*Good–Firm*		*May 24th* (8.9=37)	
679	Pete Rocket	3	7	13	27	–	37+	6–4
(634)	Friday Street	3	8	8	36	7	36	7–1
526 (577)	Shiny Hour	3	8	9	37	1½	34	4–1
	Balayer	3	7	8	22	1½	16	33–1
(473)	Clouded Vision	3	8	8	36	1	29	7–4
(295)	Pitrasi	3	7	12	26	2	(19)	20–1

Analysis: Pete Rocket had run well to finish close up third in a big field at Windsor a week before to set up a figure only a couple of pounds below that required to win this. However, an apprentice handicap at Folkestone is hardly a mortgage risking venture although the way Pete Rocket strolled home by 7 lengths one could have staked the deeds of Windsor Castle!

We have to give him full credit for this and, taking Shiny Hour's Race 526 figure as correct, we are compelled to put the winner up 10 lbs. With a 7 lbs penalty bringing him up to a rating of 36 Pete Rocket won again at Hamilton Park a couple of weeks later and confirmed our rating for this race.

Race 819	*3.0 Salisbury*	*6 furlongs*			*Good*	*May 25th*	(4.10.0=40) (3.10.0=52)	
(641)	Sanjarida	4	9	9	35	–	36	16–1
(679)	Leith Spring	3	8	6	30	Head	30	33–1
(641)	Jester's Boy	5	10	0	40	2½	33	14–1
641	Case History	4	8	2	14	2	7	11–10
711	Vernham Street	4	8	12	24	¾	17	4–1
622	Sailors Prayer	4	8	13	25	2½	(1)	11–2

Analysis: With all the doubts about Case History's figures due to the overweight carried in his last two races it was somewhat surprising to see him made an 11–10 chance to win this. Not that we ourselves had much to go on before the race. The few horses with a form figure all had plenty to do. Sanjarida had been out of the first six in Races 424 and 641, as a result of which his official rating had dropped down from 41 to 35. The gelding evidently appreciated this and as he had won over the course and distance about the same time the previous year he was not entirely one to discount. In addition he was partnered by that very good boy S. Dawson taking off another 5 lbs.

Nevertheless he had to be pushed out to beat the 3yo Leith Spring in receipt of 17 lbs but it was certainly an improved performance.

Case History did not have the best of runs to finish fourth and his jockey was subsequently fined £10 for alleged excessive use of whip. It was quite difficult to rate this race. In the end we had to accept that both Sanjarida and Leith Spring had run to their ratings and calculate to that. We would need confirmation of these figures.

Race 826	*3.15 Catterick Bdge*	*6 furlongs*			*Good–Firm*	*May 26th*	(9.7=46)	
(740)	Soba (+7)	3	8	5	30	–	40+	4–6
(624)	Calsong (+7)	3	7	11	22	4	24	11–1
240 (352)	Ritual Dance	3	9	3	42	½	42	5–1
234 (600)	Royal Revenge	3	9	7	46	3	(41)	11–2
(348)	Sovereign Royal (+2)	3	7	9	20	2½	(13)	33–1
(231)	Fandance	3	7	9	20	2	(13)	20–1

Analysis: Here we had Soba in a handicap for the first time. By her two easy wins at Thirsk and Hamilton it was already plain that she was a lot better than in her 2yo days, when *Timeform* had described her as "a fair sort, only plating class". Some plater!!

This race was difficult to rate properly. Ritual Dance had already run twice and the chances were that she was race-fit and had run to her rating of 42. We therefore elected to build the ratings round her figure.

Soba went up 10 lbs for her decisive win but there was no way of knowing whether that was the limit of her improvement. It is usually easier to be wise after the event!

Race 832	*3.0 Brighton*	*6 furlongs*			*Firm*	*May 26th*		(10.0=45)
323 (467)	Denmore	6	9	10	41	–	45	14–1
711	Bracadale	4	9	11	42	¾	44	10–11
	Chads Gamble	7	8	7	24	1½	23	12–1
323 (467)	Kassak	6	8	11	28	2½	22	8–1
641	Vorvados	5	9	9	40	1½	33	5–1
784	Byroc Boy	5	7	11	14	3	(7)	8–1

Analysis: Bracadale's performance in Race 711 ensured that he started a short priced favourite but he failed by just under a length to run to his form figure of 46. Byroc Boy was on the same handicap mark as in Race 784 but was meeting better class this time. In Race 784 he had been set to carry 8.0 in the original weights published in the *Racing Calendar* whereas in this race his original assessment had been 7.2 and one is entitled to assume that this later race is the best part of a stone higher in class, since it is obvious that the higher the class the lower the horse's weight.

To decide the form figures here we split the difference between Bracadale's official rating of 42 and our form figure of 46 and enter him at 44, using this as our guide line. Kassak's figure was in line with his "rough" estimate in Race 323 whilst Vorvados was confirmed as running about 7 lbs below his official rating. (See Race 641.)

Race 839	*3.30 Brighton*	*5 furlongs*			*Good–Firm*		*May 27th*	(8.12=35)
692	Countach	3	8	12	35	–	37	Evens
541 (739)	Rhinestone Cowboy	3	8	4	27	3	22	7–2
350 (781)	Blue Sapphire	3	7	7	16	¾	8	9–2
(473)	Stick in the Mud	3	8	7	30	5	(20)	10–1
679	Another Way	3	8	5	28	1½	(18)	9–1

Analysis: Only five runners and Countach's handicap form was superior to anything else in this race. He was an easy 3 lengths winner from Rhinestone Cowboy. The latter had been lowered in the ratings by the handicapper after finishing well behind in Race 541. Countach won 692 under a penalty and we could assume that he had improved. Blue Sapphire had not been too far behind in Race 350 for a "bracketed" rating of 8 but the form was not reliable. To assess the value of Countach's win we split 10 lbs for the 3¾ lengths between the winner and third which meant Countach going up to 37. Reference to Race 1263 shows that the handicapper put him up to 39 but he did not win. It is, of course, only possible to make these comparisons some considerable time after the event, but we do so to enable the reader to compare our decisions against those of the official handicapper.

Race 843	*2.45 Carlisle*	*6 furlongs*			*Firm*	*May 27th*		(8.9=22)
398 (684)	Crowebronze	4	7	9	8	–	11	5–1
(501)	Amanda Mary	4	7	7	6	Short-head	8	20–1
(501)	Holdall	4	8	9	22	1½	20	10–1
139	Island Walk	4	8	1	14	½	11	5–2
	Record Breaker	6	7	7	6	½	3	16–1
567	Scottish Agent	6	7	13	12	¾	8	6–1

Analysis: Carrying 4 lbs overweight Crowebronze had put up a form figure of 8 in Race 398 but it could hardly be termed a first-class pointer. Island Walk had won a similar race in very soft going at Hamilton Park (Race 139) but we had no idea how she would fare on the firm going here. According to that invaluable publication *Raceform Notebook* she did not in fact relish the ground and never got into the race. Whether or not this was so we had to take the running as it stood and split 6 lbs for the 2 lengths and a short head between the first four.

Crowebronze goes up 3 lbs, Island Walk down 3 lbs and all the rest in harmony with those amendments.

Race 855	*7.10 Ayr*	*6 furlongs*	*Good*			*May 28th*		(4.8.8=35) (3.8.8=47)	
732	Polly's Brother		4	8	8	35	–	37	4–6
174	Friendly Fun		7	8	8	35	1½	33	8–1
742	Tree Fella		5	7	10	23	Neck	20(?)	13–2
442	Bloemfontein (+6)		3	7	7	32	4	(25)	11–1
404	Primula Boy		7	9	9	50	½	(43)	14–1
732	Willie Gan (+4)		4	7	11	24	1	(17)	9–2

Analysis: This was virtually a one-horse race duly reflected in the market. At 4–6 Polly's Brother was not perhaps an attractive price but she had an undeniable chance on her form figure from Race 732.

In our analysis of that particular race we had remarked that we had to accept Willie Gan's below par performance as one of those things. At Ripon, Polly's Brother had given Willie Gan 10 lbs and finished 3¾ lengths in front of him. Today, Willie was in receipt of only 1 lb more so his chances were not bright. On our figures it seemed that Tree Fella was a few pounds overrated by the handicapper so to rate this race we took a point mid-way between his official rating of 23 and our form figure from Race 742 giving him a somewhat tentative rating of 20. We note that the resultant figures for the first two are not so far removed from their form figures obtained in earlier races and settle for that.

Race 863	*1.15 Ayr*	*5 furlongs*	*Good–Firm*				*May 29th*	(4.11.0=41)* (3.11.0=51)*	
742	Russian Winter		7	10	1	28	–	30	9–2
769	Cyril's Choice		3	11	2	53	1½	51	7–2
684	Bri Eden (+7)		8	10	10	37	4	30	5–1
742	Mary Maguire (+6)		5	9	13	26	½	18	5–1
	Music Night		5	9	9	22	1	(13)	16–1
742	Kaimlaw (+7)		8	10	5	32	2	(22)	9–2

* Higher weight scale for an amateur race.

Analysis: Our pre-race ratings gave Russian Winter (−1 from Race 458) and Cyril's Choice (+1 from Race 450) clear of the rest and they finished first and second in that order. If we apply the usual rule and split 4 lbs as an allowance for the 1½ lengths between them, we note that Bri Eden and Mary Maguire are within tolerable limits of their previous figures. Kaimlaw seems to be well below his figure from Race 742 but this was an amateurs race and we must not expect everything to add up precisely. Readers will recall however that we were reluctant to expect too much improvement from an 8yo and Kaimlaw's performance here, notwithstanding any allowance one makes for the type of race, seems to show that our prudence was justified.

Race 871	*4.30 Haydock Park*	*6 furlongs*		*Good–Firm*	*May 28th*		(8.13=41)
475	Town Flier	3	8 13	41	–	45	4–1
234	Nagalia	3	8 6	34	3	34	11–1
600	Roman Quest	3		41	1	37	13–2
234	Knight Security	3	8 5	33	Neck	28	4–1
673	Central Carpets (+7)	3	7 7	21	Neck	15	12–1
600	Swinging Baby	3	8 3	31	½	24	2–1

Analysis: Swinging Baby's best figure was established in Race 350 when her rating was "inflated" by a 7 lbs penalty and we had put in a cautionary word about taking the figure for gospel. More to the point however, she had not run anywhere near that figure in Race 600. It is, of course, quite possible that she is better suited to 5 furlongs than 6. Town Flier's (−2) from 352 (a form figure of 43 as against his present rating of 41) looked infinitely more reliable than Nagalia's figure from Race 234, obtained after deducting the "doubtful seven". At 4–1 Town Flier was good value although Central Carpets could also be fancied on his Pontefract win in Race 673 which made him (−1) here. Town Flier was always up with the leaders and ran on strongly to beat Nagalia by 3 lengths. Central Carpets could never go the pace but ran quite well to finish fifth, about 4½ lengths behind the winner. The 4 lengths between the winner and third was worth about 8 lbs, split equally (plus 4 and minus 4) between them with Nagalia staying on the same mark as her official rating. With the rest close up, the amendments to their figures were simple.

Race 884	5.0 Lingfield Park	6 furlongs			Good–Firm	May 28th	(4.9.0=26) (3.9.0=38)	
679	Premier Lass	3	9	1	39	–	42	15–8
610	Red Ellette	3	7	12	22	1	22	5–1
(611)	Och Aye (+3)	4	8	2	14	Neck	13	10–1
(739)	Love Me Do	3	7	13	23	1	19	9–1
541	Welwyn	3	9	5	43	Head	38	5–2
797	Clouded Vision	3	8	12	36	1	29	10–1

Analysis: Welwyn's neck win in Race 541 had seemed good value for a form figure of 44 and with an official rating of 43 here looked to have a favourite's chance. According to *Raceform Notebook* she "ran a fine race. . . . before the concession of weight proved the problem". Alas, we do not agree with the first part of that statement. By our figures she had run well below her form figure and the filly herself proved the point by running to a rating of 43 in Race 1117 and even to a rating of 46 in Race 1601. However, the point about the weight may have been valid. Welwyn is a robust sort of filly but 9.7 here was a different kettle of fish from the 8.1 she had carried in Race 541. This was undoubtedly a lower-class race but 20 lbs is a lot of extra to carry. Red Ellette, set to do the same as her figure in Race 610 and Premier Lass, somewhat unlucky loser of Race 679 didn't have to improve much to win this and so it proved.

Red Ellette had run a fine race however and we were reasonably confident that she had run to her rating. Leaving her unchanged we rated the rest accordingly. Clouded Vision came out precisely the same figure as in Race 797 and seemed overweighted by the handicapper. It is interesting to note that Clouded Vision subsequently won a 6 furlong maiden event in June, giving a 4 lbs beating to Blue Cloud whom we had rated at 24 in Race 1506. Thus, Clouded Vision came out as a "28" – practically the same as here.

Race 898	2.30 Doncaster	6 furlongs			Good–Firm	May 29th	(10.0=57)	
424 (658)	Camisite	4	8	13	42	–	42	13–8
467	Amorous	4	8	1	30	2	25	11–2
	First Movement	4	9	11	54	¾	48	6–1
732	Cree Song (+5)	6	9	4	47	1	40	11–4
(450)	Song Minstrel	4	7	10	25	2	18	6–1
(588)	Bold Scuffle	4	8	11	40	10	30?	9–1

Analysis: Camisite had only to go down and come back! Early birds got 2–1 about the colt who finished up at 13–8 and they were to be congratulated upon their perspicacity for he had only to reproduce his running in Race 424 to win this. Cree Song (+4) and Amorous (+5) were the only dangers of those who had run this season. Camisite, carrying 9.11, had been beaten into third place in a 7 furlong handicap at Newmarket but this 6 furlongs was more his trip. Despite what many racegoers say – there are these good things in handicaps and they very often win. In assessing this race the first two were left at their existing form figures from previous races and the beaten horses formed a queue for their adjustments as shown.

Race 915 *3.0 Chepstow* *6 furlongs* *Hard* *June 1st* (9.0=50)

(781)	Princess Virginia	3	7	13	35	–	37	11–2
775	Worlingworth	3	8	12	48	½	48	9–2
(541)	Never so Lucky	3	8	13	49	Short-head	48	7–1
(792)	Mummy's Pleasure (+7)	3	9	2	52	1½	48	5–2
663	Welsh Partner	3	9	7	57	7	(50)	2–1
(781)	Jury Palace	3	7	7	29	6	(22)	50–1

Analysis: We had a current form figure for only two of the six runners, our old "friend" Worlingworth and Welsh Partner. On his running in Race 775 Worlingworth was −3 and easily the best of the two. The race, however, went to Princess Virginia who held on well to beat our "best-in" by ½ length. In view of the close finish we split 6 lbs between the first four as shown. Worlingworth came out the same as his official rating which lends credence to it all.

Just to digress a little, we later saw Worlingworth hold on for a very gallant victory in the Sandown mile during the U.S.A. v Great Britain jockeys' match in October, 1982, as a result of which we take back all we have ever said or implied about him!

Race 930 *4.30 Leicester* *6 furlongs* *Firm* *June 1st* (4.9.0=26) (3.9.0=37)

645 (843)	Bettabet Geraghty	4	8	4	16	–	18	10–1
56 (323)	Lord Scrap	6	8	1	13	2½	9	11–4
832	Kassak	6	9	2	28	¾	22	10–1
843	Scottish Agent	6	7	12	10	½	2	10–1
134 (327)	Derring Prince (+3)	4	7	10	8	Neck	0	16–1
	Royal Trouper	3	8	12	35	Neck	27	25–1

Analysis: We have to go back to Race 187, run in April, to find Scottish Agent's best form figure of 16 and he had twice since run well below that figure so his chances did not exactly inspire confidence. Bettabet Geraghty's figure from Race 645 was fairly reliable as we knew that Welsh Noble's figure worked out well in that race. At +3 Bettabet Geraghty was, in fact, second best-in.

It was a very moderate event and Bettabet Geraghty won quite easily by 2½ lengths from Lord Scrap who was +5 from race 56. Kassak is no flying machine but seems to give his running most times so we put him in at his normal form figure of 22 and rated the rest in line with that.

Race 933	*2.45 Redcar*	*6 furlongs*		*Firm*		*May 31st*		(4.9.7=48) (3.9.7=60)
898	Song Minstrel	4	7	12	25	–	28	10–1
600	Boatrocker	3	8	2	41	1	42	4–5
711	General Wade	7	8	10	37	1	36	11–4
	Cudgel	9	9	7	48	½	45	11–1
187	Renovate	5	8	4	31	2	25	5–1
(501)	Rehoboam	4	7	7	20	2	13	33–1

Analysis: Song Minstrel's race at Doncaster (Race 898) had certainly done him the world of good for here he was, only two days later, improving about 10 lbs on his earlier run. On all rated form Boatrocker and General Wade had the best chances but the best they could do was finish second and third to the comfortable winner.

Sharing 6 lbs for the 2½ lengths between the first four seemed reasonable especially as Boatrocker and General Wade came out almost spot on with existing ratings.

Race 940	*3.15 Redcar*	*5 furlongs*		*Firm*		*June 1st*		(9.0=28)
684	Mercy Cure	6	8	5	19	–	23	13–1
752	Waresley	4	8	11	25	1½	25	6–4
	Tobermory Boy	5	9	12	40	Neck	39	20–1
458	Miss Poinciana	5	9	11	39	¾	36	5–2
863	Russian Winter (+7)	7	9	7	35	1	30	5–1
567 (752)	Northern Eclipse	5	8	12	26	2½	(19)	20–1

Analysis: One could have expected a better performance from Northern Eclipse who was here rated at −2 from Race 567 but he may not have been in racing mood that day and he tried to savage another horse after passing the post. Mercy Cure was second best-in at −1 on her race at Warwick in May (Race 483) but since that race had twice run below that figure. However, she "came good" again here and won quite nicely after having been up with the leaders all the way.

Waresley's rating from Race 752 looked reliable and it was satisfying to see that working to his figure put Miss Poinciana and Russian Winter almost exactly in line with their previous ratings.

Race 951	*2.30 Sandown Park*	*5 furlongs*			*Good–Firm*	*June 1st*	*(9.0=51)*	
692	Avonmore Wind	3	8	2	39	–	42	8–1
(541)	Alev	3	8	2	39	Head	41	20–1
541	Sylvan Barbarosa	3	9	0	51	½	51	9–4
(769)	Special Pleasure	3	9	7	58	4	51	8–1
(541)	Ghawar	3	8	2	39	2½	(32)	14–1
692	Fast Service	3	7	7	30	2	(23)	20–1

Analysis: Sylvan Barbarosa (−1), Avonmore Wind (+2), Leekmore (+3) and Fast Service (+5) were top of the figures here and they finished third, first, unplaced and sixth. Avonmore Wind's form did not look very brilliant but his form figure of 37 looked very well established and slight improvement would put him in with a chance. He had, in fact, been given a chance by the handicapper for he was here set at 39 whereas he had been rated at 45 in his previous races. Ridden for the first time by the dynamic American Steve Cauthen he had it all to do from the furlong marker but, strongly ridden by Cauthen, he got up on the line to win by a head.

We can safely leave Sylvan Barbarosa on 51 here and rating the race was no problem.

Race 987	*2.0 Epsom*	*5 furlongs*			*Firm*	*June 4th*		*(10.0=55)*
659	Steel Charger	5	9	2	43	–	48	5–1
481	Pontin Lad	4	10	0	55	Neck	59	4–1
553 (775)	Ferryman	6	9	6	47	3	44	10–1
588	Dutch Girl	5	8	3	30	Short-head	26	6–1
863	Bri Eden	8	8	4	31	Short-head	26	5–1
	Sandra's Secret	5	9	1	42	3	(35)	20–1

Analysis: We were on Pontin Lad to win this race with a rating of −2 from Race 481. Meeting Steel Charger on 12 lbs better terms for about 3 lengths seemed enough to reverse the placings although there was not going to be much in it. We had Steel Charger at +1 together with Bri Eden. Manilow, who had run well against Steel Charger in Race 659 was rated at −1 and was also to be considered. We were on our way to draw the winnings as Pontin Lad took the lead soon after half-way but, unfortunately for us, Piggott was at his brilliant best on Steel Charger and he took over close to home to win by a neck. To sort this out we split 10 lbs between the first five horses as shown. The front two went up a few pounds whilst Dutch Girl came in at her Race 588 figure. Bri Eden seemed a little outpaced on this fast track and ran a bit below par as did Manilow.

Race 997	*4.05 Epsom*	*6 furlongs*			*Firm*	*June 5th*		(10.0=49)
784 (980)	Lord Wimpy	4	8	11	32	–	34	4–1
711 (775)	Old Dominion	5	10	0	49	½	49	6–1
855	Tree Fella	5	8	2	23	¾	21	14–1
898	Amorous	4	8	9	30	Neck	27	4–1
832	Denmore (+7)	6	9	13	48	Head	44	5–1
930	Lord Scrap	6	7	7	14	Short-head	9	6–1

Analysis: Old Dominion (−1) and Lord Wimpy (−) were best in here. In finishing first and second in the reverse order they nevertheless upheld the ratings and we could be sure that any amendments using these two horses would not be far off the mark. Old Dominion is a consistent sort and by assuming that the handicapper had his measure on a rating of 49 we could make such other adjustments as were necessary.

Race 1001	*3.15 Carlisle*	*5 furlongs*			*Firm*	*June 3rd*		(10.0=31)
752	Caledonian	6	8	13	16	–	21	6–1
752	Bella Travaille	4	7	12	1	1	3	10–1
139 (567)	Bracken Gill	4	8	0	3	½	3	33–1
863	Kaimlaw (+7)	8	10	1	32	1	29	10–1
786	Brian's Star	7	8	2	5	1½	0	11–4
786	Longlands Lady	4	8	4	7	½	0	4–1

Analysis: This was a very poor race. Caledonian (−) had only to do the same figure as in Race 622 to win this race and he did! We actually had Longlands

Lady (−2) and Brian's Star (−1) best off at the weights but it really did look the sort of race to leave alone. With horses practically zero-rated one is not dealing with the aristocracy of the equine world and almost anything could happen. To rate this race after the result we took Bracken Gill as the "key". He had chased the leaders all the way and had probably run to his lowly rating. We had no confidence that we were right!

Race 1010	*4.15 Catterick Bdge*	*5 furlongs*			*Firm*	*June 4th*		**(8.6=24)**
622 (781)	Cree Bay	3	7	9	13	–	20+	14–1
(679)	Haverhill Lass	3	8	4	22	3	22	8–1
581	St Crespin Bay	3	8	6	24	¾	22	3–1
(618)	Waltham Terrace	3	7	13	17	Neck	14	20–1
511 (581)	My Fancy	3	8	11	29	Head	25	8–1
(501)	Remodel	3	7	9	13	¾	8	14–1

Analysis: In our analysis of Race 511 we stated that we took My Fancy's official rating of 31 as being correct. The handicapper had not the same confidence in himself and marked the filly down to 29 for this race. If we were right she had a chance here but neither she nor anything else ever looked like beating Cree Bay, who won by an easy 3 lengths. My Fancy ran on well from half-way and after the race went round again before her jockey got the brakes to work! She went backwards after this and her running in Race 511 was her best effort. We took St Crespin Bay as the lead here. He had run well without winning and to drop him by 2 lbs to coincide with his figure from Race 581 looked about right.

The rest were straightforward enough although we must admit that the 7 lbs plus for Cree Bay was no more than a guess.

Race 1028	*4.15 Haydock Park*	*6 furlongs*			*Firm*	*June 5th*		**(8.11=42)**
826	Ritual Dance	3	8	11	42	–	52+	9–2
871	Nagalia	3	8	3	34	6	34	4–1
871	Swinging Baby	3	7	9	26	¾	24	3–1
600 (838)	Strapless	3	8	9	40	¾	36	5–1
698	Firespark	3	7	7	24	1	18	10–1
	Central Carpets (+1)	3	7	8	25	Short-head	19	12–1

Analysis: With Ritual Dance and Nagalia both set to do the same as their latest form ratings it was difficult to choose between the two. Swinging Baby was favourite but there were some doubts about her ability to get the 6 furlongs on a galloping track like Haydock. In the race Ritual Dance surpassed herself and came home alone 6 lengths in front of Nagalia. To rate this race we took the view that Nagalia had seemed to come back to form on this course a week before and we therefore took her rating to be correct. This put the winner up 10 lbs but, as she never ran to that figure again, we probably overrated the performance. The handicapper was not so easily mis-led and put the filly up to 46 but, since he lowered Nagalia's rating by only 1 lb subsequently, one wonders whether Nagalia's connections would have taken on the winner again on only 5 lbs better terms for a 6 lengths thrashing. We doubt it!

Race 1030	*5.15 Haydock Park*	*5 furlongs*			*Firm*	*June 5th*		*(9.7=44)*
698	Errolls Boy	3	9	7	44	–	48	7–2
(646)	Hawks Nest	3	8	5	28	¾	30	15–2
475 (646)	Spanish Point	3	9	1	38	½	38	8–1
839	Countach	3	9	5	42	2	37	2–1
(256)	Mr. Gold Spur	3	7	7	16	1½	8	20–1
692	Dragunn	3	8	12	35	¾	26	7–1

Analysis: With Cool Wind not running to his earlier form, Dragunn (+2) and Errolls Boy (+3) were best in here and those punters who backed Countach down to favouritism with a 7 lbs penalty taking him up to a rating of 42 were showing optimism of the highest order.

In putting Errolls Boy up to a figure of 41 in Race 698 we had underestimated the value of that win for he is better than that. He was very confidently ridden here even though the winning margin was only ¾ length. Dragunn led for some way but faded to finish sixth. We were satisfied to accept that Countach had run to his form figure of 37 from Race 839, so set him on that figure and adjusted the rest round that. Note here that Spanish Point's rating had gone up considerably (see Race 475) following a convincing 1½ lengths win over Hawks Nest (received 3 lbs) is a maiden event at Newcastle in May.

Race 1064 *7.25 Hamilton Park* *5 furlongs* *Good–Firm* *June 8th* **(10.0=40)**

797 (889)	Pete Rocket	3	9	10	36	–	40	5–2
673 (811)	Magnamala	3	8	2	14	1	15	5–1
	Benfen	3	9	7	33	2½	29	4–1
(853)	Linpac Belle	3	8	10	22	1½	16	10–1
261 (450)	Here's Sue	3	9	7	33	Head	27	7–2
(927)	Letsgomo	3	8	4	16	1	9	5–1

Analysis: Pete Rocket duly confirmed our estimate of his win at Folkestone two weeks before but not without a spot of drama! Unseating his jockey on the way to the post, he bolted as far as the starting gate and then back again to the stands before he was caught. His pre-race adventure must have affected his performance here and Magnamala, who at (−2) was a big danger, got to within a length of the rapidly tiring winner before time ran out. To decide the form level here we took the average between Magnamala's handicap rating of 14 and our form figure of 16, called it 15, and calculated from that point.

Race 1065 *7.50 Hamilton Park* *6 furlongs* *Good–Firm* *June 8th* **(10.0=24)**

671	April Lucky	9	9	10	20	–	24	5–1
139 (658)	Mott the Hoople	4	9	7	17	1½	17	11–2
(282)	Star Heading	4	8	4	0	2½	0	25–1
523 (947)	The Huyton Girls	4	9	13	23	Head	17	12–1
863	Mary Maguire	5	9	3	13	¾	6	13–2
1001	Bracken Gill	4	8	7	3	¾	0	6–1

Analysis: Mary Maguire was best-in here at −5 but any confidence was somewhat tempered by the knowledge that the form figure had been established when carrying 6 lbs overweight in a "bumpers" race (863). On the other hand her previous form showed her to be fairly well treated. Danger threatened from April Lucky (−1) and Mott the Hoople (−1) and they were in fact first and second.

Mary Maguire ran well to the final furlong but made no progress from there. A disappointing run but she made amends by winning at Pontefract in July (Race 1498). Mott the Hoople had run a good race and his figure of 17 remained unchanged and served as the basis for the rest.

Race 1074	*4.45 Yarmouth*	*5 furlongs*			*Firm*	*June 8th*	(4.9.5=37) (3.9.5=46)	
659 (987)	Manilow	6	9	5	37	–	44+	5–2
523 (684)	Humble Blue	4	8	6	24	4	24	7–1
458	Balatina	4	7	11	15	Neck	14	4–1
940	Mercy Cure (+7)	6	8	6	24	10	(17)	10–3
375	Feather Sound	3	9	3	44	$1\frac{1}{2}$	(37)	3–1
	Dalegarth	4	10	0	46	5	(39)	14–1

Analysis: On our ratings this was due to be a desperately close affair with a difference of only 1 lb between five horses. One would not have thought so at the finish however, as the winner won by 4 lengths and a neck with the remainder of the field 10 lengths away. Manilow had disappointed his backers in Race 987 after a promising run in Race 659. Maybe he did not like Epsom but whatever the reason for his previous defeat he was superb here. Up and away like a flash he made all the running to win very easily. Humble Blue had been given a close race for second race by Balatina and had probably been "pushed" to his best figure as a consequence. Taking his rating as a guide made the first three appear on acceptable marks but we could not fathom why the also-rans had been ten lengths away!

Race 1092	*4.45 Beverley*	*5 furlongs*			*Good–Firm*	*June 10th*	(4.9.0=17) (3.9.0=26)	
1010	Cree Bay (+7)	3	8	8	20	–	23	8–1
1001	Bella Travaille	4	7	12	1	$1\frac{1}{2}$	0	10–1
339 (909)	El Presidente	4	9	1	18	$\frac{1}{2}$	15	10–1
398 (671)	Courageous Buzby	6	9	3	20	2	14	10–1
752	Rambling River	5	9	7	24	$\frac{1}{2}$	17	9–2
1001	Caledonian (+7)	6	9	6	23	$\frac{3}{4}$	16	9–2

Analysis: Our guess for Cree Bay in Race 1010 was not far out and with a penalty putting his rating on the 20 mark he was (−+) with us. Rambling River was (−2) on his performance in Race 567 but had run well below that since in Race 752. Courageous Buzby was another with a chance on his form figure from Race 398 but that was back in April. Little did we or anyone else know that Cree Bay was in the early stages of a magnificent run that was to win him six races out of seven, finishing on a rating of 40 and at 8–1 here he must have been a peach of a bet! Assessing the race seemed straightforward enough and we shared 6 lbs between the first three for the total of 2 lengths separating them.

Race 1095 *3.0 Newbury* *6 furlongs* *Good–Firm* *June 9th* (9.6=49)

600	Prevail	3	9	6	49	–	50	11–8
915	Princess Virginia (+7)	3	8	13	42	1	40	11–2
(541)	Cheri Berry	3	9	1	44	3	(37)	10–1
541	Silojoka	3	9	7	50	1½	(43)	4–1
871	Town Flier (+7)	3	9	5	48	2½	(41)	4–1
(781)	High Poppa	3	8	6	35	10	(28)	25–1

Analysis: On her running in Race 541 Silojoka had a fine chance of winning this race but after showing good speed for a long way she could find no extra and finished a well beaten fourth. Next time out (Race 1350) she relished the easier ground on a rating of 47 and put up a form figure some 6 lbs better than she did here. Such is the perversity of life! Her running here left us a bit non-plussed as to the correct approach for rating this race. After some thought we averaged the official handicap rating of Princess Virginia (42) and her most recent form figure (37), called her a "40" and hoped for the best. This meant that Prevail had improved about 5 lbs on his York figure but the colt had been well backed to win this and looked worth the increase.

It was some comfort to note that the handicapper had him on an official rating of 49 after this (see Race 2147) and to discover that we were on the right track without, however, knowing it at the time.

Race 1117 *4.25 Sandown Park* *5 furlongs* *Good* *June 12th* (8.10=43)

951	Alev	3	8	6	39	–	43	8–1
884	Welwyn	3	8	10	43	1½	43	8–1
(481)	Haditos	3	9	6	53	½	51	20–1
600	Ellerene	3	9	7	54	½	50	11–4
(769)	Tower Of Strength	3	8	0	33	Neck	28	8–1
(781)	Blue Cloud	3	7	7	26	Dead-heat	21	20–1

Analysis: Alev handsomely confirmed his 41 form figure from Race 951 with a good win here on a handicap mark of 39. He was thus (−2) with us and not a bad bet at 8–1. Ellerene was favourite and not without justification. He had twice run to form figures of 54 (Race 353) and 53 (Race 600) and was here on a handicap mark of 54. Spanish Point, who was out of the first six here, was in with a weight of 8.0 and, on the evidence of Race 1030, was very well handicapped since he had a handicap rating of 33 here, whereas he had apparently recorded a form figure of 38 in Race 1030. Unfortunately, he ran nowhere near that figure either here or any other time for the rest of the season. It is perhaps significant that the handicapper had seemingly had second thoughts about Spanish Point and the colt had been "demoted" 5 lbs in the ratings. This explains why he was on a rating of 38 in Race 1030 and on 33 here. We were convinced that Welwyn had run below form in Race 884 (see our analysis for that race) and decided to take the handicap rating of 43 as being at its correct level, especially as it fitted in with our own form figure in Race 541. With Welwyn as the basis we rated the race out as shown.

Race 1127	*3.0 York*	*6 furlongs*		*Good–Firm*	*June 12th*		(9.1=53)
663	Celestial Dancer (Disq)	3	8 12	50	–	54	11–4
863	Cyril's Choice (Placed 1st)	3	9 1	53	½	55	4–1
1095	Prevail (+7) (Placed 2nd)	3	8 13	51	½	51	9–2
769 (982)	Blue Emmanuelle (+7) (Placed 3rd)	3	8 4	42	½	40	13–2
663	On Return (Placed 4th)	3	9 5	57	4	(50)	7–1
871 (1013)	Roman Quest	3	8 3	41	6	(34)	20–1

Analysis: If ever there was an unlucky loser it was Celestial Dancer here. Likely to improve after his initial outing in Race 663, where he had set a form figure of 52, he looked a good favourite on a handicap mark of 50. Always going well his rider forced his way through to win but in going for a gap that closed on him was a certainty to lose the race in the enquiry that followed. There is no doubt he was the best horse on the day. Prevail was in good form having won two races and it seemed likely that he had run to his rating of 51 which included a 7 lbs penalty. The ratings were calculated from Prevail's figure with the fifth and sixth losing 7 lbs. Blue Emmanuelle's amended figure was well in advance of his Race 769 rating but he had won a useful handicap over 7 furlongs at Epsom earlier in June and had improved. He later confirmed this by going on to win two more handicaps over that distance.

Race 1134	3.45 Bath	5½ furlongs			Firm	June 12th		(9.3=49)
997	Old Dominion	5	9	3	49	–	49	5–4
(1044)	Durandal (+1)	5	7	13	31	1	28	16–1
819	Sailor's Prayer	4	7	7	25	1	19	15–2
(329)	Epsom Imp	9	8	13	45	1	36	14–1
784	Dewberry (+1)	4	7	8	26	½	16	6–1
832	Byroc Boy (+10)	5	7	7	25	Head	15	14–1

Analysis: We remarked upon Old Dominion's consistency in our analysis following Race 997, and those fortunate punters who got the early 5–2 about an eventual 5–4 chance were helping themselves to a good thing set to do no more than he had already done on three occasions in Races 323, 711 and 997. It was no "push-over" however and Durandal, showing considerable improvement on earlier form, gave the favourite a good race until the last hundred yards. We saw no reason at all to alter Old Dominion's established rating and revised his victims in due proportion as shown.

Race 1138	6.40 Carlisle	6 furlongs			Firm	June 12th		(9.0=38)
673	Cedrella	3	7	13	23	–	24	12–1
698 (740)	Ben Jarrow	3	8	1	25	¾	25	9–1
(747)	Western Hero	3	8	5	29	1½	27	20–1
855	Bloemfontein	3	8	3	27	1½	22	11–2
679	In Slips	3	8	8	32	Head	26	6–4
(747)	Majestic Tower	3	8	2	26	2	(16)	14–1

Analysis: We could have no real confidence in our pre-race ratings here, yet the two top-rated finished first and second albeit the wrong way round! Ben Jarrow had a form figure of 30 from Race 698 and, handicapped at 25 here, was thus (−5), whilst Cedrella's form figure from Race 673 was a very doubtful (22) and being set to do 23 in this race was therefore (+1). In our opinion, however, there was absolutely no justification for In Slips being a short priced favourite. He had twice obtained a form figure of 26 and was now set to do at least 6 lbs better than that. And, apart from our ratings, he had failed to beat Bloemfontein in Race 442 and was now only 3 lbs better off for 1½ lengths, so if In Slips was a 6–4 chance then Bloemfontein must have had better prospects than shown by its starting price of 11–2. In the event Bloemfontein finished fourth, a head in front of In Slips thus confirming exactly the form shown in Race 442. There are times when we wonder what form book the punters read! The standard here was not good and to re-rate these we allowed 7 lbs for the just under 4 lengths between the first four, but used Ben Jarrow's official rating of 25 as "par" for the course. We were not complacent enough to accept that our Race 698 form figure for Ben Jarrow was the correct one since it had been "uplifted" by a 7 lbs penalty and we would have liked confirmation of any apparent improvement.

Race 1145	*7.45 Leicester*	*6 furlongs*			*Good–Soft*		*June 12th* (10.0=59)	
997	Amorous	4	7	13	30	–	34	11–4
1074	Humble Blue	4	7	7	24	2	24	9–2
898	Bold Scuffle	4	8	9	40	1½	38	12–1
832	Bracadale	4	8	13	44	2	40	3–1
467 (775)	Sparkling Boy	5	9	12	57	½	52	7–2
1065	April Lucky (+6)	9	7	9	26	1½	19	9–1

Analysis: On the face of it the form figures of Amorous (25, 25 and 27) did not look good enough to win this race from a handicap mark of 30 but win it he did and was also favourite to do so! Perhaps the softish going helped him but it certainly put paid to the chances of Bracadale. With a form figure of 46 from Race 711 and set to do 44 by the handicapper, Bracadale seemed to have a fine chance. In the race, however, he was never going well at any stage. His subsequent form proved him to be a better horse on firm going, notably in the Goodwood Stewards Cup (Race 1926), where he ran a good second to the brilliant Soba for a form figure of 46.

Humble Blue had been the subject of a hefty sort of gamble here and had run a good race. We therefore took his handicap rating as the key. This tied up with his performance in Race 1074 and looked reliable.

Race 1159	*3.30 Nottingham*	*6 furlongs*			*Firm*	*June 14th*	(4.9.0=30) (3.9.0=41)	
566	Broon's Secret	8	9	9	39	–	41	8–1
997	Lord Scrap	6	7	11	13	Neck	14	5–1
933	Renovate	5	9	1	31	Head	31	14–1
933	General Wade	7	9	6	36	1	33	5–2
679 (862)	Northorpe (+7)	3	8	3	30	Head	26	13–2
1092	Courageous Buzby	6	8	4	20	2	14	13–2

Analysis: Broon's Secret, General Wade and Crowebronze were all set to do the same as their previous form figures here and of the three General Wade was the one most favoured by punters, being backed down from 5–1 to 5–2 favourite. Yet here was Broon's Secret with his usual boy claiming 7 lbs and three times a course and distance winner generously priced at 8–1! Granted he had not run for about five weeks but there was no excuse for this!

In a finish of inches one can take the handicap ratings to be near enough and we took the third horse Renovate as the guide.

Lord Scrap had improved on previous form figures and duly confirmed this with a very well backed win at Brighton two weeks later (Race 1430).

Race 1167	*8.35 Windsor*	*6 furlongs*			*Good–Firm*		*June 14th*	(9.0=41)
(760)	Tamdown Flyer	4	9	0	30	–	34	9–4
819	Sanjarida	4	9	9	39	1½	40	9–2
107 (551)	Dawns Delight	4	9	5	35	2	32	16–1
819	Vernham Street	4	8	4	20	Neck	16	10–1
671	Stern	6	8	0	16	¾	11	25–1
(192)	Graceful Boy	7	7	7	9	3	(2)	25–1

Analysis: In a nineteen runner handicap our top-rated horses occupied four of the first five places but they did not, unfortunately, include the winner! Tamdown Flyer had excellent 7 furlong form and in a non-handicap event at Thirsk in April he had proved himself about 9 lbs superior to Willie Gan whose best figure with us was 23 in Race 645. If this 7 furlong form was any guide then this put Tamdown Flyer on an approximate form figure of, say, 32. So, with a handicap rating here of 30, he was not without a chance.

Whilst we are pointing this out after the race, the same deductions could have been made before the race and go to show how our form figures can be used to provide an indirect assessment of an animal's chance. After all, the handicapper must work in the same way. To assess this result we allowed 9 lbs for the 4½ lengths separating the first five horses and split this by giving 4 lbs to the winner, deducting 5 lbs from the fifth horse and the others in proportion.

Race 1174	4.45 Thirsk	6 furlongs	Firm	June 15th				(4.9.0=36) (3.9.0=47)
826 (1009)	Soba (+7)	3	8 13	46	–	52	6–5	
1092	Caledonian (+7)	6	8 0	22	2	22	10–1	
301 (863)	Solar Grass (+7)	7	7 7	15	1	12?	25–1	
930 (1065)	Bettabet Geraghty	4	8 0	22	3	(15)	10–1	
(602)	Straekar	3	9 3	50	3	(40)	15–2	
855	Primula Boy	7	10 0	50	1	(40)	14–1	

Analysis: Under normal circumstances we would be surprised if a horse won a spring handicap by 2 lengths when a 7 lbs penalty had put it on a rating of (+6), i.e., set to do 6 lbs more than its previous form figure but Soba of course, was no ordinary filly and was improving by leaps and bounds. The handicapper had by no means caught up with her although she was now on an official rating of 39 compared to 23 at the start of the season. Before the season was out she was to go up to a rating of about 75, roughly 4 st improvement! It was difficult to assess the value of this race. Caledonian had won on a figure of 21 in Race 1001 so, assuming he had run roughly to that we took him as the key.

But Soba was getting away from us all the time!

Race 1195	3.45 Ascot	6 furlongs	Good–Firm	June 18th				(4.8.12=55) (3.8.12=65)
(873)	Battle Hymn	3	7 9	48	–	50	14–1	
898	Camisite	4	8 4	47	1½	45	14–1	
424 (864)	Murillo	6	8 12	55	Head	52	9–1	
775	Gamblers Dream	5	8 2	45	1½	40	12–1	
(650)	Doc Marten	4	8 9	52	Short-head	47	18–1	
(905)	Basil Boy	3	7 9	48	Short-head	43	33–1	

Analysis: The Wokingham Stakes at Royal Ascot is one of the hottest sprints of the season and is full of horses with form so exposed that the handicapper is unlikely to be far out. Consequently, our form figures gave us no encouragement for any horse based on recent form and we would not, of course, expect anything else. To assess the race for future guidance we simply took the distance separating the first three to represent 5 lbs, split this between them as shown and tied the remainder in. Comparison to previous form figures showed this treatment to be within the realms of reality.

Race 1200	2.40 Beverley	5 furlongs			Good–Firm	June 16th	(4.9.0=35) (3.9.0=43)
1145	Humble Blue	4	7	12	19	–	25	3–1
1092	Rambling River	5	7	13	20	1½	22	10–1
933	Cudgel	9	9	6	41	¾	41	8–1
732 (1082)	Karens Star	5	7	11	18	Head	17	14–1
(1082)	Starlust	3	8	13	42	Neck	40	14–1
987	Dutch Girl	5	8	9	30	2	25	4–1

Analysis: On past form figures Humble Blue (−5) and Cudgel (+4) had the race between them. They were both apprentice ridden and lived up to their ratings by finishing first and third, split by Rambling River who was taking a long time to find his best form.

A little experimentation showed that, taking Cudgel's running as the touchstone, the resultant form figures for the rest were very much in line with previous performances including those of the winner.

Race 1205	5.05 Beverley	5 furlongs			Good–Firm	June 16th	(4.9.0=11) (3.9.0=19)
622 (1001)	Blochairn Skolar	4	8	3	0	–	3	5–1
1092	Bella Travaille	4	8	4	1	1	1	5–4
(1010)	Will George	3	8	6	11	4	5	5–1
(943)	Milly Monroe	3	8	10	15	½	8	10–1
	Sew Nice	3	9	2	21	2	(14)	20–1
	Rivalry	4	8	6	3	1	0	12–1

Analysis: A very poor race and we could really only guess that the second had run to her lowly rating. There could be no reliance on these figures for the future.

Race 1212	3.15 Hamilton Park	6 furlongs			Good	June 17th	(4.9.0=26) (3.9.0=36)
577 (980)	Senorita Querida	3	9	7	43	–	47	4–1
1065	Mott the Hoople	4	8	5	17	1½	17	15–8
732	Little Atom	5	8	4	16	½	14	5–1
1138	Bloemfontein	3	8	4	26	½	22	10–1
(843)	Meritous	7	8	4	16	1½	10	12–1
671 (1065)	Secret Express (+3)	6	7	10	8	1	0	12–1

Analysis: On our pre-race figures there was little to choose between Mott the Hoople (−1), Senorita Querida (+1) and Little Atom (+1). Mott the Hoople's best figure had been recorded at this racecourse back in April (Race 139) but he had run to the same figure as required to do here again at Hamilton Park only nine days before (Race 1065) and, ridden by a 5 lbs claiming boy, was a worthy favourite. However he did not win. He was well placed all the way and looked the likely winner with just about a hundred yards to go but Senorita Querida, who had been kept behind for most of the trip, came with a good turn of foot close home to run Mott the Hoople out of it by 1½ lengths. He had run a good race though and we were inclined to accept that his handicap rating of 17 was correct. Fitting the rest to that made Bloemfontein come out at 22, a figure he had recorded twice before and we should not therefore be too far out.

Race 1216	*2.15 Ayr*	*6 furlongs*	*Good*	*June 18th*					(4.9.0=24) (3.9.0=34)
332 (1046)	In Rhythm	5	8	11	21	–	24	4–1	
(1139)	Prionsaa	4	8	1	11	1½	11	7–1	
	Pagapas Bay	5	10	0	38	1	36	5–1	
1064	Benfen	3	8	13	33	1	29	6–1	
(931)	Pampered Gipsy	3	7	9	15	Short-head	11	12–1	
940	Northern Eclipse	5	8	10	20	1½	(13)	8–1	

Analysis: In Rhythm's form figure from Race 332 gave him a clear top rating of (−2) here. There was, however, a snag in that it had been recorded nearly two months before. He had not been eating the oats of idleness since then however. He had been badly away when favourite to win a 7 furlong handicap at Thirsk early in June and not too far away when sixth over the same distance at Lingfield ten days before this. The chances were that he would be in a fit enough state to run to his best and with that good boy K. Willey riding he did not look a bad bet at 4–1. Apprentice handicaps are not exactly the best of betting mediums but Willey made no mistake, bringing In Rhythm with a well timed run in the last furlong to win comfortably by 1½ lengths.

There was not too much to go on here for rating purposes, but if we assume that the winner had indeed run to his previous best then we were not too far away with Benfen on the same rating as before.

Race 1230	*3.0 Ascot*	*5 furlongs*			*Good–Firm*		*June 19th*		**(9.7=66)**
	(300)	New Express	3	7	9	40	–	44	9–1
	1127	Celestial Dancer	3	8	8	53	½	55	2–1
	1030	Errolls Boy	3	7	13	44	2	41	13–2
	769	Lindsey	3	8	1	46	Head	42	9–1
577	(663)	Four for Music	3	8	1	46	4	(39)	16–1
	663	Never Talk	3	9	7	66	Neck	(59)	20–1

Analysis: In assessing Race 1030 we decided that we had underestimated Errolls Boy's rating in his previous race in putting him on the 41 mark and moved him up to 48. At the time it tied in with the remaining runners and in estimating the chances for this race we had no reason to believe that Errolls Boy was not in with an excellent chance at (−4). In fact, with Steve Dawson claiming 5 lbs he looked a good bet at 13–2 but, after leading for most of the way, he found little under strong driving and only just held on for third place. He subsequently won the 5 furlong Singleton Handicap at the main Goodwood meeting from a handicap rating of 45 and we can only assume that he ran below form in this race – the very competitive James Lane Handicap.

We had no firm figure for the winner New Express, although he had given Carreg Cennen a 5 lengths "thrashing" at level weights in a 5 furlong maiden event at Wolverhampton and, since we had that horse rated at a somewhat doubtful 40 (he had carried 7 lbs extra) in Race 556, New Express, set to do the same 40 here was in with a favourite's chance! Easy to see now – at the time we were not happy about using collateral ratings on form showed in a maiden event at Wolverhampton as any guide to a ten thousand pounder at Ascot! Which only goes to show how wrong one can be. To rate this race we split 7 lbs for the 2½ lengths between first and third, which put Celestial Dancer only 1 lb higher than in Race 1127 and Errolls Boy back on the 41 mark. Lindsey was only a head behind Errolls Boy and "loses" his 3 lbs minus, plus 1 lb for the head putting her on a new figure of 42. We were not too happy about that as it was some way below her figure of 48 from Race 577 – but that had been over 6 furlongs. It is, perhaps, significant that the only race Lindsey won during the season was over 6 furlongs, incidentally from a rating of 45.

Race 1242	*7.0 Warwick*	*5 furlongs*			*Good*	*June 19th*	(4.9.0=26) (3.9.0=34)	
1074	Balatina	4	8	3	15	–	18	8–1
1134	Byroc Boy	5	8	2	14	Neck	16	11–1
1092	Cree Bay (+7)	3	8	0	20	½	20	11–4
684	Colonial Line	4	7	12	10	1	8	4–1
195 (483)	Eagles Quest	4	8	3	15	½	12	12–1
819 (1046)	Case History	4	7	9	7	Head	4	12–1

Analysis: We were not to know that Cree Bay was to win his next four races of course, but even with a 7 lbs penalty he looked a good thing with an assessment of (−3). He was rightly favourite and ran a good race although unable to cope with the well handicapped Balatina (−) and Byroc Boy (−1). Colonial Line (−) was also in the shake-up so there was not too much wrong with the form. We decided to take Cree Bay's running as being equal to his rating and assessed the rest in line with that.

Race 1256	*8.35 Wolverhampton*	*5 furlongs*			*Good*	*June 21st*	(9.0=33)	
987	Bri Eden	8	8	13	32	–	34	9–2
(784)	Telegraph Boy	4	7	7	12	1½	10	5–1
752	Miss Import	4	8	11	30	4	(23)	5–1
100 (1092)	Kings Offering (+1)	7	7	11	16	Short-head	(9)	10–1
684 (930)	Curzon House (+10)	5	7	7	12	½	(5)	20–1
711	Royal Diplomat	5	7	12	17	3	(12)	6–1

Analysis: With the form of Kings Offering and Curzon House being poor, the race looked between Bri Eden and Miss Import both assessed at (+1) i.e., set to do only 1 lb more than they had done before. At 9–2 the field it was an open race but even so our front two finished first and third split by Telegraph Boy for who we had no form rating. Looking at the result we did not much like the 5½ lengths between the first three but we could not ignore it and decided to share 9 lbs between them as shown. Note, however, that we do not put the 8yo winner up too much (but see below) so credit him with just 2 lbs, taking the view that Miss Import ran a little below form. This is, perhaps, confirmed by the running of Bri Eden and Miss Import in Race 684 where the former had given the filly 3 lbs and beaten her two necks. Here he had been set to allow 2 lbs and had increased the margin to 5½ lengths.

(Our reluctance to put Bri Eden up too much was perhaps faulty judgment since he did in fact improve considerably and went on to reach a handicap rating of 47 and to win from that as well (Race 2041). In general one is reluctant to accept that an old horse has suddenly improved but to be fair to ourselves Bri Eden had not yet shown much improvement at the time. This was to come later.)

Race 1263	*4.0 Brighton*	*6 furlongs*			*Good–Firm*	*June 21st*	(9.7=44)	
(911)	Tender Trader	3	7	9	18	–	25+	4–1
1028	Ritual Dance (+7)	3	9	7	44	4	48	4–1
1074	Feather Sound	3	9	7	44	1½	44	10–1
(1080)	Out of Hand (Disq)	3	8	13	36	Head	35+	7–1
1030	Countach	3	9	2	39	2	35	7–1
(739)	Hoyden (+1)	3	7	7	16	4	(9)	12–1

Analysis: Ritual Dance was a certainty here with a form rating of (−8) from Race 1028 and, with the boy claiming 5 lbs, was a "gift" at 4–1. Unfortunately for us the Geoff Lewis trained Tender Trader, winner of a "seller" at Chepstow at the end of May, had apparently "come on a ton", for he was very well backed to share favouritism with our good thing and duly murdered her by no less than 4 lengths! He went on to win again, this time at Bath (Race 1473) and obviously had the proverbial "stone in hand". Taking the third horse as our key horse and leaving him at 44 made sense of it all – Countach was only about 2 lbs adrift – whilst Tender Trader went up 7 lbs, which seemed quite acceptable judging by the way he had won. May the fates preserve us from "dark" horses like this!

Incidentally, Out of Hand's saddle slipped two furlongs out and his rating was almost certainly better than appeared. He did in fact win at Yarmouth (at 33–1!) in Race 2690 when set to do a handicap rating of 32. Which shows the blessing of a long memory.

Race 1270	*4.30 Brighton*	*5 furlongs*			*Good*	*June 22nd*	(4.9.0=30) (3.9.0=38)	
134 (711)	Charles Street	5	8	9	25	–	33+	10–1
930 (997)	Kassak	6	8	8	24	7	22	7–1
1242	Colonial Line	4	7	8	10	2½	5	4–1
(1110)	Little Starchy	4	9	3	33	¾	27	9–1
1134	Dewberry	4	8	2	18	1½	(11)	5–1
839 (1200)	Blue Sapphire	3	7	7	17	2½	(10)	33–1

Analysis: Charles Street had started slowly and finished tailed off in Race 711 but with a form figure of 25 from Races 56 and 134 had only to run to that to have a good chance here. Colonial Line was a danger on his Race 684 running and was in fact co-favourite with Go Total, who also had an excellent chance on his Race 523 running at Chester – but perhaps not so good on his performances on more "normal" tracks. He also prefers a firmer surface than he got here.

With N. Dawe claiming 5 lbs as his rider, Charles Street was always going well and ran right away from Kassak to win by 7 lengths with Colonial Line, also ridden by a 5 lbs claimer, a further 2½ lengths away.

Accurate rating of this race was well-nigh impossible.

However, as we said in Race 930, Kassak may not be the best of sprinters but he seems to give his running most times especially at Brighton where he has won twice and so we took his performance to be his "usual" 22, and rated the rest round that with complete lack of confidence!

Race 1273	*3.45 Pontefract*	*6 furlongs*			*Good–Soft*	*June 21st*		**(10.0=44)**
784 (1159)	Musical Minx	4	8	3	19	–	21	11–2
786	H R Micro	4	7	10	12	½	12	8–1
843 (1159)	Crowebronze	4	7	9	11	Dead-heat	11	8–1
1145	Bracadale	4	10	0	44	1½	41	7–2
933	Song Minstrel	4	8	13	29	¾	25	3–1
398 (1204)	Blessed Silence (+3)	4	7	7	9	Head	4	10–1

Analysis: In our form assessments for this race 3 lbs would have covered the first four, with H R Micro, Crowebronze and Song Minstrel being "best-in" in that order. Musical Minx had a bit to find on his running in Race 784 and had also finished down the field in Race 1159. She had swerved away any chance she had in that race however and it had also been on firm going. Here at Pontefract it was soft and it obviously suited her well for she made all the running to win all out by ½ length. H R Micro and Crowebronze dead-heated for second place so we accepted their ratings as correct and used them as the basis for our calculations.

Race 1317	*2.30 Newcastle*	*6 furlongs*	*Good–Soft*	*June 24th*	(4.9.0=30) (3.9.0=40)				
1216	Benfen	3	8	7	33	–	35	6–1
1065	Mary Maguire	5	7	13	15	4	13	20–1
1212	Little Atom	5	8	0	16	1½	13	20–1
843 (1013)	Holdall	4	8	2	18	1	14	25–1
	Chimango (+1)	4	7	8	10	¾	5	25–1
930 (1159)	Scottish Agent (+1)	6	7	8	10	Neck	4	8–1

Analysis: Mary Maguire, −3 from Race 863, Holdall, −2 from Race 843 and Caledonian, −2 from Race 1174 had the best chances here. Caledonian led early on but dropped away to finish eighth and the best of these was Mary Maguire who ran quite well to finish second to Benfen.

The last named had not seemed to be much better than our rating of 29, which he had recorded twice, but he improved on that to win very easily by 4 lengths. In assessing this race we cannot allow too much for the distances involved because of the going. The problem here lay in deciding which horse to use as the key. It seemed evident that Benfen had improved, but how much? In the end we decided to raise the rating by 6 lbs – put him on 35 and rate downwards from there. We were not at all sanguine about being right but one often gets races where it is difficult to assess with confidence.

Race 1326	*7.35 Newcastle*	*5 furlongs*	*Good–Soft*	*June 25th*	(4.10.0=71) (3.10.0=79)				
1174	Soba (+12)	3	8	0	51	–	58+	6–1
114 (588)	Touch Boy	6	8	6	49	3	49	20–1
987	Sandra's Secret	5	7	13	42	Short-head	41	7–1
(1187)	Sweet Monday	4	10	0	71	¾	69	9–1
855 (1174)	Friendly Fun	7	7	7	36	3	31	8–1
(1196)	Blue Singh	4	8	5	48	1½	41	11–8

Analysis: Among the also-rans here was Manilow, about whom the official handicapper appeared to have taken the same view as us about his performance in Race 1074 for he had subsequently put the 6yo on the 44 mark. In this race however, he was set to carry 7.13, which included a 7 lbs penalty, putting him on a handicap rating of 42. In our assessments therefore he was −2, 1 lb in front of Soba who was −1.

As at Epsom however, Manilow put in another "bad one" whereas the filly won pulling up by 3 lengths. Blue Singh was a short priced favourite in this race on the strength of very good performances in top-class stakes events but his running here only served to show that form displayed in such races is not a reliable guide when allied to handicaps.

Sandra's Secret had given Touch Boy a good fight for second place and we considered that the latter had probably run to his handicap rating of 49. Even in the going Soba looked worth at least 7 lbs for the easy 3 lengths and she was put on the 58 mark with a plus.

We awaited her next races with great interest.

Race 1347B	*9.15 Doncaster*	*5 furlongs*			*Good–Soft*	*June 26th*		(9.0=52)
951	Avonmore Wind	3	8	3	41	–	44	7–4
(407)	Laurence Mac (+1)	3	7	7	31	$2\frac{1}{2}$	31	10–1
951 (1082)	Special Pleasure	3	8	12	50	2	47	20–1
(940)	Master Blow	3	7	8	32	5	(25)	14–1
(747)	Hunter Hawk (+15)	3	7	8	32	$1\frac{1}{2}$	(25)	16–1
1030	Dragunn	3	7	7	31	Neck	(24)	7–2

Analysis: Special Pleasure and Avonmore Wind met in Race 951 when the latter, in receipt of 19 lbs, finished just over $4\frac{1}{2}$ lengths in front. Special Pleasure was here conceding only 9 lbs so there was not going to be too much in it. We had them rated equal at −1 but, ridden by Steve Cauthen, going for his fifth winner of the evening, Avonmore Wind went past the pace-making Special Pleasure for a comfortable $2\frac{1}{2}$ lengths win from Laurence Mac. It was not easy to tell whether Avonmore Wind had improved or if Special Pleasure had run below form and we decided to split 6 lbs equally between the two of them for the $4\frac{1}{2}$ lengths by which they were separated. Avonmore Wind was later allotted 7.7 in the Goodwood Stewards Cup and reference to our weight equation for the race (1926) will show this to be equivalent to a handicap rating of 44 so presumably the handicapper had taken the same view of the colt.

Race 1350	*4.0 Lingfield Park*	*6 furlongs*			*Good–Soft*	*June 25th*	(4.9.7=52) (3.9.7=62)	
1095	Silojoka	3	8	6	47	–	49	13–2
1230	Lindsey	3	8	5	46	1½	45	9–2
1195	Doc Marten	4	9	7	52	Head	50	10–3
475 (980)	Milk Heart	3	8	3	44	2	39	10–1
1270	Kassak	6	7	7	24	Head	19	5–1
832	Vorvados	5	8	4	35	1½	28	10–1

Analysis: Vorvados had registered a form figure of 39 in Race 107 and needed only to reproduce that figure to have a fine chance here. He had failed to run to that level in three races since then and did not appear to be particularly fancied. Silojoka had also disappointed in Race 1095 but her Race 541 figure of 50 put her on a form assessment rating of −3 and she made handsome amends at the rewarding odds of 13–2.

In view of the softened ground the 1½ lengths win would not be worth more than between 2 to 3 lbs but Lindsey could not have pulled out any more and Silojoka was probably full value for the win. We therefore split 3 lbs between the pair with the rest in proportion.

Vorvados continues to run well below his best figure.

Race 1356	*3.0 Lingfield Park*	*5 furlongs*			*Good–Soft*	*June 26th*	(10.0=59)	
987	Pontin Lad	4	10	0	59	–	59	4–1
467 (1195)	Barnet Heir	4	8	7	38	Head	37	9–2
1167	Vernham Street (+4)	4	7	7	24	2	20?	20–1
1134	Epsom Imp	9	8	13	44	3	(37)	14–1
	Pit Stop (+3)	6	7	7	24	2	(17)	25–1
1216	Pagapas Bay	5	8	7	38	1½	(31)	7–1

Analysis: Alev, hero of Race 1117, was favourite here with a 3 lbs penalty bringing his weight up to 8.3 and was −1 on our form assessments for this race. For reasons unknown to us Alev was never going well and finished last of the ten runners. Barnet Heir was top of our figures with a form figure of −3 but this was on form shown on May 1st and he had done nothing in three races since. Pontin Lad was third best-in and on his running in Race 987 he had a bright chance of setting up the same 59 rating.

With Alev performing so deplorably Pontin Lad and Barnet Heir had the race between them with a head in Pontin Lad's favour at the end. We took

Pontin Lad to have run to his rating, deducted 1 lb from Barnet Heir and that 1 lb plus a further 3 lbs from Vernham Street.

Note the query for the overweight.

Race 1364	*3.45 Chepstow*	*6 furlongs*			*Good*	*June 26th*		(9.3=28)
(739)	Tiger Trap	3	9	3	28	–	29	12–1
(927)	Minnie Love	3	8	2	13	Short-head	13	16–1
(1245)	Pokerfayes	3	8	11	22	1	19	25–1
(577)	Caran D'ache	3	8	3	14	½	10	33–1
(911)	Free Range	3	8	0	11	3	4	33–1
(1242)	Lawers (+2)	3	8	4	15	1½	(8)	25–1

Analysis: The vast majority of the fourteen runners were un-rated by us and assessing the race for the future was mostly guesswork allied to the judgment of the handicapper.

In running Tiger Trap to a short-head we hazarded a guess that Minnie Love had run to her figure and left her on the 13 mark, with the winner going up 1 lb for the short-head. The rest were marked down accordingly.

Race 1371	*3.35 Newmarket*	*6 furlongs*			*Good–Soft*	*June 26th*		(8.4=46)
(1187)	Jacquinta	3	8	4	46	–	51	5–2
	Lucayan Lady (+1)	3	7	7	35	Short-head	39	50–1
915	Mummy's Pleasure	3	8	5	47	2	48	14–1
1230	New Express (+6)	3	8	4	46	4	41	9–4
1095	Town Flier	3	8	2	44	½	37	33–1
1138	Ben Jarrow (+11)	3	7	7	35	Head	27?	50–1

Analysis: This was not one of our best efforts! We had Mummy's Pleasure and Town Flier equal best in at −1 and as can be seen, they finished third and fifth respectively. However, we thought that New Express, the favourite at 9–4 had a bit to do on our assessment of +2 and since he finished a well beaten fourth it was probably about the only thing we got right!

Jacquinta, the short-head winner, was demonstrably about 2 lbs behind Battle Hymn on earlier running and, as that animal had won the Wokingham Handicap at Royal Ascot to set up a form figure of 50 (see Race 1195), Jacquinta was not overburdened with a handicap rating here of 46. Mummy's Pleasure had been re-handicapped since Race 915 where we had given her a figure of 48 and was now officially rated at 47. That was good enough for us although we preferred to use our own figure of 48 as the "correct" one and do our calculations round that.

Race 1377	2.45 Hamilton Park	6 furlongs			Good	June 28th		(9.0=13)
1216	In Rhythm	5	9	6	19	–	21	9–4
1273	H R Micro	4	8	13	12	¾	12	10–3
	Oyston Estates	6	8	8	7	2	3	20–1
1212	Secret Express	6	8	1	0	1½	0	9–1
(1154)	Westering Breeze	4	8	5	4	½	0	12–1
1065	Bracken Gill	4	8	3	2	6	0	12–1

Analysis: Another scintillating bet! Here we have In Rhythm, with no penalty for winning an apprentice handicap (Race 1216) set to do 5 lbs less than our form figure for that race. Ridden once more by K. Willey who claims the "five" he was a really sound bet at 9–4. But . . . he did not look like it at halfway! Outpaced from the start he was struggling with 2 furlongs to go but once he got into his stride he took off after H R Micro, who had gone clear and catching her in the last furlong went on to win by ¾ length.

Such races, though most exciting, are heart-stopping for the punter!

The second placed had run to a figure of 12 in Race 1273 and we felt able to accept that she had done the same here. The rest were very lowly rated and not worth too much burning of the midnight oil.

Race 1386	4.0 Nottingham	6 furlongs			Good–Soft	June 28th		(9.0=51)
187 (641)	Winter Wind	6	9	2	53	–	53	8–1
1195	Camisite	4	8	10	47	Dead-heat	47	9–4
1174 (1195)	Primula Boy	7	8	11	48	2½	45	16–1
641 (1196)	Kathred	4	8	5	42	1½	37	25–1
898	Cree Song	6	8	7	44	1	38	12–1
1159	Renovate (+8)	5	7	12	35	Neck	29	6–1

Analysis: Of the two dead-heaters, we had Winter Wind second best in at (–), i.e., set to do the same as in Race 187. That was way back in April however and "top of the figures" was Kathred at (−3) from Race 424. That too was at the end of April and she had not run to that figure since and had in fact finished bang last in the Wokingham Handicap at Royal Ascot. This did not augur well for her chances however and she was neglected in the market at 25–1.

In the event she ran quite well to finish fourth about four lengths behind the dead-heaters. We can do no more than to accept that the two had run to their handicap ratings – Winter Wind "tied in" with us anyway – and adjudicated from that basis.

Race 1393	*8.35 Windsor*	*6 furlongs*	*Good–Soft*	*June 28th*	(8.7=40)

166 (475)	Skyboot	3	7 13	32	–	34	8–1
577 (769)	Kash-In	3	8 6	39	2	39	7–1
(435)	Hello Sunshine	3	8 6	39	1½	38	7–1
1159	Northorpe	3	8 7	40	¾	38	12–1
1117 (1230)	Ellerene	3	9 7	54	3	(49)	4–1
1095	Princess Virginia	3	8 6	39	Short-head	(34)	9–2

Analysis: The official handicapper had put Skyboot up to a rating of 41 after his second to Sonseri at Kempton Park in April (Race 166), but he had certainly not run up to that figure when last of seven behind Purnima in Race 475. We had put the colt up to 37 after Race 166 and his subsequent failure was no real surprise since we were of the opinion that the handicapper had put him too high. In this race the official had dropped Skyboot to a very lenient 32 and he was of course (−5) with us. Incidentally, Northorpe, rated here at the 40 level, had been assessed at 23 in Race 1159 although a penalty had taken him up to 30. The penalty had been earned by a 6 lengths win in a moderate maiden event at Ayr in May and the handicapper had obviously taken a serious view of that win. He was not so far out as the colt won at Ripon (Race 2006) on a rating of 39.

To rate this we took note of the soft going and divided only 4 lbs for the approximate 4 lengths between the first four as shown.

Race 1410	*3.15 Yarmouth*	*5 furlongs*	*Good*	*June 30th*	(4.8.3=22) (3.8.3=30)

1242	Balatina (+7)	4	8 3	22	–	25	7–2
419 (1195)	Over the Rainbow	5	9 8	41	1	41	5–1
(1237)	Rain Dancer (+2)	3	7 8	21	4	(14)	6–1
1205	Bella Travaille (+11)	4	7 7	12	Neck	(5)	20–1
1010 (1242)	Haverhill Lass (+2)	3	7 10	23	2	(16)	20–1
940 (1134)	Russian Winter	7	8 11	30	½	(23)	11–2

Analysis: Nothing came right in this Yarmouth race! Russian Winter (−) and Haverhill Lass (+1) had chances on their running in Races 863 and 1010 respectively but, unfortunately, both horses had blotted their copy-books in races since with no good reason. Neither got into the race behind Balatina who showed improvement to win from a handicap mark of 22, an assessment of (+4) on our scale. He was on the crest of a wave however and went on to win again at Brighton a week later (Race 1541). Over the Rainbow had run well to finish ninth in the Wokingham Stakes at Ascot and we took his rating to be correct at 41. Balatina goes up 3 lbs for the length win but, with the rest of the runners at least 4 lengths away, we deducted the usual 7 lbs.

Race 1411	*3.45 Yarmouth*		*6 furlongs*		*Good*	*June 30th*		(9.1=44)
(1310)	No Contest (+7)	3	9	7	50	–	53	10–3
(781)	Transflash (+4)	3	7	8	23	2½	20?	20–1
556 (1181)	Curve the Wind	3	9	1	44	4	(37)	Evens
1030	Hawks Nest	3	7	12	27	1	(20)	7–2
221 (521)	Illicit	3	8	13	42	Head	(35)	10–1
(1364)	Spectral (+7)	3	7	12	27	6	(22)	14–1

Analysis: Since Race 556 where he finished a respectable third to On Return to earn an assessment of 37, Curve the Wind had won the 7 furlong Ashtead Stakes at Epsom and as a result had gone up in the official ratings. He was now on the 44 mark and looked to have too much to do. Hawks Nest had run well when second to Errolls Boy in Race 1030 and with an assessment of (−3) looked to have an excellent chance. The snag however lay in the distance of this race. Race 1030 had been over 5 furlongs whilst this was a furlong further. Hawks Nest clearly showed that he did not stay the trip and he was beaten after being with the leaders for 5 furlongs. No Contest had already won two races over 7 furlongs and had almost certainly improved. Dividing 6 lbs for the 2½ lengths between the first two put No Contest up 3 lbs on the 53 mark and we were satisfied with that. Curve the Wind and the rest go down 7 lbs.

Race 1419	*5.0 Carlisle*		*6 furlongs*			*Good*	*June 30th*		(8.0=8)
	1377	Oyston Estates	6	7	13	7	–	9	10–1
86	(134)	Jeckel	4	8	5	13	½	13	16–1
	1174	Solar Grass	7	7	9	3	1	0	8–1
	1317	Chimango	4	7	8	2	Head	0	8–1
	1273	Blessed Silence	4	7	12	6	Neck	1	20–1
	1273	Crowebronze	4	8	3	11	1	3	7–1

Analysis: Favourite at 5–2 for this race was Benfen who, with 9.6 on his back including a 7 lbs penalty, had the equivalent of a handicap rating of 38. (As a 3yo 8.0 would = 18 therefore 9.6 would equal 38, or 18 + 20). Since his best form figure was 35 his chance was not as good as his starting price indicated. Mark you, the level of the ratings clearly pointed to the class of the animals concerned and lowly-rated Crowebronze probably had shown the most consistent figures. With the boy claiming 5 lbs she had as good a chance as anything but was never nearer than at the end of the race. Jeckel had given the winner a good shake-up and we took its rating as the key. With a couple of zero ratings the race will be of little use to us in the future.

Race 1425	*5.0 Carlisle*		*5 furlongs*			*Good*	*July 1st*		(8.1=29)
1242	(1366)	Cree Bay	3	8	1	29	–	33	4–5
	1371	Ben Jarrow	3	7	10	24	1½	24	5–1
786	(1237)	Royal Question (+14)	3	7	7	21	3	12?	8–1
	(1200)	Sammy Waters (+1)	3	8	2	30	1½	19	11–1
	1064	Magnamala (+8)	3	7	7	21	2½	4	10–1
	(672)	Sweet Satisfactions (+3)	3	7	9	23	1	4	16–1

Analysis: This race seemed to lay between Ben Jarrow (−3), Cree Bay (+6) and Magnamala (+6) and on the face of it Ben Jarrow looked good value at 5–1. However, Cree Bay was on top form again and won quite comfortably. After his win in Race 1092 with a form assessment of 23, Cree Bay had run a little below form in Race 1242 but had then gone on to win the Pontypridd Club Stakes over 5 furlongs at Chepstow. Here with a handicap rating of 29 he seemed to have a lot to do. Ben Jarrow ran very well to lead inside the final furlong but then Cree Bay came along to win comfortably by 1½ lengths. This was clearly a good performance and in taking Ben Jarrow as the key horse we are able to give the winner full value for the winning distance. Royal Question, carrying 14 lbs overweight (!) goes down 9 lbs for the 3 lengths she finished behind Ben Jarrow but she was to prove later (Races 2166 and 2333) that she was better than that. On the evidence of this race we could only demote her, the only alternative being to put both Cree Bay and Ben Jarrow up to a somewhat dubious level. One must not treat handicapping as a purely mathematical exercise and judgment must come into it.

Race 1430	*3.45 Brighton*	*6 furlongs*			*Good*	*July 1st*		(9.3=24)
1159	Lord Scrap	6	8	5	12	–	18	9–4
1242	Eagles Quest	4	8	8	15	3	14	11–2
1350	Kassak	6	9	3	24	Neck	22	13–2
1270	Colonial Line	4	8	3	10	4	(3)	8–1
(1359)	Warooka	5	7	8	1	½	(0)	50–1
1273	Musical Minx (+7)	4	9	5	26	2½	(16)	12–1

Analysis: Lord Scrap was best in here with an assessment of (−2) from Race 1159 where he had been rated by us at 14 and was now set to do a figure of 12. At 9–4 he was not a bad bet and he duly made all the running to win by a very comfortable 3 lengths. Eagles Quest had been 15 with us in Race 195 but only 12 in Race 1242 and the problem now was in deciding which of these two ratings to work to here. Kassak helped to solve the dilemma. He usually runs to his level and we elected to use his usual rating of 22 as a basis here. Eagles Quest accordingly goes down 1 lb and Lord Scrap goes up to the 18 mark, making an overall difference of 7 lbs between the two horses for the 3 lengths that separated them at the finish. We note later that Lord Scrap is re-handicapped by the official at 17 (Race 2100). We will not argue about one pound!

Race 1445	*5.15 Beverley*	*5 furlongs*			*Good–Soft*	*July 3rd*		(8.9=32)
1005 (1327)	Sew Nice	3	7	8	17	–	26	10–1
(1343)	Lucky Dutch	3	8	9	32	5	32	11–10
(1341)	Staly's Pet	3	7	8	17	3	13	5–1
581	High Authority	3	7	11	20	2	14	8–1
1010 (1205)	Waltham Terrace (+2)	3	7	7	16	Short-head	10	7–1
(1138)	Miss Abwah (+4)	3	7	7	16	¾	9	12–1

Analysis: We had no reliable assessments here for this race and the winner Sew Nice had received a bracketed 14 in Race 1205. Set to do only 3 lbs more here we could not be unduly shocked to see her improve upon her previous run but she did more than could have been expected. Making all the running she stormed home well clear of her field to win by a very easy 5 lengths. There was not overmuch to guide us in assessing this result but we took the view that, as Lucky Dutch had been well backed for no real reason apparent in the form books, the colt must have shown something at home. It could not have been too much for he was well beaten but we nevertheless took his handicap rating as the mainstay for re-assessments. Sew Nice went up 9 lbs but she was to prove later that she had in fact come on considerably (see Races 2255 and 2734) where she ran to a rating of 28.

Race 1456	*3.15 Haydock Park*	*5 furlongs*			*Good–Firm*		*July 3rd*	(10.0=49)
1326	Touch Boy	6	10	0	49	–	52	5–2
1145 (1317)	Bold Scuffle	4	9	2	37	Neck	39	6–1
1377	H R Micro (+2)	4	7	7	14	2½	11	6–1
742 (1270)	Go Total	6	9	5	40	Short-head	37	4–1
(1386)	Alpine Rocket	5	9	4	39	2½	(32)	10–1
(1200)	Miss Nelski	5	8	3	24	½	(17)	12–1

Analysis: Bold Scuffle's figure of 38 in Race 1145 had been made in soft going and was well in front of his firm going figure from Race 898. He had the going on the firm side here but ran a really good race to run Touch Boy to a neck. The latter had been set to do the same as in Race 1326 but that too had been on softish going. On the form shown in Race 1377 H R Micro had a chance and he led to the distance until passed by Bold Scuffle who in turn gave way to the winner.

We split 6 lbs for the neck and 2½ lengths between the front three, giving 3 lbs to the winner, taking 3 lbs off the rating of H R Micro, whilst Bold Scuffle goes up 2 lbs. This is calculated by adding the 3 lbs given to the winner less 1 lb for the neck beating.

Race 1462	*4.10 Sandown Park*	*5 furlongs*			*Good–Soft*		*July 2nd*	(8.1=35)
1350	Vorvados	5	8	1	35	–	40	10–1
1134 (1159)	Sailor's Prayer (+7)	4	7	7	27	1½	28?	25–1
659	Pusey Street	5	7	9	29	Short-head	29	8–1
301	Brentex	4	7	12	32	½	30	5–1
1270	Little Starchy	4	7	13	33	3	(25)	14–1
659	New Embassy	5	8	3	37	1½	(27)	9–1

Analysis: "Vorvados is a remarkable animal on his day." So said *Raceform Notebook* about this performance and we could not agree more. On his running in Race 107 he was a good thing for this with a form assessment of (−4) but his performances since then of (33), 33 and 28 did not inspire any real confidence. The going was no real excuse. It had been softish when he had been comprehensively beaten behind Silojoka in Race 1350 and the ground was subsequently on the firm side when he won at Newmarket (Race 1968) and at Doncaster (Race 2617). He has also won at 5 furlongs and 6 furlongs and it would not therefore appear that the distance makes much difference. One could write the result off as "one of those things" but such inconsistency is confusing to handicappers, official or otherwise. Incidentally, he won three times when ridden by Willie Carson, and the Portland Handicap at Doncaster (Race 2617) when Lester Piggott was aboard, so maybe he responds to the master touch!

We took Pusey Street's running as the guide and constructed the ratings round that. Sailor's Prayer gets a query for the overweight but his figure nevertheless set the seeds for the "disaster" which followed in Race 1683, of which more later.

Race 1473	*3.30 Bath*	*5½ furlongs*		*Good*		*July 3rd*		*(9.7=53)*
1263	Tender Trader	3	7	8	26	–	28	2–1
(1371)	Golden Green	3	9	2	48	Neck	49	20–1
1371	Mummy's Pleasure	3	9	1	47	Neck	47	10–3
(82)	Lady Cox	3	8	9	41	1½	38	14–1
797 (889)	Shiny Hour	3	7	11	29	½	25	12–1
1127	Cyril's Choice	3	9	7	53	½	48	3–1

Analysis: Shiny Hour's form figure of 34 in Race 526 had been confirmed in Race 797 although the 8½ lengths beating by Pete Rocket in the latter race left one wondering! He had also been well beaten in a 7 furlong handicap at Warwick at the end of May so the general picture was not one of improvement. He had been downgraded by the handicapper by 5 lbs and his showing here left us in no doubt that he was no longer the horse he had been at Salisbury on May 5th and he never ran to that figure again.

Apart from Shiny Hour the race lay between Mummy's Pleasure and Tender Trader (−1 and +1 respectively) and they finished third and first in a finish of necks with Golden Green. Tender Trader was on the up and up and had improved on his figure in Race 1263. Rating this was quite straightforward using Mummy's Pleasure as the key.

Race 1482	*8.20 Nottingham*	*6 furlongs*			*Good–Firm*		*July 3rd* (8.0=28)	
541 (1167)	Purnima	3	8	3	31	–	34	6–4
1393	Northorpe	3	8	6	34	1	34+	Evens
(546)	The Bystander (+15)	3	7	7	21	6	(11)	66–1
(1316)	Tywith Belle (+1)	3	8	0	28	½	(18)	20–1
839	Another Way	3	7	8	22	2½	(12)	8–1
(1015)	Rhy-Yan Tudor (+7)	3	7	7	21	1	(11)	25–1

Analysis: With three horses carrying a combined total of 23 lbs overweight any handicap becomes a mockery and the extended distances and the starting prices returned go to make this race a non-event as far as we are concerned. Only the first two are of real interest. We have to go back to Race 475 for Purnima's figure of 29 whilst we have already made comment about Northorpe's climb in the ratings in our analysis of Race 1393. His figure there was good enough to win this from a mark of 34 and the way the race was run he was probably unlucky not to do so. Denied any sort of run when Another Way hung badly to the right and nearly brought down Rhy-Yan Tudor, Northorpe got going again far too late to catch Purnima who was making the best of his way home.

To rate this we take Northorpe's rating to be about right but give him a plus sign to remind us that he may well be better than that.

Purnima goes up 3 lbs for the length but the rest are pure guesswork.

Race 1491	*3.0 Edinburgh*	*5 furlongs*			*Good*	*July 5th*		(9.0=28)
1256	Miss Import	4	9	1	29	–	34	4–1
(1154)	Pergoda	4	8	2	16	2	17	8–1
1200	Rambling River	5	8	6	20	3	15	5–1
1001 (1092)	Brian's Star	7	7	7	7	1	2	8–1
1200 (1256)	Karen's Star	5	8	3	17	½	11	20–1
1159	Broon's Secret	8	9	13	41	2	34	9–1

Analysis: Rambling River was getting rather exasperating! His form figures to date read 16, 19, 26, 16, 17 and 22, the highest performance being that at Edinburgh in Race 567. Here his official rating stood at 20 and if we heeded the best figure, stood at a form assessment of −6. Miss Import, Karen's Star and Broon's Secret were all on the (−) mark and could obviously be given a chance. Rambling River looked a good each way bet at 5–1 and in fact he ran well for a long way until lack of pace found him out. Readers will see that he finished the season on a rating of 32 (Race 2855) but that was still in the future at this stage. He did however win from a rating of 18 in Race 1878.

Taking 10 lbs as representing the 5 lengths between the placed horses, we gave 5 lbs to the winner, deducted a similar amount from Rambling River whilst Pergoda goes up 5 lbs less 4 lbs for the 2 lengths beating – a net increase of 1 lb.

Race 1498	*3.45 Pontefract*	*6 furlongs*			*Good–Soft*	*July 5th*	(4.10.0=47) (3.10.0=56)	
1317	Mary Maguire	5	7	8	13	–	17	8–1
1174 (1317)	Caledonian	6	8	2	21	1	22	12–1
871 (1419)	Knight Security	3	8	2	30	Head	30	7–1
1167 (1404)	Dawn's Delight	4	9	2	35	2	31	10–1
1200	Cudgel	9	10	0	47	Neck	42	5–1
1256	Royal Diplomat	5	7	11	16	4	9	10–1

Analysis: Mary Maguire had on four occasions set up form figures as good as or better than she was required to do here. Ridden by the 5 lbs claimer A. Nesbitt, she was a splendid value bet at 8–1. Caledonian's figure of 22 put up behind Soba in Race 1174 also put him in with a chance, whilst Dawn's Delight had figures of 35 in Races 62 and 107 but had run below that in Race 1167.

It all worked out pretty well according to our calculations and adjustments were easy, taking Knight Security as the guide. He had obviously been ridden right out in an effort to get second place but in missing this by a head he had almost certainly run up to his official rating.

Race 1506	*8.35 Windsor*	*5 furlongs*			*Good–Firm*	*July 5th*	(8.5=24)	
292 (1370)	Superb Singer (+5)	3	7	7	12	–	17?	33–1
1364	Minnie Love	3	7	8	13	1½	14	7–2
610 (997)	Hit the Line	3	8	5	24	Neck	24	11–2
1117 (1230)	Blue Cloud	3	8	5	24	2	18	12–1
128 (679)	Fast Lad	3	9	7	40	Short-head	33	5–1
(716)	Agreloui	3	8	11	30	Short-head	23	25–1

Analysis: Superb Singer had been tailed off in a Newmarket "seller" some nine days earlier and was apparently unfancied at 33–1. Racehorses are not given to reading the form-book or, as far as we know, having a quick look at the bookmakers' boards on the way down to the start, so Ken Ivory's filly saw no good reason for not seeing this lot off, which she did by 1½ lengths. Such stuff is despair made of!

Perhaps the only crumb of comfort was that in Race 292 we had assessed her quite satisfactorily at a form rating of 12 and here she was set to do no more than that figure. Some form students would say that the form is there if one goes back far enough but there are limits to human credulity and we would not dream of taking any credit for this.

Taking Hit the Line's handicap rating as correct looked a reasonable approach and tied in with our figure from Race 610. We took her as the key to this but in any case we did not have much else to go on. Superb Singer goes up 5 lbs with a question mark for the 5 lbs overweight, since this involves the filly going up 10 lbs more than her original handicap rating.

Race 1511	*8.0 Wolverhampton*	*5 furlongs*			*Good–Firm*	*July 5th*		(9.0=30)
1256	Bri-Eden (+7)	8	9	7	37	–	41	3–1
1256	Telegraph Boy	4	7	9	11	1½	11	7–2
424 (784)	Dungeon Ghyl	4	9	0	30	2	24	16–1
139	Winner Takes All (+5)	5	7	9	11	Short-head	4	16–1
(909)	Young Inca	4	7	8	10	Short-head	3	33–1
1356	Vernham Street	4	8	4	20	¾	12	7–2

Analysis: The best documented form we had was for Telegraph Boy (+1) and Bri-Eden (+3) and they finished first and second though not in that order.

In Race 1256 Telegraph Boy had been officially rated at 12 and we had given him a form figure of 10. Here he was on a level of 11 and with no need to indulge in any nit-picking we took his figure as correct. Bri-Eden had beaten Telegraph Boy (received 20 lbs) in that race also and by the same 1½ lengths margin. Here Bri-Eden was conceding 26 lbs so clearly had to go up on our figure in that race. An assessment of 41 looked about right.

Race 1525	*4.40 Newmarket*	*6 furlongs*			*Good*	*July 6th*		(9.7=65)
1230	Celestial Dancer	3	8	12	56	–	60	85–40
428	Master Cawston	3	8	5	49	1½	49	8–1
1371	Lucayan Lady (+3)	3	7	7	37	2½	31	3–1
(1195)	My Dear Fellow	3	8	10	54	¾	47	33–1
769 (1327)	Fidalco	3	7	7	37	Neck	29	33–1
(1386)	Chris's Lad	3	9	7	65	Short-head	56	33–1

Analysis: On her running in Race 1371, where she had been a bit backward, Lucayan Lady could be expected to improve but although she had every chance here and with a form assessment of (−2) she never really looked like winning at any stage. Certainly the 3 lbs overweight made no difference to the result.

Celestial Dancer and Master Cawston were the only two other runners with good figures and they duly finished first and second. Master Cawston had been in front a furlong out and was very strongly ridden when challenged by the winner and it looked best to take his rating of 49 to be the constant factor here.

Race 1541 *3.15 Brighton* *5 furlongs* *Good–Firm* *July 7th* (4.9.8=38) (3.9.8=45)

1410	Balatina (+7)	4	8	6	22	–	25	6–4
1356	Barnet Heir	4	9	8	38	1	38	6–4
1430	Kassak	6	8	8	24	Neck	23	8–1
1506	Hit the Line	3	8	1	24	3	(17)	8–1
(1242)	Russian Debonair	3	7	8	17	2½	(10)	20–1
329 (1511)	Star of Enzo	4	9	0	30	1	(23)	25–1

Analysis: Barnet Heir had two good figures to his name, 41 over 6 furlongs in Race 467, and 37 over 5 furlongs in Race 1356 and was set here to do 38. He was co-favourite with Balatina whose figures had been getting better all the time. Also in with a chance were Hit the Line and Kassak. Barnet Heir led until well inside the last furlong when Balatina came along in fine style to win by a length. Hit the Line was running for the second time in three days and may have been feeling the strain for she could keep on only at one pace at the finish. Kassak had once again run his usual game race at Brighton but this time we decided to split his handicap mark of 24 and our usual figure of 22 and call him 23 to avoid the possibility that we might be 2 lbs adrift. After the first three we deduct the usual 7 lbs because of the 3 lengths and more that the rest were in arrears.

Race 1548 *8.40 Warwick* *5 furlongs* *Good–Firm* *July 7th* (9.5=38)

(256)	Return to Me	3	9	5	38	–	41	5–4
(781)	Listen to Me (+1)	3	7	10	15	3	12	25–1
(1138)	Dark Mystique	3	8	0	19	2	11	10–3
(1230)	Pass No Remarks	3	9	5	38	Head	29	5–2
(1363)	Fast Service	3	8	4	23	25	(13)	9–1

Analysis: The five runners were all "unknown" to us and our interest in the race therefore purely academic. With something like 30 lengths between the first and last horses any rating has to be mostly guesswork. Listen to Me had not had to be pushed to hold on to second place and the distance she was beaten by the winner could well have been less. In a case such as this we allow 2 lbs per length and share the resultant 6 lbs equally between the front two. Dark Mystique, on the other hand, had been ridden out to snatch third place and we allow 5 lbs for the 2 lengths behind the second horse plus the 3 lbs we have already taken from Listen to Me – a total deduction of 8 lbs.

Race 1582	*2.45 Ayr*	*6 furlongs*			*Good*	*July 10th*		(4.8.11=55) (3.8.11=64)	
1386	Camisite (+4)	4	8	7	51	–		58	7–1
(1187)	Great Eastern	5	9	10	68	1½		71	9–2
1195	Murillo	6	8	11	55	1½		54	6–1
855 (1236)	Polly's Brother	4	7	9	39	Head		37	8–1
1326	Soba (+9)	3	8	0	53	½		50	4–5
1386	Primula Boy	7	8	4	48	5		(41)	12–1

Analysis: Although she was carrying 9 lbs more than her original handicap mark Soba was (−5) with us on her form in Race 1326 and looked a certainty. Evidently the punters thought so too and she was backed from 11–8 against to odds-on. Whether it was partly the effects of her long journey in a horse-box or whether the slight lameness she showed after the race manifested itself earlier and caused Soba to run below form we cannot say. Certainly she was never able to get clear of her field in her usual tearaway style and although she struck the front just after halfway she had nothing left when the rest came at her during the latter stages of the race. Several well known pressmen of our acquaintance had been shrewd enough to take some fancy ante-post prices about the filly for the forthcoming Goodwood Stewards Cup to be run just over a fortnight later and their feelings as she limped away afterwards can be imagined!

We took Polly's Brother as the key horse. He was in good form and had run his heart out to be beaten only a head for third place. His previous outing had earned him a 37 with us and we elected to keep him on that figure and calculate the rest from that.

Race 1590	8.20 Chester	5 furlongs			Good	July 9th		(9.7=50)
1347	Special Pleasure	3	9	7	50	–	54	5–4
1117 (1356)	Haditos	3	9	7	50	2	50	5–1
1347	Dragunn (+2)	3	8	4	33	5	(26)	7–1
1411	Curve the Wind	3	9	1	44	1½	(37)	5–2
673 (1030)	Cool Wind (+1)	3	7	8	23	Short-head	(16)	15–2

Analysis: Although Cool Wind was best-in here he was not running to his early figure (see also comments to Race 1030) and on recent form the race lay between Special Pleasure and Haditos. They were first and second 5 lengths clear of the other three runners and we took Haditos as having run to her figure, crediting Special Pleasure with 4 lbs for the 2 lengths win. The rest come down 7 lbs.

Race 1595	3.45 Chester	6 furlongs			Good	July 10th		(4.9.3=35) (3.9.3=44)
997 (1174)	Tree Fella	5	8	4	22	–	27	13–2
832 (1145)	Denmore	6	9	13	45	2½	45	11–2
1159	General Wade	7	9	2	34	Short-head	33	7–2
(1386)	Havon Cool	6	10	0	46	1½	42	5–1
1456	Alpine Rocket	5	9	7	39	Neck	34	7–2
1371	Town Flier	3	9	3	44	2½	(37)	9–2

Analysis: That wily old campaigner General Wade was co-favourite with Alpine Rocket for this and did at least have a few fair performances to his credit whereas his betting market companion seemed to have a lot to find if his performance in Race 1456 was any criterion.

In that race we had assessed his showing at (32) and here he was set to do 39, a not inconsiderable factor. The winner Tree Fella had not been able to match strides with Soba in Race 1174 but the rating of 21 he achieved in Race 997 run at Epsom gave him a good chance, as did an earlier race here (Race 523).

There were several horses that could be fancied however and the open nature of the betting was justified. With the result in the book we noted that Denmore had been set to do the same figure by the handicapper as our assessment in Race 832 and we took this figure as the guiding star despite his failure in Race 1145. Chester sprints are notoriously unsatisfactory events and we were not inclined to make too many drastic changes on the evidence of this race. Town Flier, for example, should have done better but took so long to get into his full stride that the race was over before he got into contention.

Race 1601	*3.45 Lingfield Park*	*6 furlongs*			*Firm*	*July 9th*		(8.0=19)
1117 (1230)	Welwyn	3	9	7	40	–	46	2–1
556 (1506)	Preparation	3	8	5	24	$2\frac{1}{2}$	24	5–2
1411	Transflash	3	8	0	19	4	(12)	6–4
(1364)	Caesar's Ghost	3	7	8	13	5	(3)	25–1
(1473)	Open the Box	3	9	7	40	$2\frac{1}{2}$	(30)	14–1
1030	Mr Gold Spur	3	7	7	12	$\frac{1}{2}$	(2)	25–1

Analysis: On recent form there were only two horses to be considered, namely Welwyn (−3 from Race 1117) and Transflash (−1 from Race 1411) but how punters could make the latter a 6–4 favourite beats us!

If a second in a £4600 event at Sandown does not represent better form than the same placing in a £2500 race at Yarmouth then form students are all wasting their time! As far as we were concerned Welwyn's rating was well substantiated and he had run to practically the same figure in Race 541. Transflash's figure on the other hand was rather doubtful. In Race 1411 it had been inflated by the 4 lbs overweight and prior to that he had done no better than to finish seventh of nineteen in a maiden race at Bath, a venue which, whilst delightful, is not exactly famous for attracting the cream of bloodstock.

With five previous races to go on we reasoned that if the handicapper had not got Preparation's measure by now he never would and so she went into the book at 24. Welwyn had won easily and we had no qualms about putting his rating up 6 lbs for the $2\frac{1}{2}$ lengths on firm going.

Transflash gets 7 lbs knocked off and the rest "lose" 10 lbs for being too far away to take any interest. Incidentally, Transflash subsequently ran unplaced in maiden events at Epsom and Yarmouth whilst Welwyn went on to win two good sprints at Goodwood (Races 1946 and 2402) proving yet again that because a horse is favourite he is not necessarily the form horse.

Race 1609 *4.45 Lingfield Park* *5 furlongs* *Firm* *July 10th* (10.0=44)

1430	Colonial Line	4	7	7	9	–	12	11–4
(1256)	Quae Supra	5	7	8	10	¾	11	9–1
1074 (1326)	Manilow	5	10	0	44	1½	41	3–1
(1242)	Boldly Go (+6)	4	7	7	9	Neck	5	33–1
1419	Jeckel	4	7	11	13	¾	8	2–1
	Jack Splendid (+8)	7	7	7	9	½	3	25–1

Analysis: We have to go back to Races 483 and 684 to get Colonial Line's best figures which gave him excellent prospects but he had been running a little below that level in recent events. Manilow (−) and Jeckel (−) had good enough figures to earn respect and the punters got it about right with 9–1 bar these three, of which Colonial Line came out best.

The finish was quite well contested and we shared 6 lbs for the 2¼ lengths between the first three.

Race 1613 *3.0 York* *5 furlongs* *Good–Firm* *July 9th* (8.8=44)

940 (1326)	Tobermory Boy	5	8	4	40	–	41	10–1
1386	Cree Song	6	8	8	44	Short-head	44	5–1
588 (1462)	Ponchielli	4	10	0	64	2	59	3–1
1001 (1491)	Kaimlaw	8	7	7	29	1	22	6–1
(1273)	Kabour (+10)	4	7	7	29	½	21?	33–1
1456	Miss Nelski (+5)	5	7	7	29	1½	(19)?	16–1

Analysis: Since running second to Susarma in Race 588 Ponchielli had been flying high. In the very hot Temple Stakes run over the Sandown 5 furlongs he had run quite well to finish sixth some 5½ lengths behind the winner and was then taken to Chantilly where he finished second to Kind Music beaten a length. He was then brought back to handicap company and with 9.11 on his back was made favourite in Race 1462 at Sandown finishing eighth. None of this high living had apparently escaped the handicapper's eagle eye and, from a rating of 59 in May he was now on the 64 mark. With Maestro Piggott aboard he was a well backed second favourite but he was unable to go with the leaders and ran on gallantly enough to take third place.

Favourite for this event was Bold Scuffle and with a form assessment of (−2) he should have been thereabouts but running in blinkers he ran no sort of race to finish last but one of the eight runners. On his performance in Race 940 Tobermory Boy (at +1) was not without prospects of success whilst

Cree Song had put up a good show in Race 732 (+1). Any horse which goes off at such a blinding pace as Cree Song did here and only gets caught on the line can almost always be taken to have run up to his rating and this we did here, calculating the rest from his 44 assessment.

Race 1623	*4.35 York*	*6 furlongs*		*Firm*	*July 10th*		(9.2=48)
(1341)	Expressly Yours (+2)	3	7 8	26	–	30	25–1
1473	Cyril's Choice	3	9 7	53	1½	53	4–1
1473	Golden Green	3	9 2	48	2	43	5–2
(1425)	Biddable	3	7 8	26	3	(19)	20–1
1393	Princess Virginia	3	8 7	39	3	(29)	4–1
(1230)	Strath of Orchy	3	9 1	47	1½	(37)	9–2

Analysis: Cyril's Choice (−2), Golden Green (−1) and Princess Virginia (−1) could all be fancied here but the 25–1 chance Expressly Yours brought smiles to the bookmakers' faces. The nearest we had to any sort of figure for the winner was from Race 1138 where she had finished seventh to Cedrella from a handicap mark of 29. Here she had been downrated to 26 and showed her appreciation by landing this prize of just over £3000.

Cyril's Choice had run below his Race 1127 figure in his next race (1473) and we therefore took the handicapper's mark as the correct one for assessing the first three whilst the rest go down by the usual 7 lbs.

Race 1626	*3.0 Salisbury*	*6 furlongs*		*Good–Firm*	*July 10th*		(4.8.9=34) (3.8.9=43)
1350	Milk Heart	3	8 10	44	–	48	11–2
1145 (1195)	Amorous	4	8 9	34	2	34	13–2
1167 (1195)	Sanjarida	4	9 0	39	½	37	8–1
1350	Lindsey	3	8 12	46	¾	43	7–2
1430	Lord Scrap (+7)	6	7 9	20	7	(13)	9–2
1511	Dungeon Ghyl	4	8 5	30	½	(23)	7–1

Analysis: Reference to Race 1350 reveals that Milk Heart and Lindsey had met before. On that occasion Lindsey was set to concede 2 lbs and did so by a head and 2 lengths. From that result we estimated that Lindsey was some 6 lbs the better horse. On exactly the same terms here, however, the placings were reversed with Milk Heart finishing some 3¼ lengths in front. Both races were over 6 furlongs and both horses appear to act on any going.

We have to accept the result as it stands and shared 7 lbs out among the first four as shown above.

Race 1631	*3.0 Edinburgh*	*5 furlongs*			*Good*	*July 12th*	(4.10.6=22) (3.10.6=29)	
1377	Bracken Gill (+7)	4	9	7	9	–	13?	8–1
(1212)	Melba Toast	8	9	7	9	4	5	9–2
339 (1595)	Silent Tears (+9)	5	9	7	9	1	2?	14–1
1001 (1575)	Longlands Lady (+7)	4	9	7	9	1	0?	3–1
1138	In Slips	3	10	6	29	Short-head	(20)?	11–10
100 (1419)	String of Stars (+9)	4	9	7	9	1½	0?	50–1

Analysis: A poor race with amateur riders on lowly rated animals. The 3yo In Slips had the enormous burden of 10.6 to carry and even with that talented rider Elain Mellor in the saddle one has to wonder at the starting price of 11–10. He was never in the race which went to the 4 lengths winner Bracken Gill who, like most of the rest of the field, was carrying overweight. Rating this was a very dubious exercise, 8 lbs was shared between the first two for the 4 lengths that separated them whilst In Slips goes down 9 lbs. But the entire race was guesswork both before and after.

Race 1640	*4.45 Pontefract*	*6 furlongs*			*Firm*	*July 12th*	(9.0=17)	
(1204)	Royal Duty	4	9	8	25	–	28	6–1
1498	Mary Maguire (+9)	5	9	5	22	1	22	8–1
1613	Kabour	4	9	2	19	¾	17	10–1
1419	Crowebronze	4	8	8	11	2½	(6)	11–1
1317	Holdall	4	8	11	14	Short-head	(8)	12–1
(1518)	Chad's Gamble	7	9	7	24	Short-head	(17)	8–1

Analysis: Holdall's figure of 20 in Race 843 had been made to look adrift in Race 1317 where he had been well beaten. On that running he was about 9 lbs superior to Crowebronze to whom he was now set to concede 3 lbs. Neither was fancied however and the race went to Royal Duty who had won a 7 furlong handicap at Beverley in June. With a 9 lbs penalty Mary Maguire had run surprisingly well and since she may have improved we took her figure as being the correct one. We would be happy with further confirmation of course.

(4.9.0=29)
Race 1655 *3.0 Leicester* *5 furlongs* *Firm* *July 13th* (3.9.0=36)

1425	Cree Bay (+7)	3	8	8	30	–	37	5–1
1410 (1553)	Bella Travaille (+6)	4	7	7	8	1½	11	25–1
1462	Brentex	4	9	3	32	1½	31	5–1
1462	Pusey Street	5	9	0	29	Neck	27	6–1
1356 (1462)	Epsom Imp	9	9	10	39	½	35	16–1
1541	Barnet Heir	4	9	7	36	¾	30	9–2

Analysis: Our pre-race ratings for this race gave the best chances to Cree Bay (−3), Barnet Heir (−2), Pusey Street (−) and Balatina (−). At 5–1 Cree Bay looked good value and he won his third race on the trot with very little trouble. Brentex had been hard ridden to get third and we calculated his form assessment of 31 by taking the average between his official rating of 32 and our latest form figure of 30. This was unlikely to be far out. Cree Bay goes up another 7 lbs but had not finished yet! (See Race 1786.)

Race 1680 *3.30 Bath* *5 furlongs* *Good* *July 14th* (9.0=24)

581 (1506)	Lochtillum	3	8	6	16	–	17	25–1
(1415)	April Memories	3	8	6	16	Neck	16	7–1
1506	Minnie Love	3	8	3	13	2	8	6–4
951	Ghawar	3	9	7	31	¾	25	3–1
1548	Listen to Me	3	8	4	14	¾	7	8–1
884 (1364)	Red Ellette	3	8	10	20	4	(10)	6–1

Analysis: A poor class sprint handicap at Bath with form figures for about half the runners does not sound the sort of race to go nap on and it was a pleasant surprise to have a 25–1 winner equal best in! With a form assessment of −2 from Race 581 Lochtillum had a good chance, although to be fair the figure was a bit suspect since he had carried 5 lbs overweight and readers will know by now our views on that! But at 25–1 one cannot have everything and he was worth a few bob on the Tote. With only a neck between the first two it was likely that both ratings were near enough with Lochtillum getting a 1 lb rise for the neck win.

Race 1683		6.0 Kempton Park	6 furlongs			Firm	July 14th	(4.10.0=45) (3.10.0=54)	
	1273	Bracadale	4	9	12	43	–	47	11–4
	1386	Kathred	4	9	8	39	1	40	7–1
	1410	Over the Rainbow	5	9	9	40	2½	37	5–2
	1462	Sailor's Prayer	4	8	3	20	Head	16	3–1
	1393	Kash-In	3	8	13	39	5	(29)	6–1
659	(775)	Spectacular Sky	4	10	0	45	2	(35)	16–1

Analysis: On his running in Race 1462 Sailor's Prayer was a good thing to win this. It is, of course, undeniable that Bracadale and Kathred had very good chances on their best form but one had to go back to Races 711 and 424 respectively for that. To our great consternation Sailor's Prayer never got into the race and finished just a fair fourth.

On reflection we should have known better! The Race 1462 figure had been inflated by the 7 lbs overweight and should not have been taken as holy writ! However, imagine our reaction when he came out at Ascot some nine days later and won a good handicap at 7–1 from a handicap rating of 29!! The handicapper had evidently thought the same as us and upgraded him by 9 lbs after Race 1462. In this race he was still on his old mark and should have walked it! Perhaps the sixth furlong was to blame although he had won over the distance in soft going as a 3yo.

One of the sweet mysteries of life!

Race 1706		4.45 Yarmouth	6 furlongs			Good	July 15th	(8.0=33)	
	(1469)	Looking Glass	3	7	12	31	–	34	9–4
	(1469)	Balcanoona	3	8	1	34	2	32	16–1
	1117	Tower of Strength	3	7	11	30	3	(23)	7–2
	1263	Ritual Dance	3	8	13	46	3	(36)	13–8
1263	(1428)	Feather Sound	3	8	10	43	1½	(33)	4–1

Analysis: On her figure from Race 1028 Ritual Dance had an excellent chance here but she had disappointed behind Tender Trader in Race 1263 and in fact never ran to the Race 1028 figure again. Neither Looking Glass nor Balcanoona had been noted in our book and it was difficult to rate this race correctly. We split 5 lbs for the 2 lengths separating first and second, giving the edge to the winner for what appeared to be a good performance. The rest were all doubtful.

Race 1707	6.45 Hamilton Park	6 furlongs			Good	July 15th	(4.8.11=13) (3.8.11=22)	
1205	Blochairn Skolar	4	8	2	4	–	6	11–2
1212 (1586)	Mott the Hoople	4	9	2	18	¾	18	7–2
(790)	Royal Grant	3	8	11	22	4	14	16–1
1419	Oyston Estates (+7)	6	8	12	14	1	(4)	7–4
1145	April Lucky	9	9	9	25	1	(15)	7–2
(1378)	Garthland Arms	3	7	12	9	3	(0)	10–1

Analysis: Three of the eight runners were rated equal top at (+1) and they finished first, second and fifth. Oyston Estates was favourite but with a 7 lbs penalty was (+5) with us and could get no nearer than fourth, beaten 5¾ lengths by the winner. Mott the Hoople kept on well to be second and we took his rating as being dependable, being only 1 lb different from his figure in Races 1065 and 1212. Royal Grant goes down 8 lbs for the 2 lengths behind Mott the Hoople but the rest "lose" 10 lbs.

Race 1716	8.05 Hamilton Park	5 furlongs			Good	July 16th	(8.7=28)	
863	Music Night	5	8	1	22	–	24	12–1
1511 (1556)	Bri-Eden (+7)	8	9	6	41	¾	41	11–8
174 (1556)	Sammy Bear	4	8	7	28	4	(21)	5–1
(1493)	French Touch (+8)	5	7	7	14	2	(7)	8–1
1430	Warooka (+13)	5	7	7	14	¾	(6)	14–1
1613	Miss Nelski	5	8	3	24	Head	(15)	9–2

Analysis: When a horse finishes fifth of eleven on its first outing in an event confined to amateur riders one cannot have too much confidence in its assessment. Such was the case with Music Night who had finished 7 lengths behind Russian Winter in Race 863 and "earned" a bracketed 13 with us. The race had evidently done him good and he won comfortably from the top two rated horses. We had put Bri-Eden up to 41 after Race 1511 and saw no reason to question that figure here. Music Night goes up to 24 but the rest go down considerably in view of the 4 lengths and more they were behind the winner.

Race 1724	5.15 Thirsk	6 furlongs			Good	July 16th		(4.8.2=21) (3.8.2=29)
86 (1553)	Lindy Bay (+4)	5	7	8	13	–	14	8–1
1419	Blessed Silence (+8)	4	7	7	12	Head	12?	16–1
1347	Laurence Mac	3	8	2	29	5	(22)	5–2
1200 (1595)	Starlust	3	8	13	40	2½	(33)	10–1
1640	Kabour	4	8	0	19	¾	(12)	9–2
1167	Stern (+4)	6	8	0	19	4	(12)	13–2

Analysis: There was nothing outstanding here and ifs and buts about several of the runners. Kabour's figure from Race 1613 was inflated by 10 lbs overweight whilst Blessed Silence was forced to carry 8 lbs more than his official rating. On balance the most reliable figure was that of Laurence Mac (31 from Race 1347B) and therefore −2 for this race. The colt was made favourite but unfortunately hung badly left when about to make his challenge and was a badly beaten third at the finish. Lindy Bay had gone down from an official rating of 19 in Race 86 and was now on the 13 mark after several very uninspiring performances. To rate this we took the front two as having run to their ratings, albeit with some strong misgivings about Blessed Silence.

Race 1740	2.30 Newmarket	5 furlongs			Good	July 17th		(9.7=49)
1590	Haditos	3	9	7	49	–	50	9–2
(1393)	Red Rosie	3	9	7	49	Neck	49	14–1
1590	Special Pleasure (+8)	3	9	13	55	¾	53	6–4
1473 (1511)	Mummy's Pleasure	3	9	7	49	2½	(42)	3–1
240 (1410)	Miss Trilli	3	8	4	32	4	(24)	12–1
1541	Hit the Line	3	7	10	24	½	(14)	13–2

Analysis: Miss Trilli's dismal performance in three races since Race 240 had convinced the handicapper – and us – that she was no longer the horse she appeared to be on that running and she had been dropped to a rating of 32, a downgrading which spoke volumes concerning the official view of her ability. Her form assessment with us of −13 was purely academic and such a margin was in itself a clear indication that something was wrong. Readers are warned to take more than a second look at such a figure. Handicappers do not normally let horses in with nearly a stone less than their form warrants and one is well advised to let the handicapper have the last word. Miss Trilli's official ratings had been going down steadily since her first outing and that is never a good sign unless the animal in question shows some semblance of a return to form in a recent race. Such was certainly not the case with Miss Trilli.

Disregarding the filly therefore, we have Haditos best in at −2 and was not a bad sort of bet at 9–2.

Special Pleasure had run well with an 8 lbs penalty and taking Red Rosie as the key horse made the ratings of the winner and third look about right. Mummy's Pleasure appeared to have run about 6 or 7 lbs below her best and it was pleasing to see her come back with a very good run to finish fourth in the Goodwood Stewards Cup (Race 1926).

Race 1748	*8.15 Nottingham*	*6 furlongs*			*Firm*	*July 17th*	(10.0=50)	
1626	Amorous	4	8	12	34	–	38	11–10
	Yoohoo (+1)	8	7	7	15	1½	15	16–1
1595	Alpine Rocket	5	9	1	37	1½	34	5–1
1430 (1626)	Eagle's Quest	4	7	7	15	¾	10	10–1
(1273)	Polly Royal	4	7	12	20	1½	(14)	8–1
(1522)	Steel Pass	4	10	0	50	½	(43)	3–1

Analysis: Whilst not a very good price Amorous was the best bet here. Set to do a rating of 34 he had twice run to that figure and we had made comment about his improvement in our analysis following Race 1145. The going had been on the soft side then but Amorous proved that he did not mind a firm surface winning in good style from the 8yo Yoohoo, who was running for the first time this season.

We shared 7 lbs between the first three with Amorous going up to a new rating of 38.

Race 1755	*4.15 Ripon*	*5 furlongs*			*Good–Firm*	*July 17th*	(4.9.6=33) (3.9.6=39)	
1491	Miss Import (+5)	4	9	6	33	–	35	9–4
1200	Dutch Girl	5	9	1	28	Neck	29	5–1
1491 (1655)	Rambling River	5	8	6	19	Head	19	9–1
940	Miss Poinciana	5	9	10	37	6	(30)	5–1
1230	Errolls Boy	3	9	12	45	¾	(38)	4–1
	Jose Collins	5	10	0	41	1½	(31)	14–1

Analysis: Rambling River again! As discussed in our comments on Race 1491 he had set up figures in excess of that he was being asked to do and since he was assessed at −3 he was a tempting price at 9–1. Errolls Boy was also well in on his figure from Race 1030 but he had a lot of weight to carry for a 3yo against older horses.

Miss Import was set to give Rambling River only 5 lbs more than in Race 1491 where she had beaten him 5 lengths. On those terms she was favourite to beat him again and she succeeded in doing so in a desperate finish with only a neck and a head separating the first three and the rest of the runners well beaten off.

Rating was easy. We keep Rambling River on his rating of 19 and give the first two 2 lbs and 1 lb respectively.

Race 1763	*4.15 Ayr*	*6 furlongs*			*Good–Firm*	*July 17th*		(8.9=37)
1623	Expressly Yours (+10)	3	7	12	26	–	36+	7–2
(1583)	Sew Nice (+7)	3	7	8	22	7	24	10–11
1064	Here's Sue (+1)	3	8	2	30	½	30	7–1
1138 (1489)	Western Hero	3	7	11	25	Neck	24	12–1
1127 (1453)	Roman Quest	3	8	9	37	Head	35	10–1
1010 (1491)	My Fancy (+1)	3	8	0	28	Neck	25	20–1

Analysis: The comments on Races 1445 and 1623 with reference to the respective winners make interesting reading now. In Race 1445 we had to make an educated guess at the value of Sew Nice's win when we had put her figure up 9 lbs, whilst we were only a little less in the dark with Expressly Yours for whom we had no previous figure. She had by now gone down to an official mark of 16 and even with a 10 lbs penalty was set to do 26 and was thus −4 with us, the same as Sew Nice.

The latter was 10–11 favourite with Expressly Yours at 7–2 and with so little to choose between them the "value" bet was obvious. At the end of the race, however, there was enough daylight between them to erect half-a-dozen fair sized greenhouses as Expressly Yours came right away in the last 2 furlongs. With the next five horses separated by about a length we could only accept that they had all run more or less to their ratings and that Expressly Yours had improved still further.

Here's Sue's rating of 30 was exactly midway between her official figure of 33 in Race 1064 and our form assessment of 27 in the same race and was unlikely to be far out.

Race 1767	*4.0 Ayr*	*5 furlongs*	*Good*	*July 19th*			(8.7=28)
1456	Touch Boy (+7)	6 10 8	57	–	57	4–1	
1462	Little Starchy	4 8 9	30	1	27	10–1	
1716	Sammy Bear	4 8 7	28	¾	23	11–1	
1595	General Wade	7 8 13	34	2	(27)	7–2	
1491	Pergoda	4 7 9	16	Head	(9)	5–1	
1716	Miss Nelski	5 8 3	24	½	(17)	12–1	

Analysis: Pergoda and Pagapas Bay (unplaced here) were both rated at −1 from their performances in Races 1491 and 1216 respectively. The latter had not run to that figure in Race 1356 but Pergoda's second to Miss Import in Race 1491 had been enhanced by that filly's win in Race 1755 two days before. (These two horses were later first and second again in Race 2065 where Miss Import gave Pergoda a further 7 lbs and beat him by 2 lengths as against the 1½ lengths in 1491. It was clear at that stage that Miss Import had improved whilst Pergoda virtually stood still.) On the face of it here, however, Pergoda, with a boy claiming 5 lbs looked to have a very good chance but he never really got to the leaders.

Touch Boy's performance was a surprise. We could not have given his Race 1456 win more than face value and the 7 lbs penalty taking his weight up to 10.8 seemed to give him too much to do. It did not stop him though and it looked a very good performance. Surprisingly enough, the handicapper was not over impressed because he was rated at 52 in September, only 2 lbs more than his figure here. He had, however, been well beaten in between in Race 2065. Rating was not easy. We were not inclined to put Touch Boy up too much because he had won with a 7 lbs penalty and we were not prepared to accept that we were more than that amount wrong. We therefore installed him at 57 and rated the rest from that.

Race 1780	*8.20 Windsor*	*6 furlongs*	*Good–Firm*	*July 19th*			(7.12=24)
(1370)	Trooper Sergeant	3 7 8	20	–	22	2–1	
1482	Another Way	3 7 10	22	¾	22	33–1	
109 (1696)	Gentle Star (+7)	3 7 7	19	1½	15?	16–1	
1601	Preparation	3 7 12	24	½	19	5–1	
166 (1310)	Diamond King	3 8 3	29	4	(22)	14–1	
1095	Cheri Berry	3 8 13	39	½	(32)	5–2	

Analysis: Preparation was (−) here on her running in Race 1601 where we had come to the conclusion that the handicapper had her truly weighted but she still could not win. (She did eventually, in Race 2781 from a rating of 20, so everything comes to she who waits!)

Trooper Sergeant had been running in selling class and had in fact won the Newmarket seller in which Superb Singer had finished tailed off only to re-appear to win Race 1506. There must have been something in the Newmarket air for Trooper Sergeant made all the running to win this and was 2–1 favourite to do so. Another Way had been hard ridden to get second and we took her as the key horse.

Race 1786	*4.15 Wolverhampton*	*5 furlongs*			*Good*	*July 19th*	(10.0=36)	
1655	Cree Bay (+7)	3	10	0	36	–	40	11–8
364 (1643)	Free Range	3	7	10	4	½	6	8–1
410 (1506)	Rain Dancer	3	8	10	18	7	(11)	6–1
(1489)	Venetian Joy	3	8	12	20	1½	(13)	10–1
1590	Cool Wind	3	8	13	21	Short-head	(14)	12–1
(1030)	Pitter Pat	3	8	7	15	2	(8)	20–1

Analysis: These were not a good lot and even with a 7 lbs penalty Cree Bay did not have to do too much to win this although he had to put his best foot forward to beat Free Range by ½ length.

It was possible that Cree Bay had nearly reached the limit of improvement having gone up considerably in the official ratings and it seemed unwise to put him up too much. He was therefore written in on the 40 mark with the same increase for Free Range less 2 lbs for the ½ length between them. The remainder were well beaten off and all their ratings are reduced by 7 lbs pending confirmation.

Race 1803	*3.30 Warwick*	*5 furlongs*			*Good–Firm*	*July 21st*	(9.7=39)	
(1484)	Spinner (+3)	3	7	10	14	–	17	9–2
221 (1270)	Harpers Bazaar	3	9	7	39	1½	38	5–1
1680	Lochtillum (+7)	3	8	5	23	Short-head	21	11–4
610 (1364)	Sound of the Sea	3	8	7	25	5	(18)	7–4
1364 (1453)	Pokerfayes	3	8	1	19	2½	(9)	15–2
(673)	Cawston Star	3	7	8	12	5	(2)	16–1

Analysis: Harpers Bazaar had failed in three races to produce his form figure of Race 221 and did not look a good bet to do so here. Nevertheless he ran a good race to finish second to Spinner. There was not too much between the first three and we split 5 lbs between them as shown.

Race 1821	*7.35 Hamilton Park*	*5 furlongs*		*Good–Firm*		*July 21st*	(4.9.0=23) (3.9.0=29)
1655	Bella Travaille	4	7	7	2	–	5	11–2
1613	Kaimlaw	8	9	6	29	1	29	7–1
1707	Blochairn Skolar	4	7	9	4	$\frac{3}{4}$	2	11–4
1724	Laurence Mac	3	9	0	29	$1\frac{1}{2}$	25	6–1
1767	Little Starchy	4	9	7	30	$\frac{1}{2}$	25	13–2
419 (1456)	Tom Dowdeswell	6	8	4	13	1	6	20–1

Analysis: If Bella Travaille's figure from Race 1655 was only half true she was past the post for this! Unfortunately, the figure was inflated by the 6 lbs overweight she carried that day and looked doubtful. Ridden by a 5 lbs claimer she was always going well and won nicely by a length from Kaimlaw. The latter, rated at 29, the same as his form figure from Race 1001, seemed the right sort to use as the standard for rating the rest.

Race 1827	*7.35 Hamilton Park*	*6 furlongs*		*Good–Firm*		*July 22nd*	(9.7=29)	
1425 (1623)	Ben Jarrow	3	9	4	26	–	34	6–1
1028 (1341)	Firespark	3	8	5	13	4	13	9–1
1425 (1484)	Magnamala (+6)	3	8	11	19	Head	18	6–1
(1341)	L'Angelo di Carlo	3	7	13	7	Neck	5	12–1
1763	Here's Sue	3	9	7	29	5	(22)	4–1
1498	Knight Security	3	9	4	26	1	(19)	5–2

Analysis: We could have no real confidence that the result here would be in accordance with our expectations. Firespark's best figure was over 5 furlongs, Knight Security's on soft going and Here's Sue had been well behind Expressly Yours in Race 1763. Ben Jarrow had confirmed his figure several times and proved a decisive winner. We decided here to give him full value for an improved performance and rated from Firespark downwards as shown.

Race 1835	*8.0 Sandown Park*	*5 furlongs*			*Good–Firm*	*July 21st*	(4.9.9=43) (3.9.9=49)	
1074 (1655)	Dalegarth	4	9	9	43	–	45	25–1
1511	Telegraph Boy (+2)	4	7	7	13	Neck	14	4–1
1134 (1462)	Durandal	5	8	7	27	Neck	27	9–2
1655	Pusey Street	5	8	9	29	1	26	11–4
1525	My Dear Fellow	3	9	9	49	Head	45	9–2
1195 (1386)	Gamblers Dream	5	9	11	45	Head	40	7–1

Analysis: On their best figures the race lay between Durandal (−1), Pusey Street (−), Telegraph Boy (+2) and My Dear Fellow (+2), but they were all beaten by Dalegarth who had started slowly when tailed off behind Cree Bay in Race 1655. Prior to that he had been last of six behind Manilow in Race 1074 so there was no encouragement from the form book. In a very tight finish we took Durandal as having run to his rating which was only 1 lb different from his figure in Race 1134 run on similar going.

Using him as the yardstick made the others fit in very closely with previous figures.

Race 1846	*3.15 Carlisle*	*6 furlongs*			*Firm*	*July 23rd*		(10.0=25)
1491	Karen's Star	5	9	1	12	–	14	12–1
1419	Crowebronze	4	9	0	11	½	11	11–2
(1498)	Spoilt for Choice	4	8	13	10	3	(3)	14–1
1317 (1556)	Little Atom	5	9	4	15	Short-head	(8)	12–1
1640	Holdall	4	9	3	14	8	(4)	8–1
	Bokara in Shallah	5	9	5	16	1	(6)	16–1

Analysis: Karen's Star's best figure of 17 from Race 1200 made her clear best in here at −5, the snag being that she had run below that figure in two races since, both over 5 furlongs on good going.

Here she had the same firm going as in Race 1200 and it evidently suited her for she made all the running to win by a length.

Crowebronze's rating of 11 was the same as in Race 1273 where he had been in a tight finish and we took him as the guide to rate Karen's Star. The rest were 3 lengths away – a shade too far for confident ratings.

Race 1851	*2.30 Ascot*	*5 furlongs*				*Good–Firm*		*July 23rd*		(4.8.0=29) (3.8.0=35)
1683	Sailor's Prayer		4	8	0	29		–	33	7–1
1462	Vorvados		5	8	12	41		1½	41	4–1
1350	Silojoka		3	9	2	51		Neck	50	4–1
1835	Durandal		5	7	12	27		Short-head	25	4–1
775 (1110)	Hampton Bay		3	9	7	56		3	50	11–2
1655	Brentex		4	8	5	34		1	27	4–1

Analysis: On our best figures there was little to choose between Durandal (−1), Sailor's Prayer (+1), Vorvados (+1) and Silojoka (+2), although we must admit that after Sailor's Prayer's poor showing in Race 1683 we had been inclined to revamp the ratings in Race 1462, thinking that we must be well adrift. Common sense came to the rescue however. It was far more likely that Sailor's Prayer had run a bad race than that the rest of the horses were some 12 lbs wrong and we watched the race with considerable interest even though our financial involvement was nil!

A burst watermain had put the straight course out of action and we had the odd spectacle of a 5 furlong race at Ascot being run on the round course. Whether that circumstance made any difference to the result we cannot say but Sailor's Prayer loved it! Second into the straight he took the lead a quarter of a mile from home and that was that as far as the rest were concerned.

We rated this race using Vorvados as the anchor. This put Sailor's Prayer up to 33, a figure which we still cannot believe! He never ran to within 8 lbs of that figure again and we can only conclude that the result was a bit of a fluke as far as the winner was concerned because every figure bar his looked right.

Race 1875	*1.30 Newcastle*	*6 furlongs*				*Good–Firm*		*July 24th*		(10.0=49)
1134	Old Dominion		5	10	0	49		–	55	10–3
1377	In Rhythm		5	8	4	25		4	23	3–1
1640	Mary Maguire		5	7	8	15		Head	12	Evens
671 (1640)	Java Tiger		4	8	7	28		2½	(21)	8–1
450 (1640)	Zoilo		4	7	12	19		1½	(12)	20–1
(1174)	Archimbolo		4	8	4	25		25	(15)	20–1

Analysis: Mary Maguire was easily best in here at −7 from Race 1640 but she ran well below that figure. Backed down from 2–1 to evens she was always thereabouts but pulled out nothing from 2 furlongs out. It was a disappointing performance, the more so because she subsequently recorded figures of 23 (Race 2072), 20 (2590), 20 (2663) and 22 (2883). She had been re-rated at 24 by the official handicapper by the beginning of August so she must just have had an off day. It was difficult to decide here whether to give Old Dominion full credit for the easy 4 lengths win, keeping In Rhythm on the 25 mark, or whether to split 8 lbs for the 4 lengths that separated them.

Eventually we split the difference between In Rhythm's present rating of 25 and his most recent form figure of 21, called him 23 and rated from that. Old Dominion did not run up to his new rating of 55 (see Races 2059 and 2656), whereas In Rhythm ran to within a pound or two of his rating of 23. In retrospect it appears that Old Dominion's win was worth less than it looked at the time.

Race 1878	*3.0 Newcastle*	*5 furlongs*			*Good–Firm*	*July 24th*	(4.8.3=18) (3.8.3=24)	
1755	Rambling River	5	8	3	18	–	19	7–2
1716	Bri-Eden (+6)	8	10	2	45	Head	45	10–1
1755	Dutch Girl	5	8	13	28	2½	23	9–4
1613	Cree Song	6	10	0	43	1½	36	6–1
1716	Music Night (+6)	5	8	13	28	½	20	10–1
1623	Biddable	3	7	11	18	½	8	20–1

Analysis: At long last Rambling River did what he had been threatening to do for a long time! His handicap rating of 18 was below the form figures he had set up in four races and with the good apprentice N. Day claiming 3 lbs he looked a racing certainty. He did not win like one however as, after heading the front running Bri-Eden well inside the final furlong he was all out to resist that horse's renewed challenge. The latter had been setting up improved figures and we were inclined to accept that his present rating of 45, which included a penalty, was the correct one. The trouble with this was that it made nearly all the rest appear to have run below form – not a good sign. On the other hand, with Rambling River and Bri-Eden having a battle royal up front, there was clearly no real incentive for the rest of the riders to go all out for the £364 third prize.

Race 1889	*3.15 Bath*	*5 furlongs*			*Good–Firm*	*July 26th*	(4.9.0=36) (3.9.0=42)	
(1489)	Night Clown	3	7	9	23	–	24	7–1
1623	Golden Green	3	9	6	48	Neck	48	8–1
1786	Cree Bay (+7)	3	8	12	40	3	33	7–2
1167 (1522)	Tamdown Flyer	4	9	0	36	Short-head	29	6–4
1511	Young Inca (+8)	4	7	7	15	Neck	7	50–1
1835	Pusey Street	5	8	7	29	3	(19)	5–1

Analysis: Cree Bay had been going up in the official scale and with a 7lbs penalty to carry as well it looked as if the handicapper had caught up with him at last. On his running in Race 1786 he still looked in with a chance of increasing his splendid winning run but although he ran on well from a furlong out he could not get near to challenge Night Clown. The latter had finished well behind Cree Bay in a non-handicap event at Chepstow in June but had since won a moderate apprentice event over 5 furlongs at Edinburgh.

It looked to us as if Golden Green had run right up to his best and we took his official rating of 48 as the mark from which to calculate the rest.

Race 1920	*3.15 Redcar*	*6 furlongs*			*Good–Firm*	*July 28th*	(9.8=39)	
1174 (1498)	Bettabet Geraghty	4	7	13	16	–	23	14–1
(1224)	Top o' the Lane	5	8	5	22	2½	23	8–1
1748	Yoohoo	8	7	11	14	Head	14	13–2
1498	Cudgel	9	10	0	45	6	(35)	6–1
1683	Kathred	4	9	8	39	3	(29)	3–1
	Hexgreave Star	4	8	3	20	1½	(10)	33–1

Analysis: After his win in Race 930 with a form figure of 18, Bettabet Geraghty had "caught a tartar" when tackling Soba in Race 1174. Even so he was not disgraced and finished fourth some 7 lengths behind that flying filly. Here he was rated on the 16 mark and made it all to win very comfortably. Top o' the Lane and Yoohoo had a good fight for second place and had probably run to their ratings, Yoohoo's figure being only a pound difference from that of Race 1748.

Using Yoohoo as the standard put Bettabet Geraghty up to 23 but the win looked worth it.

Race 1926	*3.10 Goodwood*				*6 furlongs*	*Good–Firm*	*July 27th*	(4.8.0=43) (3.8.0=51)
1582	Soba (+5)	3	8	4	55	–	65+	18–1
1683	Bracadale	4	8	0	43	2½	46	12–1
1525	Celestial Dancer (+3)	3	8	10	61	2	61	9–1
1740	Mummy's Pleasure	3	7	10	47	½	45	50–1
(1522)	Scarrowmanwick	4	9	6	63	2½	58	25–1
(1534)	Gabitat	4	9	7	64	Short-head	58	14–1
1582	Camisite (+7)	4	9	0	57	Short-head	51	14–1
1582	Great Eastern	5	9	11	68	Short-head	61	14–1
1623	Cyril's Choice	3	8	2	53	Head	45	16–1
1767	Touch Boy (+1)	6	8	7	50	Neck	41	7–1

Analysis: After her defeat at Ayr (Race 1582) Soba was found to have back trouble and for some while was thought to be a very doubtful runner for this race, the Stewards Cup, rightly regarded as one of the hottest sprints of the season. Holders of ante-post vouchers must have been very relieved when she appeared to have responded to treatment and was duly declared as a runner. Unfortunately their trials and tribulations were not yet over and how they felt as Soba went down to the start is not recorded. For it looked odds against her ever reaching her destination as she ducked and plunged about for practically the whole of the straight.

Her able jockey confessed afterwards that it felt like being in an American rodeo and he for one must have been very thankful when she finally got to the stalls. She had also been "unlucky" in that she had drawn the number one position, considered to be the worst possible place over the Goodwood 6 furlongs.

So the portents were not good!

She had been beaten at Ayr, plagued with back trouble, drawn the worst starting place and on top of that, no-one could be sure what had caused her erratic behaviour on the way down. Soba, of course, was completely oblivious of these and other problems besetting the minds of all who watched and showed her contempt for such mundane matters by hurtling out of the stalls like a shot from a gun to win unchallenged by 2½ lengths and breaking the course record into the bargain.

It was a superb performance and those who had backed Soba for this race before the Ayr defeat could now airily affirm their complete and utter confidence in the filly now that she was safely past the post.

On their best figures, Touch Boy, Bracadale, Soba and Great Eastern had the best chances and with Lester Piggott in the saddle Touch Boy was favourite. Lester put up 1 lb overweight but, like the rest of the field, Touch Boy was always being pushed along to keep within hail of Soba who was making her majestic way down the stands side, and had run out of steam after 4 furlongs. Bracadale, however, ran a good race to come through very late on the far side to take second place. Mummy's Pleasure, drawn three, had the unenviable task of taking on Soba from the start and she did extremely well to improve upon her figure of Race 1740.

We took the view that most of the near at hand horses had run to their assessments and Celestial Dancer's rating of 61 was used as the touchstone. Bracadale, Mummy's Pleasure and Gabitat came out within a pound or two of recent performances, whilst Soba went up 10 lbs for a smashing display which we feel privileged to have seen.

Sheer magic!

Race 1930 *2.0 Goodwood* *5 furlongs* *Good–Firm* *July 28th* (8.4=40)

1755	Errolls Boy	3	8	9	45	–	47	9–2
1230 (1356)	Street Market	3	9	5	55	Neck	56	15–2
(1462)	Fly Baby	3	9	7	57	Short-head	57	20–1
1740	Red Rosie	3	8	13	49	$\frac{3}{4}$	47	7–2
1371	New Express	3	9	0	50	$\frac{3}{4}$	46	15–8
1127	On Return	3	9	6	56	$1\frac{1}{2}$	49	10–1

Analysis: Street Market's form in Races 240 and 481 had earned him assessments of 63+ and 64 respectively but since then he had been beaten in four races as a result of which his official rating had dropped a few pounds. His defeats had been in very good company however and a couple of slow starts had not helped his cause. On his best form he was – 9 with us, followed by Errolls Boy −3, whose performance in Race 1030 merited a figure of 48 and who had been trying to concede weight to older horses on his last outing.

These two were rated clear of the field and they fought out a very close finish with Fly Baby. This was an improved performance on the latter's part and we now took her rating as being correct.

Such a stirring finish involved only minor adjustments to existing figures.

Race 1946	4.05 Goodwood	6 furlongs			Good–Firm		July 30th	(4.8.8=39) (3.8.8=47)
1601	Welwyn	3	8	5	44	–	46	5–1
1626	Sanjarida	4	8	8	39	Neck	40	6–1
1411	No Contest	3	8	11	50	5	45	9–2
1889	Night Clown (+7)	3	7	7	32	1	24	3–1
1595	Tree Fella	5	7	11	28	Short-head	20	10–1
(1236)	My Dad Tom	3	9	7	60	2	(50)	7–1

Analysis: No Contest, Welwyn and Sanjarida were best-in in that order and with Steve Dawson claiming 5 lbs Sanjarida looked a very good each way bet at 6–1. Incidentally, how Night Clown could have been favourite for this event is a mystery! He had been all out to win Race 1889 and could not really be rated any higher than 24. Here, with a 7 lbs penalty he was set to do 32 and even with the boy claiming 5 lbs was not a good bet.

Sanjarida was ridden to perfection by young Steve Dawson, being brought with a perfectly timed run close home. Unfortunately for him however, Welwyn, also held up to the last minute by Willie Carson, just got first run and held on to win a terrific race by a neck.

We took both horses to have run to their previous best figures of 46 and 40 respectively which, calculated down, put Night Clown on what we thought was his correct rating of 24. No Contest is put on the 45 mark, a figure arrived at by deducting the 8 lbs we have taken from Night Clown and adding back 3 lbs for the length between them, a net reduction of 5 lbs.

Race 1963	3.45 Doncaster	5 furlongs			Good–Firm	July 29th		(9.0=24)
1541 (1655)	Balatina	4	9	0	24	–	29	5–4
1846	Karen's Star (+7)	5	8	9	19	3	17	9–1
481 (1755)	Relative Ease	11	7	13	9	2	4	20–1
940 (1511)	Waresley	4	9	1	25	¾	(18)	5–1
1200 (1350)	Humble Blue	4	9	3	27	2	(19)	5–1
1456 (1613)	Bold Scuffle	4	10	0	38	3	(28)	7–1

Analysis: We could not entertain Relative Ease here even though he was assessed at −7 on his running in Race 481. He had carried 12 lbs overweight there and his consequent rating was wildly at variance with his previous form. In any case, at 11 years old he ought to be getting past this sort of thing. He was not though! He did manage to win a "bumpers" race at

Wolverhampton two weeks later (2221) where most of the field carried a lot of overweight.

Balatina and Bold Scuffle were rated equal at −1 and, on the face of it, the latter looked a "value" bet at 7–1. He had been far from consistent though and had failed to win a race so far this season, whereas Balatina had made very good progress and was already the winner of five races. It is, of course, easier to give plausible reasons after the event but nevertheless, on balance, the form student should always give preference to the horse that has done it rather than one who has always promised to deliver but never does. Balatina looked in some trouble 2 furlongs out however until her rider managed to squeeze through a narrow gap to go on and win by an easy 3 lengths.

Karen's Star's best figure had been 17 in Race 1200 and we decided to leave him on that figure and assess the rest round him. Balatina went up to 29 but had not yet finished!

Race 1968	*7.10 Newmarket*	*6 furlongs*			*Good–Firm*	*July 30th*	(4.8.8=39) (3.8.8=47)	
1851	Vorvados	5	8	8	39	–	40	4–1
(1533)	Queen of Scots	3	8	1	40	Head	40	3–1
1350 (1730)	Doc Marten	4	9	7	52	Short-head	51	13–2
1748 (1926)	Steel Pass	4	9	5	50	1	46	14–1
1706	Tower of Strength	3	7	7	32	2½	(25)	25–1
	Royal Kingdom	5	7	9	26	¾	(18)	25–1

Analysis: Vorvados (−2) was clear best-in here and had proved himself over 6 furlongs in Race 107. Next best was the 3yo Purnima at (+1) and with M. Hills claiming the 5 lbs allowance could have been expected to be thereabouts. Race 1482 was not the best of guides however (see analysis of that race) and Purnima had probably been lucky to win. He never showed here to finish ninth.

Queen of Scots ran her heart out and was only caught on the line. She could confidently be taken as the marker here. Vorvados and Doc Marten go to figures only a pound different from earlier runs. The form of this looked reliable.

Race 1988	*3.45 Thirsk*	*5 furlongs*			*Firm*	*July 31st*		(10.0=59)
	Doubtwash Girl	4	7	7	24	–	26	33–1
1498 (1724)	Caledonian (+3)	6	7	7	24	Head	25	9–1
1356	Pontin Lad	4	10	0	59	Neck	59	2–1
	Be Sharp (+17)	4	7	7	24	Short-head	23?	33–1
1626	Dungeon Ghyl	4	7	9	26	2	22	5–1
1878	Dutch Girl	5	7	13	30	5	(23)	5–4

Analysis: There was little to choose between our assessments for this race with Pontin Lad, Dutch Girl, Caledonian and Dungeon Ghyl having the best of it. Dutch Girl was made favourite at 5–4, a price not really justified by the form book. Her stable were apparently entertaining an angel unawares however and Dutch Girl's yard companion took the race at 33–1 with four horses going over the line together. Pontin Lad was well established at 59 and there seemed no reason to change his figure which formed the basis for rating the race. Be Sharp's assessment gets a query for the huge amount of overweight carried. In passing it can be mentioned that Doubtwash Girl never ran to this form again.

Race 1994	*8.05 Windsor*	*5 furlongs*			*Good*	*July 31st*		(4.8.12=25) (3.8.12=31)
1786	Free Range	3	7	7	12	–	17	5–1
(1900)	Mummy's Treasure	4	8	5	18	Short-head	22	9–1
1609	Quae Supra	5	7	10	9	3	6	8–1
1511	Winner Takes All	5	7	7	6	3	0	12–1
1851	Durandal	5	8	12	25	1	(18)	5–2
(1786)	Mandrake Belle	3	7	11	16	1½	(9)	33–1

Analysis: Prior to running second to Cree Bay in Race 1786 Free Range had won an apprentice selling handicap at Windsor and as a result had been promoted from a rating of 4 to the 12 she was set to do here. She had obviously found a bit of form and in the hands of Steve Dawson she battled on well to beat Mummy's Treasure by a short head. To rate this we shared 7 lbs for the 3 lengths between the second and third as shown above, whilst Free Range goes up the second's 4 lbs plus a further pound for the short head win.

Race 2003	*4.15 Folkestone*	*6 furlongs*			*Firm*	*August 2nd*		(8.10=38)
1212 (1533)	Senorita Querida	3	9	3	45	–	50	8–1
1930	Red Rosie	3	9	7	49	2	49	13–8
1548 (1774)	Dark Mystique (+8)	3	7	7	21	¾	19?	25–1
884 (1543)	Love Me Do	3	7	8	22	Neck	19	7–1
(1425)	Double Vie	3	8	2	30	1	24	20–1
1706	Balcanoona	3	8	0	28	1½	(21)	5–1

Analysis: Balcanoona (−4), Senorita Querida (−2), Another Way (−1) and Red Rosie (−) were best in here and we could be reasonably satisfied with the result. Balcanoona had tired towards the end of Race 1706 and did the same here. 5 furlongs may be her best trip. On past form Red Rosie seemed accurately assessed at 49 and we took her figure as the guideline. Dark Mystique's overweight gets a query.

Race 2006	*3.30 Ripon*	*6 furlongs*			*Good*	*August 2nd*		(9.5=57)
1482	Northorpe	3	8	3	39	–	43	3–1
(1774)	Godly (+7)	3	8	10	46	2½	44	4–1
	Gold Key (+7)	3	7	7	29	1	24	33–1
(1868)	Sparkling Form (+17)	3	7	7	29	1	23	33–1
1827 (1884)	Ben Jarrow (+7)	3	7	12	34	1	27	10–3
1230 (1582)	Four for Music	3	8	7	43	2½	35	5–1

Analysis: This was a puzzling race to sum up. Clear best-in was Four for Music but he had been a disappointment to us in Race 577 after his 5 lengths win at Newmarket in Race 428 and had not covered himself in glory since. We were also not happy with the ratings in Race 1482 but we had noted that Northorpe could well be better than we had estimated. Ben Jarrow had a 5 lbs penalty for his Hamilton win (Race 1827) but on the figure we had given him there he was not without a chance. He had also run quite well to be second in a useful handicap over 7 furlongs at Newcastle in July. Northorpe was favourite and confirmed our suggestion that he may have improved by winning in good style. Four for Music started slowly and was always well behind in company with Ben Jarrow. It now looked as if Northorpe was indeed better than our Race 1482 figure and in splitting 6 lbs for the 2½ lengths between him and Godly we gave the edge to Northorpe, putting him on the 43 mark.

Race 2041	*3.15 Ayr*	*6 furlongs*	*Good*	*August 4th*		(4.9.0=18) (3.9.0=25)

1724	Blessed Silence	4	8	0	4	–	12	5–2
1410 (1511)	Russian Winter	7	9	9	27	2½	29	13–2
1875	In Rhythm	5	9	7	25	Head	26	10–3
1707 (1774)	Royal Grant	3	8	11	22	1	20	12–1
566 (1234)	Young Croftie	5	8	0	4	1	0	20–1
1821	Bella Travaille (+7)	4	8	8	12	¾	5	5–1

Analysis: Blessed Silence was clear top rated (−8) for this although we had misgivings about the Race 1724 rating in which the colt carried 8 lbs overweight. Even so, he seemed to have enough in hand to win this. On earlier form Russian Winter was −3 with us and they finished first and second. With this race as confirmation we could now quite reasonably establish Blessed Silence on the hitherto doubtful figure of 12 with corresponding amendments to the remainder. Note that Russian Winter goes up the winner's 8 lbs less 6 lbs for the 2½ lengths, a net increase of 2 lbs, whilst In Rhythm goes up Russian Winter's 2 lbs less 1 lb for the head between them.

Readers unused to the method are urged to study this and other races in order to familiarise themselves with the procedure.

Race 2059	*3.0 Brighton*	*6 furlongs*	*Firm*	*August 5th*		(4.9.0=42) (3.9.0=49)

1926	Bracadale	4	9	4	46	–	47	5–4
1875	Old Dominion	5	9	7	49	Neck	49	7–2
1748 (1968)	Amorous (+7)	4	8	13	41	1	38	14–1
1640 (1956)	Chad's Gamble	7	7	7	21	1½	14	20–1
1626	Milk Heart	3	9	0	49	Head	42	11–2
1835 (1926)	Gambler's Dream	5	9	2	44	¾	35	8–1

Analysis: We now appeared to have overestimated Old Dominion's win in Race 1875. On that assessment he was well in here at −6 with Bracadale the danger at −1. The latter was favourite, wrongly so in our opinion but the punters had it right this time, even if only by a neck. It is interesting to look back to Race 711 where Bracadale had beaten Old Dominion ¾ length in receipt of 6 lbs. Old Dominion came out 4 lbs the better in that race and here was set to concede 3 lbs, giving him only a marginal advantage. In failing by a neck there was clear confirmation that we had read too much into his easy win at Newcastle.

Our judgment looked correct at the time but it was now plain that In Rhythm and Mary Maguire had run below form. There was confirmation of this in that In Rhythm appeared to have improved on that performance at Ayr the previous day (Race 2041) whilst Mary Maguire ran a 10 lbs better horse at Pontefract just over an hour later than this (Race 2072).

In the circumstances it looked safest to accept the official rating of 49 as being the correct one and rate the rest round that.

This is a very instructive lesson for all of us who aspire to beat the book and shows how easy it is to be misled by what looks a greatly improved performance. One must always be prepared to be proved wrong in the face of further evidence.

Race 2062	*4.30 Brighton*	*5 furlongs*			*Firm*	*August 5th*		(9.7=33)
1803	Harpers Bazaar	3	9	7	33	–	38	4–1
(547)	No Ink	3	8	2	14	6	11	50–1
556 (1366)	Carreg Cennen	3	7	12	10	1½	5	11–4
1803	Cawston Star (+3)	3	7	11	9	1½	3	50–1
1740 (2003)	Hit the Line	3	8	5	17	7	(10)	9–2
(1650)	Lotus Dancer	3	7	7	5	Neck	(0)	50–1

Analysis: In Race 556 Curve the Wind had been set to give Carreg Cennen 8 lbs and the latter, carrying 7 lbs extra thus reducing the difference to 1 lb, finished 2 lengths in front. Here, some three months later, Curve the Wind was set to concede no less than 22 lbs, Carreg Cennen having been demoted from a rating of 38 to one of 10. This was a clear sign that something was amiss (see comments on Miss Trilli in Race 1740) and cast very serious doubts about the current validity of Carreg Cennen's rating. Curve the Wind had also gone down in the official ratings and his last two performances had been "bracketed" with us. He was certainly not the 5–4 chance that the punters made him here. Harper's Bazaar had established a figure of 45 in Race 221 but had been down-rated to this level. Nevertheless, his figure of 38 from Race 1803 still looked good enough to win this. He did – and in style! He was 6 lengths to the good passing the post although he had things made easier for him when Curve the Wind reared up in the stalls and had no chance from the off. We put Harpers Bazaar back on his 38 pedestal and deducted 3 lbs from the second, thus in effect allowing 8 lbs for the 6 lengths between them. All other adjustments are open to question because of the extended distances.

Race 2065	3.45 Pontefract	5 furlongs			Firm	August 4th		(9.5=42)
1755	Miss Import (+7)	4	9	5	42	–	44	7–2
1767	Pergoda	4	7	7	16	1½	14	8–1
1878	Music Night (+7)	5	8	6	29	½	25	6–1
1767	General Wade	7	8	11	34	4	(26)	4–1
1926	Touch Boy (+7)	6	10	7	58	2½	(48)	10–3
1963	Bold Scuffle	4	8	13	36	8	(26)	8–1

Analysis: We had by now given Bold Scuffle up as a lost cause and Pergoda's form behind Miss Import in Race 1491 looked good enough here. In that race Pergoda had been in receipt of 13 lbs and finished 2 lengths in arrears at the finish – say, a relative difference of about 17 lbs between the two. Since then Miss Import had won again whilst Pergoda had failed to run to his figure behind Touch Boy in Race 1767. However, the difference in weight now was 26 lbs and it looked as if the filly had a formidable task. She was up to it though and having established an early lead she never looked like being caught. Pergoda did his best and actually got to the filly's quarters entering the final furlong but he hung off a straight line to lose by 1½ lengths. To resolve this we shared 4 lbs between the front two and handicapped the rest as shown.

Race 2072	4.15 Pontefract	6 furlongs			Good–Firm	August 5th		(9.3=29)
1640 (1920)	Royal Duty	4	9	3	29	–	31	5–2
1875	Mary Maguire	5	8	12	24	2	22	11–2
1846	Crowebronze	4	7	11	9	2	5+	11–4
1707	April Lucky	9	8	13	25	2½	(18)	6–1
1988	Caledonian	6	8	9	21	1½	(14)	3–1

Analysis: Caledonian's form figures to date read 16, (9), 21, 22, 22 and 25 and one would have thought that, set to do 21 here, he would have a good chance. Mary Maguire had been officially re-assessed by now and was on the 24 mark, not far in front of her best mark, whilst Crowebronze also had prospects on his Race 1846 figure of 11 which made him −2 here. Royal Duty had proved about 6 lbs the better horse in Race 1640 and with a difference of 5 lbs here there was not going to be much between them. (It is interesting to note that Royal Duty had been uprated from 25 to 29 by now and Mary Maguire had gone up to 24 from 22 – which included a 7 lbs penalty – and these increases had now brought them to compete against each other at about the same difference in ratings.) Royal Duty again proved the better, this time by 2 lengths and had obviously improved a bit despite his failure in Race 1920 when unplaced carrying a 7 lbs penalty. We shared 4 lbs for the 2 lengths between them which put Mary Maguire on 22, a figure well in line with our previous assessments. Crowebronze was rather unlucky in that he was slowly away. He thus gets a plus to show that he is probably better than this.

Race 2083	*3.15 Yarmouth*	*6 furlongs*			*Good–Firm*	*August 5th*		*(10.0=57)*
1706	Looking Glass (+7)	3	8	4	33	–	38	3–1
1780 (1976)	Gentle Star (+13)	3	7	7	22	2	22?	11–1
1780	Trooper Sergeant (+7)	3	8	0	29	1	26	15–8
1946	No Contest	3	9	7	50	Head	46	4–1
1631	In Slips	3	7	10	25	2	(18)	10–1
(1809)	Ardent Lady (+3)	3	7	7	22	Head	(15)	20–1

Analysis: After No Contest had won Race 1411 we put his rating up to 53. The handicapper did not share our view however as in Race 1946 the colt was still on the 50 mark, the same level as in Race 1411 except of course that that rating had been "inflated" by a 7 lbs penalty – the original rating having been 43. Thus the handicapper had put him up by 7 lbs whilst we had set the improvement at 10 lbs. The evidence of this race suggests that we were both wrong as he never ran to even the lesser of the two ratings again.

Even with a penalty Looking Glass was assessed at −1 whilst In Slips could also be fancied on earlier form. In the event Looking Glass led all the way although he was stopping fast at the finish. No Contest had nothing left at the end having been second to the winner all the way and appeared to have run about the same level of performance as in Race 1946.

In rating this race we started by putting Trooper Sergeant on the 26 mark, roughly halfway between his present rating of 29 (including the penalty) and our rating of 22 from Race 1706. Calculating from that basis put Looking Glass on the 38 mark and we were satisfied with a 4 lbs improvement from Race 1706. Gentle Star gets a query for overweight.

Race 2094	*2.30 Haydock Park*	*5 furlongs*	*Good–Firm*	*August 7th*	(4.8.7=26) (3.8.7=31)

1926	Soba (+7)	3	10	1	53	–	65+	5–4
2041	Russian Winter	7	8	7	26	2½	29	10–1
1994	Durandal	5	8	5	24	1½	23	12–1
1988	Dutch Girl	5	8	5	24	1½	19	8–1
1851	Sailor's Prayer (+4)	4	8	1	20	¾	14	7–2
(1994)	Roger Bacon	7	8	7	26	Short-head	19	20–1

Analysis: If Sailor's Prayer's figure for Race 1851 was to be believed then he could give Soba a race. On her Stewards Cup form however, Soba was −12 and (without the complication of Sailor's Prayer) was as near a racing certainty as one will ever get. The handicapper must have been having decidedly unkind thoughts about Sailor's Prayer as rating him was proving impossible. After Race 1462 the official put the colt up to 29 whereupon it disgraced itself at Kempton in Race 1683. After that disaster the handicapper put him down again for this race but in the meantime Sailor's Prayer won at Ascot from his 29 rating! Obviously, the horse has a mind of its own and we would never again rely on it to run to its figure.

To lighten the gloom however, here was Soba, a 3yo with 10.1 on her back, drawn worst of all, but leading all the way to break yet another course record. A scintillating performance and we kept her on the 65 mark she had earned in the Stewards Cup. The chances were that she was even better than this. We put Russian Winter up to 29, the same figure as in Race 2041 and handicapped the rest from that.

Race 2100	*2.30 Lingfield Park*	*6 furlongs*	*Good*	*August 6th*	(8.0=18)

1963	Balatina (+7)	4	8	13	31	–	34	3–1
1626	Lord Scrap	6	7	13	17	1	17	15–2
1242	St Terramar	7	7	10	14	2	10	20–1
1994	Quae Supra (+2)	5	7	7	11	½	6	14–1
1994 (2052)	Winner takes All (+8)	5	7	10	14	½	8	25–1
1988	Dungeon Ghyl	4	8	8	26	Short-head	20	12–1

Analysis: Our pre-race assessments showed only 3 lbs separating six of the horses taking part so it was obviously not a race to bet on. In the event Balatina continued her merry way and won her seventh race of the current season in impressive fashion. Lord Scrap was very quickly away and tried to make all the running but had to give best to Balatina. He ran on very well however and we took the view that he had probably run to his rating of 17. (See our notes to Race 1430.) The rest of the first six were rated in accordance with that, which could not be far out.

Race 2117 *8.20 Newmarket* *6 furlongs* *Good* *August 6th* (4.7.13=31) (3.7.13=38)

1851	Silojoka	3	8	12	51	–	50	11–4
(790)	Azaam	4	7	13	31	¾	28	10–1
1498	Royal Diplomat (+12)	5	7	7	25	Head	21?	16–1
1920	Bettabet Geraghty (+7)	4	7	7	25	1½	18?	7–1
1920	Yoohoo (+9)	8	7	7	25	¾	17?	20–1
1525 (1924)	Lucayan Lady (+3)	3	8	6	45	7	(35)	2–1

Analysis: Four of the first six had carried overweight but Silojoka at +1 was a good bet on our assessments. Rating this accurately was a problem with all that overweight complicating the issue but we saw no reason to change Silojoka from her Race 1851 figure of 50. The rest were straightforward enough but watch the overweight!

Race 2136 *4.45 Redcar* *5 furlongs* *Good* *August 7th* (7.9=24)

1740	Miss Trilli	3	7	9	24	–	31	7–4
(1897)	Turtle Hill (+3)	3	7	7	22	3	22	5–2
2006	Gold Key (+3)	3	7	7	22	3	(15)	9–4
2006	Sparkling Form (+13)	3	7	7	22	5	(12)	6–1
(1814)	Sallwah (+6)	3	7	7	22	½	(12)	33–1

Analysis: On her best form, as in Race 240, Miss Trilli was the racing certainty of all time, especially as the other four runners were all carrying overweight to a greater or lesser degree. Unfortunately, her official rating had been going down since the start of the season, a circumstance not likely to give one excessive confidence in her chance. She won of course – she could hardly do anything else – but it seemed as if she had beaten nothing of consequence. We decided to give her full value for the 3 lengths she had beaten Turtle Hill and gave somewhat doubtful assessments to the rest. Amazingly enough, Turtle Hill later won the Raffingora Sprint Stakes (non-handicap) at Beverley, from My Dear Fellow (gave 3 lbs) who had previously finished second in the Portland Handicap at Doncaster on a rating of 44 only to be subsequently disqualified! Results in weight-for-age races are sometimes quite impossible to explain.

Race 2147	*3.30 Newcastle*	*6 furlongs*			*Good–Firm*	*August 9th*		(9.7=62)
1926	Celestial Dancer	3	9	7	62	–	68	3–1
2094	Soba (+8)	3	9	13	68	Short-head	73	9–4
1926	Cyril's Choice	3	8	11	52	2	52	12–1
1127 (1453)	Prevail	3	8	8	49	½	47	16–1
1968	Queen of Scots	3	7	11	38	1½	34	4–1
1835	My Dear Fellow	3	8	8	49	3	(42)	20–1

Analysis: In the Goodwood Stewards Cup Soba had beaten Celestial Dancer by 4½ lengths in receipt of 6 lbs. Here Soba was set to concede 6 lbs, a turnover of 12 lbs so it was going to be close. It certainly was! Soba went off in her usual tearaway style and everything except Celestial Dancer was soon flat to the boards in an attempt to keep up. To his credit Celestial Dancer not only kept with Soba but was able to find sufficient to tackle the filly in the last hundred yards and win by the shortest of short heads. A very game performance on the part of two fine sprinters.

How to rate this? Cyril's Choice is a consistent sort and his official rating of 52 would not be far away. We therefore use his figure as the yardstick. Soba now goes up to 73 – some advance since the start of the season!

Race 2160	*3.45 Nottingham*	*6 furlongs*			*Good*	*August 9th*		(4.8.10=41) (3.8.10=48)
1946	Sanjarida	4	8	8	39	–	42	6–1
1613	Tobermory Boy	5	8	10	41	½	42	9–1
2003	Senorita Querida (+7)	3	9	0	52	1	50	10–1
1968	Doc Marten	4	9	7	52	Neck	49	7–2
1525 (1968)	Chris's Lad	3	9	7	59	Neck	55	16–1
1920	Kathred	4	8	8	39	2	(30)	9–1

Analysis: Recent form pointed to the chance of several horses here and there was nothing to choose between Sanjarida, Music Night (unplaced) and Tobermory Boy. On earlier form we could also include Kathred, Cudgel (unplaced) and Broon's Secret (also unplaced) and, all in all, a race to watch! Broon's Secret's best form was the best part of two months ago but was backed as if there was to be no settling day. He ran a good race for 4 furlongs but from there on never really looked like winning.

We had been reasonably well satisfied with the rating we had given Senorita Querida in Race 2003 and she seemed to be in good form here, having run a good race after missing the break. We took her figure as par for the course and note that in doing so we bring the rest in line with current figures. This is always a sign that ones assessments are reliable.

Race 2166	*7.0 Nottingham*	*5 furlongs*			*Firm*	*August 10th*		*(8.6=17)*
1425	Royal Question	3	8	2	13	–	20	7–2
1803	Spinner	3	8	3	14	2½	15	9–4
1410 (2083)	Haverhill Lass	3	8	6	17	Head	17	14–1
1827	Magnamala	3	8	8	19	½	17	10–1
(1911)	Janlarmar (+7)	3	7	10	7	1	0	8–1
350 (811)	Transonic	3	8	5	16	¾	10	25–1

Analysis: The question of overweight is certainly a vexed one and we had further experience of this in Race 1425 where Royal Question, carrying no less than 14 lbs extra, had run quite a good race to finish third to Cree Bay and Ben Jarrow. There we had given her a figure of 12 which was still 5 lbs ahead of her official standing of 7, but both here and in Race 2333 she was to prove much better than that, the only consolation being that the handicapper had also been well adrift in his estimation. We have to take overweight into account of course and the query about the assessment is to remind us not to take the figure as gospel until it is confirmed. Royal Question did that here in no uncertain manner, beating the well handicapped Spinner by 2½ lengths.

Haverhill Lass had run to a much higher figure than her rating here but that was in Race 1010, two months before, and she had disappointed in three races since then. She had run quite well here however and may have found her correct level. We, therefore, took her official rating of 17 as being the right one and worked from that. We may have over-rated Spinner's win in Race 1803 a little and 15 is probably nearer the correct mark.

Race 2182	*5.15 Catterick Bridge*	*5 furlongs*	*Good–Firm*	*August 11th*	(4.8.11= 7) (3.8.11=12)				
1988	Be Sharp	4	8	11	7	–	17+	3–1	
(2034)	Everyman (+7)	3	8	12	13	4	16	7–2	
1456 (1846)	H R Micro	4	9	2	12	1	12	7–1	
1963	Karen's Star (+7)	5	9	9	19	½	17	4–1	
(37)	Some Cherry	6	8	6	2	Short-head	0	25–1	
1377 (1575)	Westering Breeze	4	8	5	1	Head	0	16–1	

Analysis: As if to confirm our remarks following Race 2166 here we had another winner in Be Sharp who had carried considerable overweight in a previous race (1988) and received an "inflated" figure as a result.

In that race she had carried 17 lbs overweight to return a rating of 23. If she reproduced that figure here at Catterick she was simply thrown in with an official rating of 7, lessened still further by a good boy claiming 5 lbs. Such stuff as dreams of avarice are made of!

It was really no race. Be Sharp simply bolted out of the stalls to make all the running and win very easily by 4 lengths.

H R Micro's figure of 12 was pretty reliable and we took the rating as the key for re-assessment.

Race 2185	*7.0 Catterick Bridge*	*6 furlongs*	*Firm*	*August 12th*	(9.0=25)			
1445 (1725)	Staly's Pet	3	8	1	12	–	16	14–1
(1983)	High Port	3	9	4	29	1½	29	16–1
(1725)	Premiere Danseuse	3	8	13	24	1½	21	5–2
1138 (1325)	Majestic Tower	3	8	7	18	Neck	14	33–1
(1715)	Houghton Weaver	3	9	3	28	1½	21	8–1
1786 (1976)	Pitter Pat	3	7	12	9	2½	(2)	20–1

Analysis: Of the few horses in this race with an unbracketed figure and therefore reasonably reliable, Here's Sue (−2) and Staly's Pet (−1) were best in. Here's Sue was nearer last than first but Staly's Pet took the lead in the last half-furlong to win by a very comfortable 1½ lengths. Three of the first four had no previous rating with us and we shared 7 lbs for the 3 lengths separating them.

Race 2190	*2.30 Salisbury*	*6 furlongs*			*Good–Firm*	*August 11th*		(9.0=43)
1626 (1926)	Lindsey	3	9	2	45	–	49	6–1
1780	Cheri Berry	3	8	2	31	4	30	13–2
884 (1608)	Clouded Vision	3	8	2	31	2	27	8–1
2003	Red Rosie	3	9	5	48	Neck	44	11–2
2003	Balcanoona	3	8	3	32	2½	(25)	16–1
1482 (1968)	Purnima	3	8	5	34	1	(27)	13–2

Analysis: On best running this race lay between Red Rosie, Lindsey and Cheri Berry, although the latter's figures were "bracketed for doubt". Red Rosie's form was well established whilst Lindsey, although outclassed in the Goodwood Stewards Cup, had run well in previous races. Red Rosie was made favourite but after being well away and leading to halfway she could find no more. Lindsey was very hard driven to wrest the lead from Red Rosie and ran on well to win by an easy 4 lengths from Cheri Berry. With 6 lengths separating the first and third there was a problem with the rating.

It was clear that we could not take Red Rosie's normal figure of around 49 as the key since that would push the leaders up too much. A better solution was to accept that Red Rosie had run below form and share the poundage equivalent to the 6 lengths between the first four.

But how much?

With the winner going away to win by 4 lengths it was likely that there was no great incentive for the rest to be pushed unnecessarily and so we decided to call it 4 lengths in all and allow 8 lbs for the total share-out. So, 4 lbs is added to the winner, the same amount deducted from the third and fourth who had finished together, and 1 lb deducted from the second. Calculation will show that we have therefore allowed an overall 5 lbs for the 4 lengths between the first and second and 3 lbs for the 2 lengths dividing the second and third.

It may sound complicated but a close study of the figures will familiarise the reader with the process. To a certain extent it is trial and error but one hopes to be right more often than one is wrong.

Race 2212	4.0 Newbury	5 furlongs		Good		August 14th			(10.0=46)
2117	Royal Diplomat	5	7	7	11	–	14	6–1	
(1946)	Copper Beeches	5	8	9	27	¾	28	20–1	
1889	Pusey Street	5	8	8	26	Head	26	6–1	
1889	Young Inca	4	7	7	11	Short-head	10	20–1	
1821 (2050)	Little Starchy	4	8	8	26	¾	24	7–1	
1851 (1994)	Brentex	4	8	10	28	1½	(21)	9–1	

Analysis: Backing horses who have previously run well carrying a lot of overweight has almost got the makings of a profitable system! Once more we have a winner who, carrying 12 lbs extra, had set up a rating well in excess of its previous form. Royal Diplomat had run to a figure of 21 in Race 2117 and there really did not look much wrong with the assessment. Here he was on an official rating of 11, ridden by our young friend Steve Dawson claiming another 5 lbs and 6–1 co-favourite. Not a bad bet in the circumstances.

Just under 2 lengths separated the first five and to share 5 lbs between them was reasonable. (Note that this was an improvement on Young Inca's previous form and the gelding confirmed this with a useful 11–2 win in Race 2468 to return the same figure as here.)

Race 2219	4.20 Ripon	6 furlongs		Good		August 14th			(8.0=21)
2182	Karen's Star	5	7	9	16	–	18	4–1	
2117	Yoohoo (+1)	8	7	7	14	1	13	10–1	
1707 (1847)	Oyston Estates (+3)	6	7	7	14	3	(7)	8–1	
1724 (1920)	Stern (+4)	6	7	8	15	½	(8)	16–1	
2065 (2160)	Music Night	5	8	2	23	1	(15)	10–1	
2072	April Lucky	9	8	3	24	2½	(14)	16–1	

Analysis: Best in here were Yoohoo (−3), Music Night (−2) and Karen's Star (−1). The last named duly won the race but whether he deserved to keep it is quite another matter. According to *Raceform Notebook* he hampered at least five of the remaining runners when hanging badly to the right, so much so in fact, that he crossed from one side of the track to the other. The Stewards' decision to let Karen's Star keep the race is called by *Raceform Notebook* "one of the most disgraceful decisions ever". We did not see the race but on the face of it assessing the form for the future must be a very doubtful process.

Nevertheless we cannot "twist" the result to suit our figures and we adjudicate it as it stands. We can always bear the circumstances in mind for the future.

We take Yoohoo's figure of 14 as about right as it ties up with our ratings from Races 1748 and 1920 and use that as our guide.

An unsatisfactory result for all concerned except the lucky backers of Karen's Star.

Race 2221	*1.30 Wolverhampton*	*5 furlongs*		*Good*	*August 14th*		(4.9.7=13) (3.9.7=18)
1963 (2182)	Relative Ease (+12)	11	9 7	13	–	17?	20–1
2041	Bella Travaille (+9)	4	9 7	13	½	16?	14–1
1256	Kings Offering (+8)	7	9 7	13	1½	14?	12–1
1631	Bracken Gill (+9)	4	9 7	13	½	13?	12–1
1994 (2159)	Free Range (+7)	3	9 7	18	1½	15?	10–1
1994	Mummy's Treasure (+5)	4	9 7	13	Neck	9?	15–8

Analysis: No-one in their right mind would have entertained the thought of having a bet in the race, an amateur riders' event with many of the horses carrying a lot more avoirdupois than allotted by the handicapper. One of those "non-events" as far as we were concerned and rating the race is a pretty futile exercise. We make the attempt however and share 8 lbs between the first six for the approximate 4 lengths that separated them.

Race 2254	*5.15 York*	*5 furlongs*		*Good*	*August 17th*		(8.11=42)
2094	Russian Winter	7	7 10	27	–	30	15–2
1878	Rambling River	5	7 7	24	Short-head	26	16–1
1326 (1755)	Friendly Fun	7	7 12	29	1	29	20–1
1755 (1875)	Miss Poinciana	5	8 1	32	1	30	9–1
2094	Durandal (+2)	5	7 10	27	Head	24	12–1
2065	Miss Import (+7)	4	8 11	42	Short-head	39	8–1

Analysis: On best form, some admittedly a few weeks old, those with the best chances were Miss Poinciana (−4), Russian Winter (−2), Friendly Fun (−2) and Miss Import (−2) and they all finished in the first six. Even Rambling River could have been included at (−2) on his running in Race 567 but he had not been running to that figure recently although he had won at last in Race 1878 from a rating of 18. With less than 2½ lengths between the first six we split 6 lbs between them as shown. The clue here for the future was Rambling River's return to his best figure and, after running second at Beverley in Race 2388, he won a good race at Newcastle (Race 2441) from a rating of 21 at the nice price of 11–2.

Race 2255	*2.0 York*	*6 furlongs*	*Good*		*August 18th*			(9.0=53)
2147	Cyril's Choice	3	8	13	52	–	57	4–1
1930	On Return	3	8	13	52	2½	53	18–1
1683 (2190)	Kash-In	3	7	13	38	1½	36	20–1
1763	Sew Nice (+11)	3	7	8	33	Neck	30	20–1
1317 (1920)	Benfen	3	7	10	35	Short-head	32	15–2
2160	Chris's Lad	3	9	6	59	½	55	18–1

Analysis: Cyril's Choice had been very consistent and was one of several horses with a chance here, including Prevail, who was unplaced, Kash-In and Benfen. Cyril's Choice and Prevail had the best recent form and on the placings in Race 2147 Cyril's Choice had slightly the best of it. In the race Prevail got behind early on and only appeared on the scene when the race was over to finish seventh just behind Chris's Lad, whereas Cyril's Choice came through a furlong out to win comfortably.

We shared 9 lbs for the approximate 4½ lengths between the first six, giving the slight edge to Cyril's Choice with a rise of 5 lbs.

Race 2291	*4.45 Yarmouth*	*6 furlongs*	*Good–Firm*		*August 18th*			(9.0=39)
2083	Trooper Sergeant	3	7	13	24	–	28	7–4
2083	Looking Glass (+7)	3	9	2	41	5	38	6–1
(1110)	Dayton Legacy	3	7	9	20	2½	(13)	12–1
(2182)	Par Pak	3	7	10	21	2½	(11)	25–1
2083	Gentle Star (+7)	3	7	11	22	Head	(12)	8–1
(2201)	Blue Cloud	3	7	12	23	1½	(13)	14–1

Analysis: At the previous Yarmouth meeting Looking Glass, over the same distance and on similar going (Race 2083), had proved about 12 lbs superior to Trooper Sergeant but was now required to concede 17 lbs. On such terms the latter was deservedly favourite to reverse the placings and did so decisively by 5 lengths. Gentle Star had split the pair in that race carrying 13 lbs more than her official handicap mark and was again carrying overweight, this time only 7 lbs. She never got into the race however.

To rate this we took the view that Looking Glass had run to his Race 2083 figure and judged the 5 lengths to be worth no more than 7 lbs. Thus

Looking Glass goes down 3 lbs whilst Trooper Sergeant goes up 4 lbs. In view of the extended distances the remaining ratings were somewhat speculative.

Race 2303	*3.45 Chester*	*6 furlongs*			*Yielding*	*August 20th*		(8.10=24)
86 (226)	Dhuard	5	8	8	22	–	28	16–1
1212 (2226)	Meritous (+1)	7	7	13	13	3	16	13–2
1920 (2160)	Cudgel	9	10	0	42	3	42	16–1
2072	Crowebronze	4	7	12	12	½	11	12–1
2219	Music Night	5	8	10	24	Neck	22	14–1
(2087)	Rich Virginia (+3)	6	7	7	7	¾	4	25–1

Analysis: Chester spring handicaps are difficult to assess both before and after and many form experts take the view that any performance on this track can be ignored. We would not ourselves go as far as that but this particular race was run on yielding going and with 6 lengths between the first three there could be no confidence in our ratings. Before the event we could point to at least seven horses with good chances on our figures, including the winner on his performance in Race 86. This, however, had been back in March. He later won a seller at Pontefract in April but is certainly better than selling plate class.

We took Crowebronze as the key horse here. At his best he runs to a figure of about 11 and putting him in at that level makes Cudgel and Music Night pretty much in line with previous assessments.

Dhuard goes up 6 lbs for the 6 lengths he finished in front of Cudgel and we note the improvement from Meritous who had been +3 here, i.e. with 3 lbs more than previous form warranted. He did not run for us again but on his next two outings won twice over 7 furlongs.

Race 2328	*2.45 Ripon*	*6 furlongs*			*Good*	*August 21st*		(4.8.10=53) (3.8.10=59)
2147	Soba (+10)	3	9	7	70	–	75+	9–4
1582	Polly's Brother	4	7	12	41	2½	40	8–1
1498 (2160)	Dawns Delight (+3)	4	7	7	36	Neck	34	33–1
2160	Kathred	4	7	10	39	1½	33	16–1
2059	Bracadale (+10)	4	8	10	53	Short-head	47	17–2
(1926)	Milk of the Barley	5	10	0	71	1½	63	20–1

Analysis: How Soba could have been allowed to start at 9–4 for this race is a mystery! Indeed, she was 7–2 at one time and at that price was an absolute gift. On her performance in Race 2147 she was −3 with us and once more she put up a superb performance to beat a good field of sprinters by an easy 2½ lengths.

We built our figures round Dawns Delight here. On his best form he is around the 32–35 mark and as he had run well here we hazarded a guess at 34 and rated from there.

Readers will doubtless be interested to learn that, nearly at the end of the flat-racing season, Dawns Delight won at Doncaster (Race 3201) from a rating of 31 at no less than 50–1!

Race 2333 *2.45 Hamilton Park* *6 furlongs* *Good* *August 23rd* (8.4=22)

2166	Royal Question (+6)	3	8	1	19	–	24	9–2
2185	High Port	3	8	5	23	½	26	5–1
(2159)	Legal Sound	3	7	10	14	1½	13	6–1
1216 (2178)	Pampered Gipsy (+3)	3	7	7	11	1	7	8–1
1763	My Fancy	3	8	3	21	3	(10)	12–1
2185	Majestic Tower	3	8	0	18	Head	(7)	14–1

Analysis: On our rating from Race 2185 High Port looked a good bet at 5–1 for we had him clear at −6. As the race was run he may have been unlucky not to score. He was quite badly hampered after the field had gone a furlong and had to be switched to avoid further trouble. He ran on very gamely and was only beaten ½ length by Royal Question who was making the best of her way home.

In retrospect, however, High Port may well have been too high in the weights since he could not win from the same level of 23 in Race 2484. It now looks as if Race 2185 had been no sort of guide to the future and that we had the level too high. One finds these things out later!

On her figure from Race 2166 Royal Question was also in with a chance at −1 and she duly confirmed the improvement she had appeared to demonstrate in Race 1425.

To assess this race we took the difference between High Port's previous performance and his present rating and write him in at 26. Unlucky or not, he had been beaten and the chances were that we had him too high.

Race 2338	*2.30 Windsor*	*5 furlongs*			*Good–Firm*	*August 23rd*		(8.10=37)
1205 (2166)	Will George (+14)	3	7	7	20	–	30?	33–1
1994	Mandrake Belle (+9)	3	7	7	20	3	21?	33–1
1889 (2291)	Night Clown	3	7	12	25	½	24	8–1
2136	Miss Trilli (+7)	3	8	4	31	Head	29?	4–1
2221	Free Range (+6)	3	7	7	20	1	15?	10–3
(2003)	Sound of the Sea (+2)	3	7	7	20	½	13?	10–1

Analysis: Not a very inspiring sort of race and our pre-race figures gave no encouragement. We were certainly not enamoured of Miss Trilli who, however, even with a 7 lbs penalty, was set to do more than she had done in Race 2136. She ran quite well though and that after having been slightly hampered in the final furlong.

Will George had a figure of 5 from us in Race 1205 and in the original handicap had been rated at 6 for this race. Unfortunately, or so it seemed at the time, he had to carry no less than 14 lbs overweight but it made not the slightest difference! Up with the pace all the way he quickened well in the last hundred yards to win by an ever increasing 3 lengths.

Rating this accurately was difficult. Five of the first six were carrying overweight and we decided to take the only one – Night Clown – that had carried its true impost. He had run to a figure of 24 in Race 1889 and we used that figure as the basis here.

Will George went up 10 lbs to a figure of 30 for his easy win and in consequence we did not faint with surprise when he won the last sprint handicap of the season from a rating of 24 at 33–1.

Race 2353	*3.15 Yarmouth*	*6 furlongs*			*Good–Soft*	*August 24th*		(7.12=35)
(1897)	Famous Star	3	8	3	40	–	41	5–2
2291	Looking Glass (+6)	3	8	3	40	Neck	40	9–1
(2080)	Big Land	3	7	7	30	3	27	33–1
2006 (2131)	Ben Jarrow (+6)	3	8	3	40	2	34	12–1
2291	Trooper Sergeant (+6)	3	7	7	30	2½	(22)	8–13
915 (2291)	Worlingworth	3	8	9	46	½	(36)	14–1

Analysis: Looking Glass and Trooper Sergeant renew acquaintance yet again. The former was the better horse of the two – of that there was no doubt – but by how much? In Race 2083 we made him 12 lbs superior and in

Race 2291 the difference was 10 lbs. Here, with both carrying a 6 lbs penalty for their respective wins, Looking Glass was set to concede 10 lbs which, on our reckoning brought them together. As such the betting on the two was ridiculous! Trooper Sergeant was favourite at 8–13 whilst Looking Glass was 9–1. Amazing!

Looking Glass did not win but failed only by a neck to hold Famous Star after attempting to make all the running. Trooper Sergeant ran very badly finishing the best part of 8 lengths behind his old rival.

True, the going was soft on this occasion whereas it had been firm on their last two meetings but, at the subsequent Stewards' Enquiry, it was stated that Trooper Sergeant had struck into himself so perhaps that was the answer. To us it looked as if Looking Glass was going the right way and so we calculate from his figure, noting in doing so that Ben Jarrow comes out the same as his Race 1827 figure, a factor which is always some encouragement that one is on the right lines.

Race 2388	*3.45 Beverley*	*5 furlongs*			*Good–Firm*	*August 26th*		(4.8.2=18)
2221	Mummy's Treasure	4	8	3	19	–	22	12–1
2254	Rambling River	5	8	5	21	½	22	9–2
752	Mel's Choice	4	8	1	17	Head	17	9–1
1835 (2212)	Dalegarth	4	10	0	44	Neck	43	20–1
2182	H R Micro	4	7	9	11	½	9	20–1
	Nice Value	8	8	4	20	1	17	25–1

Analysis: Twenty-four runners in a Beverley sprint handicap is no race to be thinking in terms of a good thing but Rambling River looked something to bet on here. Set to do a rating of 21 he had several times done better than that, notably in Race 2254 only nine days before when he seemed to have returned to his best. Well, he ran a good race but found Mummy's Treasure, racing on the opposite side of the track, just too good for him at the weights. He was, however, to make amends in Race 2441.

With just over 2 lengths between the first six, rating this was simple enough and we share out 6 lbs as shown. The winner comes out on the same figure as in Race 1994 and we would refer the reader to our notes on Race 2221 where Mummy's Treasure had been 15–8 favourite when finishing sixth.

Race 2404	*3.0 Goodwood*	*6 furlongs*			*Good–Firm*	*August 27th*	(4.8.11=42) (3.8.11=48)	
1946	Welwyn	3	8	8	45	–	47	4–1
2212	Copper Beeches	5	7	7	24	½	24	9–2
2059	Gamblers Dream	5	8	10	41	½	40	15–2
2255	Chris's Lad	3	9	4	55	1½	50	8–1
2160	Sanjarida	4	8	11	42	Head	37	11–2
(2254)	Hollywood Party	3	9	6	57	Neck	51	16–1

Analysis: With an assessment of −4 from Race 2212 and ridden by young Steve Dawson claiming 5 lbs, Copper Beeches looked well worth the rent but well though he ran, Welwyn (second best at −1) would not be denied and after a ding-dong struggle throughout the last 2 furlongs proved the stronger to win by ½ length. There would be no need for handicappers if all finishes were like this and we merely share out 3 lbs between the first three as shown.

Race 2415	*3.0 Newmarket*	*6 furlongs*			*Good–Firm*	*August 27th*	(4.8.5=36) (3.8.5=42)	
1926	Camisite	4	9	12	57	–	61	10–1
(2056)	Off the Hook	3	8	5	42	1	44	13–2
2117	Silojoka	3	8	13	50	½	50	7–1
2083	No Contest	3	8	9	46	2½	40	20–1
2328	Kathred	4	8	6	37	½	30	10–1
2117 (2290)	Azaam (+1)	4	7	11	28	1	21	7–1

Analysis: Kash-In (−3), Camisite (−1), Silojoka (–), No Contest (–), Azaam (–) and Doc Marten (–) all had chances here. We were a little disappointed with Kash-In who, on previous form, had an excellent chance to win this good sprint. She had never shown her best form on firm ground however and was never dangerous at any stage. Silojoka is well established at 50 and we took his rating as the key to the race.

Race 2441	3.20 Newcastle	6 furlongs			Good	August 30th		(4.9.4=40)
2388	Rambling River	5	7	13	21	–	25	11–2
2328	Bracadale	4	10	0	50	1	51	5–1
2328	Polly's Brother	4	9	5	41	Neck	41	4–1
2219	Yoohoo (+2)	8	7	9	17	¾	15	14–1
1273 (2303)	Song Minstrel	4	8	6	28	Short-head	25	16–1
2072	Mary Maguire	5	7	12	20	½	16	20–1

Analysis: Rambling River paid for all past disappointments here at the nice price of 11–2. Rated at 21 he really had to win this race to make sense of the assessments and he did so in good style.

He looked a good bet at the weights but like all the good things of life there was a snag – and it looked a big one! All his best form had been over 5 furlongs and he had never won at any further than that. In addition, the Newcastle track is notably unkind to short-runners and Rambling River had several times shown distinct signs of tiredness at the end of races over even the minimum distance.

A great pity really for it took the gilt off what looked a first-class wager. But Rambling River made nonsense of all the quaverings by not only staying the stiff 6 furlongs but was actually going away at the finish.

With no great distance between the first five we share 7 lbs among them as shown.

Race 2455	4.0 Woverhampton	5 furlongs			Good–Soft	August 30th		(3.9.1=41)
2166	Haverhill Lass (+3)	3	7	8	20	–	23	10–1
679	Parabems	3	7	8	20	½	21	7–1
577 (769)	Bernard Sunley	3	8	7	33	Short-head	33	13–2
1590 (2333)	Dragunn	3	7	12	24	1½	20	10–1
1680 (1976)	April Memories (+1)	3	7	7	19	Short-head	15	7–2
2338	Mandrake Belle (+8)	3	7	7	19	Short-head	14	16–1

Analysis: At (−2) Haverhill Lass, Bernard Sunley and Mandrake Belle were best-in. We would have to go back to Race 1010 for Haverhill Lass's best figure, whereas Mandrake Belle, a colt despite his feminine sounding name, had run right up to his figure at Windsor only a week before. At 16–1 he looked a very good each way bet even though he had to carry 8 lbs more than his long handicap weight. Unfortunately for his backers however, Mandrake Belle, after being very smartly away, veered halfway across the course after 3 furlongs and, according to *Raceform Notebook*, gave away more distance than he was beaten by.

Haverhill Lass had kept to the straight and narrow however and held on well to win a closely contested event. Bernard Sunley, having his first race for some time, was bang on top of the first two and we put him in at his official rating of 33 for the standard here. In passing, it should be pointed out that he did not run to anywhere near that figure on his next outing in Race 2655 and he may need the soft going he had here.

Parabems was also re-appearing after a long break and ran well to what is probably her correct figure. (See earlier comments about this filly.)

Race 2468	*3.45 Chepstow*		*5 furlongs*		*Good*	*August 31st*		(4.9.4=29)
2212	Young Inca	4	7	10	7	–	10	11–2
1835	Telegraph Boy	4	8	1	12	1	12	5–2
2100 (2370)	Quae Supra	5	7	11	8	Short-head	7	9–1
2212	Brentex	4	9	3	28	Head	27	11–1
(2221)	Ascot Blue	9	8	8	19	Neck	17	16–1
1609 (1994)	Manilow	5	10	0	39	1	36	12–1

Analysis: On his best form Manilow was well in here but he had not been running well and the handicapper had "demoted" him by some 5 lbs since early in June. Certainly, Young Inca (−3) looked a much better proposition, having shown signs of improvement in Race 2212, the danger being the favourite Telegraph Boy who was assessed at (−1) from Race 1835. In a good race home Young Inca was all out to hold off Telegraph Boy by a length with Quae Supra, Brentex and Ascot Blue all in a heap for third place.

With only a shade over 2 lengths between them we split 6 lbs between the first six as shown. Take particular note here, however, that we give Young Inca the full 3 lbs for the length advantage over Telegraph Boy. The reason for this is that with three horses breathing down his neck Telegraph Boy was almost certainly ridden out to the full and the winner must be well worth the distance by which he won.

Race 2480	*3.05 Epsom*	*5 furlongs*		*Good*		*August 31st*		(4.8.6=35) (3.8.6=39)
1878	Bri-Eden	8	9	3	46	–	49	5–1
1655 (2212)	Barnet Heir	4	8	7	36	Short-head	38	9–1
1740 (2254)	Special Pleasure	3	9	6	53	½	53	14–1
2338	Free Range (+1)	3	7	7	26	2	23	20–1
2062	Harper's Bazaar	3	8	6	39	Head	36	10–1
987 (2212)	Ferryman	6	8	11	40	Neck	36	8–1

Analysis: Several of the animals in this race had run in Race 987 at the Epsom Derby Meeting. Second, third and fifth respectively had been Pontin Lad (10.0), Ferryman (9.6) and Bri-Eden (8.4). Today they were set to carry 10.0, 8.11 and 9.3 in that order. Time had not stood still for Bri-Eden however and he had since won three races and finished second in the other two in five races since June. The handicapper had taken note of all this of course and had elevated Bri-Eden from a rating of 31 in June to his present figure of 46. Ferryman could not hold a candle to this excellence and had not managed a place in four races since.

Pontin Lad had also gone on to better things, though not to the same extent as Bri-Eden. He won a useful sprint in softish going at Lingfield (Race 1356) and ran well to be third to Doubtwash Girl in Race 1988. On recent form, therefore, the race looked between Pontin Lad, Barnet Heir, Special Pleasure, Bri-Eden and Harper's Bazaar.

Pontin Lad unfortunately ran nowhere near the same race as at the Derby Meeting, finishing out of the first seven but all the rest showed up well.

It looked reasonable to allow 7 lbs to compensate for just under 3 lengths between the first six and that amount was distributed as shown.

Race 2484	*2.0 Ripon*	*6 furlongs*		*Good*		*August 30th*		(9.3=42)
2255	Benfen	3	8	10	35	–	39	5–1
2333	High Port	3	7	12	23	1	24	6–1
2291	Gentle Star	3	7	8	19	2½	16	10–1
350 (2388)	Mrs Love It (+2)	3	7	8	19	1½	15	33–1
2353	Big Land (+7)	3	7	11	22	1	18	10–1
2136	Gold Key (+6)	3	7	7	18	½	13	20–1

Analysis: This race served to confirm that we had indeed overrated Race 2185 and that High Port in particular was at least 5 lbs too high. A rating of 24 was clearly much nearer the mark.

Looking Glass was made 2–1 favourite here on the strength of previous form. He was set to carry 8.11 which on our scale meant a rating of 36, some 4 lbs below his best figure obtained in Race 2353.

To the dismay of his backers, however, he was slowly away and never got into the race at any stage. The first three were rather strung out and rating this is a bit tentative. We therefore split only 7 lbs for the 3½ lengths involved. Similarly for the others, and we note that Gold Key has twice now run well below his figure from Race 2006.

Race 2494	*4.30 Ripon*	*5 furlongs*		*Good–Soft*		*August 31st*		(4.9.0=29)
2254	Friendly Fun	7	9	0	29	–	31	3–1
2182	Westering Breeze (+8)	4	7	7	8	1	8	33–1
1821 (2094)	Kaimlaw	8	8	9	24	¾	23	12–1
2254	Miss Poinciana	5	9	3	32	¾	30	11–4
2072 (2388)	Caledonian	6	8	7	22	1½	18	16–1
1846 (2388)	Little Atom	5	7	11	12	1½	7	25–1

Analysis: Friendly Fun had not been running up to his earlier form and had dropped 7 lbs in the official ratings. To show his appreciation of that fact and relishing the soft surface, he led all the way to win by a length but with absolutely nothing in hand.

On his best figures Kaimlaw was well in here at −5 but had shown his best form this season on firm going. That circumstance was not responsible for his defeat here however since he went on to win Race 2728 in yielding going. He had not run too well in his last two outings and this run could have meant that he was coming back to form. He disappointed on his next outing (when out of the first six in Race 2663) but, as mentioned above, came back to his best the next time out. Horses are not machines and we must allow an 8yo to have a few funny ways!

To rate this, we took Miss Poinciana as the key. She had run well at York in Race 2254 and we set her in at her 30 rating and assess the others from there.

Race 2516	3.0 York	5 furlongs			Good		September 2nd		(7.11=41)
2255	On Return	3	8	8	52	–		56	11–1
1889	Cree Bay	3	7	11	41	1		43	4–1
1930 (2254)	Errolls Boy	3	8	4	48	1		48	10–1
2190	Lindsey	3	8	5	49	½		47	9–1
1347 (1926)	Avonmore Wind (+1)	3	8	3	47	1		43	6–1
1548 (2254)	Return to Me	3	7	11	41	1½		35	13–1

Analysis: There was little to choose between five of the runners for this race with On Return at −1 from Race 2255 being best-in. With the good boy M. Hills claiming 5 lbs she was not a bad each-way bet at 11–1. She made nearly all the running and won well enough but Lindsey was probably the unlucky horse of the race. She missed the break and found herself with too much to do at the critical stage of the race. Errolls Boy was also not too smartly into his stride but soon made up the ground and probably ran to his rating. In taking his figure as the guide here we note that Lindsey had only run a mere 2 lbs below her best figure so perhaps she was not so unfortunate as it looked. Readers can note the implications of this. Ones figures will very often show the truth of a race regardless of what ones binoculars or the post-race reports seem to suggest.

Race 2523	3.45 Haydock Park	5 furlongs			Good		September 3rd		(4.9.3=41)
2388	Mel's Choice	4	7	7	17	–		20	5–2
2494	Miss Poinciana	5	8	8	32	½		33	5–1
2065	Touch Boy	6	10	0	52	1½		50	6–1
(2441)	Fairgreen	4	7	9	19	¾		16	25–1
2160 (2254)	Tobermory Boy	5	9	3	41	1		36	6–1
1920 (2379)	Hexgreave Star	4	7	11	21	½		15	25–1

Analysis: On his performance in Race 1767 Touch Boy was clear best-in here at −5 although he had not however run to his rating in Race 2065. Tobermory Boy and Mel's Choice were also in with a chance and the latter did best of the two, making all the running to hold off the strong challenge of Miss Poinciana who had run well in Race 2494 a few days earlier.

Sharing 6 lbs between the first four produced final assessments that were acceptable, with the exception of Touch Boy who appeared to have run below form. He was subsequently very unlucky not to win the Portland Handicap at Doncaster for the second time. (See comments on Race 2617.)

Race 2548	*2.45 Thirsk*	*6 furlongs*	*Good–Firm*			*September 4th*	(4.9.5=47) (3.9.5=52)	
2255	Cyril's Choice (Disq)	3	9	9	56	–	60	9–4
1491 (2160)	Broon's Secret (+1)	8	8	11	39	1½	39	9–1
2441	Song Minstrel	4	8	0	28	Head	27	8–1
2353	Famous Star (+7)	3	9	0	47	1½	42	5–1
2441	Rambling River (+10)	5	8	10	38	Neck	32	6–1
2441	Yoohoo (+10)	8	7	9	23	Head	16?	7–1

Analysis: Cyril's Choice (−1) had run a good race at York (2255) and looked to have a favourite's chance here. Broon's Secret was actually best-in at −2 but on a figure attained back in June. Others with good chances were Music Night and Bettabet Geraghty both at (−).

The race itself was more like the Battle of Waterloo than a horse-race. Cyril's Choice came through to win his race inside the last furlong but in doing so went across to the right and interfered with Song Minstrel who had to be snatched up. Music Night was also almost brought to his knees but was probably beaten at the time.

Cyril's Choice was inevitably disqualified for this but he was not the only culprit. Broon's Secret went away to the right away from his rider's whip and interfered with the horses on that side whilst the waving whip itself made Rambling River have second thoughts about the fun of it all when about to make his challenge. There was no real justice in that Broon's Secret got the race upon the disqualification of Cyril's Choice and can be considered very lucky to get the race in such circumstances.

For the purpose of this book we take the result as it originally stood and use Broon's Secret as the key. The only satisfaction we got from the race came from the fact that our top two had originally been first and second.

Race 2561	*3.0 Nottingham*	*6 furlongs*	*Good–Firm*			*September 6th*	(4.9.3=27) (3.9.3=32)	
2006 (2255)	Northorpe	3	9	9	38	–	43	6–1
2041 (2469)	In Rhythm	5	8	12	22	¾	25	7–1
(2000)	Rocky Green	3	7	7	8	4	(0)	7–2
2333	Pampered Gipsy	3	7	8	9	Short-head	(0)	15–2
(1647)	Coasting Breeze (+5)	4	7	10	11	¾	(4)	33–1
2480	Free Range	3	8	10	25	Neck	(18)	15–2

Analysis: Despite the nineteen runners which went to the post this was really a four-horse race. On our figures Northorpe (−5), In Rhythm (−4) and Pampered Gipsy (−2) were the only horses to be considered from a form assessment point of view. However, Rocky Green had come out about the same horse as Pampered Gipsy over 7 furlongs at Folkestone and presumably had about the same chance as that colt.

What the punters thought is clear and Rocky Green was backed from 6–1 down to 7–2 favourite. He ran a reasonable sort of race but he and the rest of the field were well behind the first two at the finish.

We kept Northorpe at his Race 2006 figure of 43 and rated from there. This put In Rhythm within a pound of his last figure so there was probably not much wrong with the figures so far. The remainder were far enough behind to make their ratings a little doubtful.

Race 2590	*4.30 Pontefract*	*6 furlongs*			*Firm*	*September 7th*		(4.10.0=38) (3.10.0=43)
2415	Off the Hook	3	9	13	42	–	52	2–1
2441	Mary Maguire	5	8	10	20	4	22	12–1
2494	Caledonian	6	8	12	22	Neck	23	33–1
1595 (2059)	Denmore	6	10	0	38	¾	37	14–1
(2178)	Leap Bridge	4	8	4	14	Head	12	33–1
1846 (2379)	Spoilt for Choice	4	7	11	7	Head	4	33–1

Analysis: On earlier form Denmore was "thrown in" here with a form assessment of −7 from Race 1595 (Chester!) but had done nothing in two races since including the Goodwood Stewards Cup. He did not appear to be fancied but actually ran quite well to join a group of horses fighting for the minor placings 4 lengths behind the easy winner Off the Hook. The latter had run a good race behind Camisite at Newmarket in Race 2415 and was plainly on the upgrade.

Rating this throws a very interesting light on the treatment of such races. Here we have a group of horses – the second to the sixth – who have finished on top of each other and we therefore share a poundage equivalent between them, in this case 5 lbs, and only then adjust the winner's figure by an amount equal to the winning distance, plus the amount given to the second horse, in this case 2 lbs.

On the Hook therefore goes up to 52, being 8 lbs for the 4 lengths plus Mary Maguire's 2 lbs – a total increase of 10 lbs. Readers are urged to make sure that the principle is thoroughly understood.

Race 2596	*3.15 Salisbury*	*5 furlongs*			*Good–Firm*		*September 8th*	(4.8.12=32)
2388	Mummy's Treasure (+7)	4	8	6	26	–	27	7–1
2480	Ferryman	6	9	1	35	Neck	35	7–1
2212	Pusey Street	5	8	7	27	$\frac{3}{4}$	25	7–1
2468	Brentex	4	8	5	25	2	19	15–2
2468	Manilow	5	9	5	39	Short-head	33	14–1
1117 (2404)	Alev	3	9	4	41	1	34	16–1

Analysis: With a 7 lbs penalty Mummy's Treasure seemed to us to have a bit to find but the Mummy's Pet colt had found his form with a vengeance and in a really stirring finish held on to win despite the very strong challenges of both Ferryman and Pusey Street.

Ferryman had been dropped in the official ratings for reasons which were noted in Race 2480 but was probably now running to his correct rating and we take his figure of 35 as the landmark.

Race 2617	*4.0 Doncaster*	*5½ furlongs*			*Good–Firm*		*September 9th*	(4.9.0=41) (3.9.0=44)
1968	Vorvados	5	8	13	40	–	42	6–1
2147	My Dear Fellow (Disq)	3	9	0	44	Neck	45	20–1
2548	Famous Star (+7)	3	9	3	47	1	46	13–2
2523	Touch Boy	6	9	11	52	Head	50	9–2
2404	Gamblers Dream	5	9	0	41	1½	37	7–1
2415	Kathred	4	8	10	37	$\frac{3}{4}$	32	16–1

Analysis: The Portland Handicap is one of the hottest sprint handicaps of the season and the handicapper has "got it all together" by then. He has a season's form to go on and one can be well satisfied if ones pre-race assessments throw up the winner in the top four. We were lucky in that we did better than that and our top three were as follows:

Vorvados	−1	(Won 6–1)
Tobermory Boy	−1	(8th)
My Dear Fellow	−1	(2nd disq)

Ridden by Lester Piggott Vorvados was held up and rather fortunate to find a gap close to home and catch and beat My Dear Fellow by a neck. Unfortunately My Dear Fellow hung to the right and gave Touch Boy a bump for which he was subsequently disqualified. Touch Boy was unlucky, for the hefty bump that he got from My Dear Fellow practically stopped him in his tracks as he was making his challenge to win this race for the second time.

Once more, we take the original result for our assessments and handicap by sharing 4 lbs for the approximate 1½ lengths between the first four with the fifth and sixth horses adjusted accordingly.

Race 2643 *4.25 Goodwood* *6 furlongs* *Good–Firm* *September 11th* (5.9.1=31) (3.9.1=36)

2590	Off the Hook	3	10	0	49	–	52	11–8
(2537)	Roman Ruler	3	8	5	26	Head	28	11–2
(2469)	Susans Sunset	4	7	12	14	1	14	11–1
2404	Copper Beeches	5	8	13	29	1½	26	3–1
2065 (2468)	General Wade	7	8	13	29	Short-head	26	10–1
1601 (2190)	Open the Box	3	8	2	23	2½	(16)	20–1

Analysis: Off the Hook confirmed the improvement shown in Race 2590 and ran right up to the figure we had given him on that occasion. The rest were not too far away however and we shared 6 lbs between the first five horses, putting the winner up to a new figure of 52.

Although in the end he only won by a head, Off the Hook with 7 lbs knocked off for P. Bloomfield, was a good bet at the early 15–8 which was available.

Race 2648 *4.0 Goodwood* *5 furlongs* *Good–Firm* *September 13th* (4.8.8=27) (3.8.8=30)

2212 (2596)	Little Starchy	4	8	6	25	–	29	12–1
2480	Barnet Heir	4	9	0	33	¾	35	9–4
1755 (2596)	Jose Collins	5	9	2	35	1	34	10–1
2100 (2480)	Balatina	4	9	2	35	1½	30	5–1
1748 (2480)	Polly Royal	4	7	12	17	Head	11	33–1
2561	Free Range	3	7	9	17	Short-head	11	16–1

Analysis: With a form assessment of −5 from a twice achieved figure of 38, to say nothing of a much earlier 41+ in Race 467, Barnet Heir was justly favourite as far as we were concerned. It is true that he had not run to the Race 467 figure since but with only a rating of 33 to run to, he looked "nailed on". He does not win a race very often, however, and although he ran well, he could not hold Little Starchy who, on the form showed in Race 1767, was −2. On the −3 level we had the 3yo Special Pleasure who, with 10.0 to carry, was rated at 50. She had finished ½ length behind Barnet Heir in Race 2480 at Epsom and was meeting that horse on the same terms allowing for the 1 lb difference in the WFA Scale from August to September.

Ridden by Lester Piggott, we expected a good showing from the filly but after 3 furlongs she was done with. It was now quite obvious that we had put Barnet Heir too high and we split the difference between our figure of 38 and the official rating of 33, set him in at 35 and rate the rest from that.

Race 2655		*4.15 Chepstow*	*6 furlongs*		*Good–Firm*		*September 11th*	(4.9.3=23) (3.9.3=28)
2219 (2469)	Stern (+7)	6	8	12	18	–	22	7–2
1780	Preparation	3	8	10	21	Neck	24	10–1
2561	In Rhythm	5	9	3	23	4	20	5–1
1364 (2417)	Caran D'Ache	3	8	4	15	2	10	6–1
2468	Quae Supra	5	8	3	9	3	(2)	8–1
2455	Bernard Sunley	3	9	8	33	Head	(26)	14–1

Analysis: Stern was carrying a 7 lbs penalty for a win in a 7 furlong handicap here in August and, if the gelding's form in Race 2219 was anything to go by, he had to find something to win this. In the Chepstow race he had In Rhythm (gave 11 lbs) some 5½ lengths behind and today was in receipt of 5 lbs. It could therefore be argued that he ought to beat In Rhythm again and true enough he did.

This time In Rhythm was a neck and 4 lengths behind and it was clear that Stern had improved on our figure. It was, however, the third time he had won at Chepstow and it may well be that he reserves his best efforts for this track.

The neck and 4 lengths between the first and third was worth about 7 lbs which we allocated by giving 4 lbs to the winner and deducting 3 lbs from the third horse. Preparation and the rest fit in as shown.

Race 2656	*4.45 Chepstow*	*5 furlongs*			*Good–Firm*	*September 11th*	(4.9.3=39)	
2100	Lord Scrap	6	7	9	17	–	20	6–4
2059 (2328)	Old Dominion	5	10	0	50	2½	47	9–4
2182	Some Cherry (+4)	6	7	7	15	2½	(6)	33–1
2468 (2596)	Ascot Blue	9	7	8	16	¾	(6)	7–2
1821 (2523)	Tom Dowdeswell (+6)	6	7	7	15	Short-head	(5)	33–1
1609 (2468)	Jack Splendid (+15)	7	7	7	15	2	(5)	33–1

Analysis: Race 2059 had convinced us that we had put too high a value on Old Dominion's win in Race 1875 and the result of this race further strengthened that view. In this apprentice handicap Lord Scrap, best in at −1 from his win at Brighton (1430), was ridden by Steve Dawson and justified his favouritism with an easy win.

The 2½ lengths between the pair was worth 6 lbs and was shared equally as shown. The rest were very doubtful.

Race 2663	*3.15 Hamilton Park*	*5 furlongs*			*Good*	*September 13th*	(4.9.10=42) (3.9.10=45)	
2523	Hexgreave Star	4	8	2	20	–	27	7–1
2065	Pergoda	4	7	10	14	1½	17	12–1
2590	Mary Maguire	5	8	2	20	Neck	22	9–2
1767 (2178)	Miss Nelski	5	7	9	13	2	10	12–1
2221 (2494)	Bella Travaille (+3)	4	7	7	11	Short-head	8	12–1
2333	Royal Question	3	8	3	24	Short-head	20	6–1

Analysis: The size of the fields and some of the results were taking on an autumnal look and this certainly was not a betting race as far as our figures were concerned. Kaimlaw, Pergoda, Mary Maguire, Royal Question and Music Night, an unlucky horse in Race 2548, all seemed to have reasonable chances. Kaimlaw was with the leaders for most of the way but could not quicken when it mattered.

All the others, however, were beaten by Hexgreave Star who had not in fact been beaten that far when sixth to Mel's Choice in Race 2523 but was +5 with us on that running.

Mary Maguire's figure of 22 from Race 2590 looked pretty reliable and she was written in at that to form the key for the remainder. This put Pergoda back on 17, his figure from Race 1491, and seemed some confirmation that we might be correct in using Mary Maguire's figure as the yardstick.

Race 2690	*4.15 Yarmouth*		*6 furlongs*		*Good*	*September 14th*		*(9.2=45)*
1263 (2590)	Out of Hand	3	8	3	32	–	37	33–1
2117	Lucayan Lady (+2)	3	8	6	35	1½	36	11–2
2353 (2617)	Worlingworth	3	8	10	39	Short-head	39	15–2
775 (2484)	Hampton Bay	3	9	2	45	Short-head	45	33–1
1968 (2083)	Tower of Strength	3	7	11	26	Head	25	33–1
2484 (2592)	Big Land (+3)	3	7	7	22	¾	19	16–1

Analysis: Readers with retentive memories may recall that, in Race 1263, Out of Hand had been unlucky to have his saddle slip two furlongs from home. Despite that handicap he earned a figure of 35 and here he was on a rating of 32, thus being −3 with us.

At 33–1 we could not believe it! He had run unplaced in Race 2590 on a rating of 32 but that had been his first outing since the Brighton escapade some 2½ months before. Northorpe, at −5 from Race 2561 was the obvious danger but we were not too sanguine about his figure from Race 2006 by now because Gold Key had twice run below its figure from that race and In Rhythm (in Race 2655) had not really franked the form. All in all, Out of Hand looked a peach of a bet but we must confess that we did not have the courage of our convictions and let the race go by. When Shakespeare said "Nothing venture – nothing win" he must have had sprint handicaps in mind!

Our old friend Worlingworth had shown up well and we took his present rating as being near enough for our purposes. Northorpe showed up well for 4 furlongs but then dropped out of contention. Maybe he had had enough for the season for he ran well below form in a later race (3231).

Race 2717	*2.0 Brighton*		*6 furlongs*		*Firm*	*September 16th*		*(8.13=31)*
2338 (2655)	Sound of the Sea	3	7	12	16	–	22	14–1
(2592)	Moufide (+2)	3	7	7	11	2½	11	4–1
2480	Harpers Bazaar	3	9	7	39	½	37	6–1
(2624)	Webbs Jewel (+2)	3	7	12	16	4	9	16–1
2190 (2473)	Clouded Vision	3	8	11	29	Head	(22)	10–1
2338	Night Clown	3	8	11	29	2	(22)	5–1

Analysis: When Will George won Race 2338 he had carried 14 lbs overweight and our resultant figure of 30 had a question mark. He had won easily enough but with five of the first six carrying overweight we were in some doubt about the assessments. With 8.6 to carry here, equivalent to a rating of 24, he seemed none the less to have good prospects of success even if we had been a little over-zealous in our estimate. This was a higher class of event however and he just could not keep up with the rest after 3 furlongs had been covered. As mentioned in Race 2338, he later won at Doncaster to return a figure of 27 with us so perhaps we were not so far out and he just had an off day.

This was yet another big price winner. Sound of the Sea had been about 5 lengths behind Will George in Race 2338 at level weights and was set to receive 8 lbs today which did not really look enough to bring them together. Sound of the Sea did not appreciate all this of course and proceeded to lead all the way to win by an easy 2½ lengths.

We took Harpers Bazaar as the key horse here. He had run to a figure of 36 in Race 2480 and returned 38 in Race 2062 and to write him in at 37 could not be far out. We note that, although bracketed, Night Clown's figure of 22 is only 2 lbs below its figure in Races 1889 and 2338.

Race 2728	*4.30 Ayr*	*5 furlongs*			*Yielding*	*September 15th*			*(9.0=32)*
2494 (2663)	Kaimlaw	8	8	6	24	–		26	10–1
1216 (1709)	Prionsaa (+3)	4	7	8	12	2½		11	20–1
2254 (2523)	Russian Winter	7	9	0	32	1		30	6–1
1767 (2663)	Sammy Bear	4	8	4	22	½		19	14–1
2523	Miss Poinciana	5	9	0	32	¾		28	7–4
2523	Fairgreen	4	8	1	19	¾		14	6–1

Analysis: On his best form Kaimlaw was let in quite lightly here and was −5 with us but readers are asked to refer to our analysis following Race 2494. On going as soft as this he could not be a good bet but it made no difference to the old boy! He was smartly away and duly made all the running to win well by 2½ lengths.

In such going we are never keen on making too many drastic amendments and we allow only 3 lbs for the winning distance, sharing it as shown with the others altered in proportion. Russian Winter comes out the same as his Race 2254 win and we are satisfied to leave it at that.

Race 2734	*4.30 Ayr*	*6 furlongs*	*Yielding*	*September 16th*					(9.7=38)
1347B(1763)	Master Blow	3	8	1	18	–	21	12–1	
2484	Benfen	3	9	7	38	1½	39	7–4	
2255 (2388)	Sew Nice	3	8	11	28	¾	28	9–2	
2484	Mrs Love It	3	8	0	17	6	(10)	4–1	
1763 (2625)	Roman Quest	3	8	11	28	2½	(21)	6–1	
2643	Open the Box	3	8	6	23	1½	(16)	6–1	

Analysis: We had Roman Quest on −7 here on earlier form but he seems always to get so far behind and recent races over 7 furlongs and 1 mile had probably been more suitable trips than the 6 furlongs he was being brought back to here.

Master Blow had run to a (doubtful) figure of 25 in Race 1347B and on that running he too was −7. Since that race he had been last of seven behind Expressly Yours in Race 1763 when on a handicap rating of 25 and as a result had gone down about 7 lbs in the official scale. On that level he had quite a reasonable chance and under strong driving from John Lowe he won fairly comfortably from Benfen. The latter had been made favourite and had run to a figure of 39 in Race 2484. We, therefore, took this figure as the touchstone for the first three horses home. The rest all "lose" 7 lbs without any great conviction that the resulting figures are correct.

Race 2737	*3.05 Ayr*	*6 furlongs*	*Yielding*	*September 17th*					(4.7.11=40) (3.7.11=44)
2617	Famous Star	3	7	7	40	–	46	13–2	
2441	Polly's Brother	4	7	12	41	Head	46	9–1	
2415	Camisite	4	9	0	57	2½	59	9–2	
1926 (2203)	Scarrowmanwick	4	9	6	63	Head	64	14–1	
2059	Milk Heart (+1)	3	8	1	48	Head	48	5–1	
1582	Murillo	6	8	12	55	Neck	54	8–1	

Analysis: Like the Portland Handicap run at Doncaster, the Ayr Gold Cup is a very closely knit handicap coming as it does towards the end of the season with form very well exposed. The best chance for we unofficial handicappers lies in circumstances where horses have shown better form than was available to the handicapper prior to the publication of the weights. Such was the case here and Famous Star at −6 and Camisite at −4 were clearly well in. Polly's Brother, Milk Heart and Bracadale were also fairly treated.

As far as we were concerned it was a two-horse race and with Paul Eddery, a 3 lbs claimer, on Famous Star he looked a good bet at 13–2. In the event, however, Eddery could not do less than the 7.7 allotted and it nearly lost him the race. Polly's Brother came with a storming run which only failed by a head, the post coming just in time for Famous Star.

Assessing this race illustrates most interestingly the method adopted and shows how one has to keep pre-race ratings in mind when arriving at the final figures.

We had Famous Star at 46 prior to this race and we assume that figure to be correct for the time being. Putting him on that mark and allowing Polly's Brother 1 lb for the head defeat puts him on the 46 mark also and again we accept that for now. This is a rise of 5 lbs and, going on from there, we add that 5 lbs to Camisite but then deduct 3 lbs for the 2½ lengths in soft going, taking him to 59, a net rise of 2 lbs. We give Scarrowmanwick that 2 lbs less 1 lb for the head behind Camisite, thus giving him a final rating of 64. Then we come to Milk Heart. The adjustment of 1 lb increase to keep him with Scarrowmanwick less 1 lb for the head between them leaves him on his official mark of 48, exactly the same as our figure when he won Race 1626. Murillo loses 1 lb for the neck behind Milk Heart and also comes out at precisely the same as his last performance in Race 1582.

There are, thus, two minor discrepancies. Camisite has run 2 lbs below his previous best figure but we can live with that but Scarrowmanwick appears to have improved some 6 lbs on his last running with us in Race 1926. However, it came as a pleasant piece of confirmation when he gave Soba such a close race in the Coral Champion Sprint stakes three weeks after this.

Readers are urged to study this race very thoroughly as it really shows what private handicapping is all about and how one constantly searches for confirmation of ones figures. When it all fits together like a jig-saw one can be well satisfied with the final result.

Race 2770	*4.0 Bath*	*5 furlongs*	*Firm*	*September 20th*				(4.8.11=26) (3.8.11=29)
2656	Lord Scrap	6	8	1	16	–	20	11–4
2468 (2596)	Young Inca	4	7	10	11	Neck	14	7–1
2596	Brentex	4	8	11	26	1	26	10–1
1541	Kassak	6	8	7	22	2	17	11–1
2663	Bella Travaille	4	7	7	8	Head	2	16–1
2254 (2596)	Durandal	5	8	9	24	Head	17	14–1

Analysis: Lord Scrap's success in Race 2656 had earned him an assessment of

20 with us and, set to do only 16 here, was thus −4 and a fine bet at 11–4 with our friend Steve Dawson claiming the 5 lbs allowance. A good boy like Dawson is worth a small fortune to trainers and when his mounts are well in on the figures are well worth a financial interest. Such was the case in this race and although the winning verdict was only by a neck the winner always seemed to have the race well in hand as soon as he took the lead from the front running Young Inca.

We keep Lord Scrap on the 20 mark and rate the others from that. Brentex consequently comes out the same as his official handicap mark of 26 and we are content to leave it at that.

Race 2781	*3.45 Leicester*	*6 furlongs*		*Good–Firm*	*September 20th*	(4.9.9=33) (3.9.9=37)	
2655	Preparation	3	8 6	20	–	24	7–2
2655	Stern (+7)	6	8 11	21	½	23	5–1
2255 (2415)	Kash-In	3	9 4	32	Head	33	16–1
2548	Song Minstrel	4	9 2	26	Neck	26	11–2
2100 (2469)	Winner Takes All (+1)	5	7 9	5	Neck	4	20–1
2648	Polly Royal	4	8 7	17	¾	14	14–1

Analysis: Another big field of nineteen runners, not a good medium for investment, but the form worked out extremely well.

Our top three were Preparation (−4), Kash-In (−3) and Winner Takes All (−3). Stern and Preparation, of course, had been first and second in Race 2655 when Preparation had come out 2 lbs the better. Here she was receiving 5 lbs because of Stern's 7 lbs penalty and the two ran almost to the ounce.

It was a tremendous race and the winner broke the track record with another five horses breathing down her neck. Preparation and Stern had confirmed the form of Race 2655 so well that there seemed little point in changing the filly's assessment of 24. The remainder were amended strictly in line with her figure as shown.

Race 2840	*4.20 Ascot*	*5 furlongs*	*Good–Soft*	*September 24th*	(4.8.8=33) (3.8.8=35)					
2596 (2770)	Pusey Street	5	8	2	27	–	26	9–1		
2770	Young Inca (+6)	4	7	7	18	Short-head	16	20–1		
2094 (2596)	Sailors Prayer	4	8	4	29	2	25	20–1		
(2648)	Morse Pip	3	8	2	29	¾	24	20–1		
2388 (2596)	Dalegarth	4	9	4	43	2½	(36)	20–1		
2404	Sanjarida	4	9	2	41	Neck	(34)	12–1		

Analysis: As we pointed out in our comments following Race 2094 we would never again rely on Sailors Prayer to run to its rating. He was, of course, a snip if he reproduced his Ascot form of Race 1851 but the odds were against it. Apart from that capricious beast there were several horses with a chance on the book and Pusey Street was only one of them. The mare had run quite a good race when seventh to Lord Scrap in Race 2770 and on her best figure from back in July she was −2 for this. She had been running a few pounds below her best level recently but did not need to find much here.

It was perhaps significant that she was being ridden by an apprentice for the first time this season and with M. Hills claiming 5 lbs she was quite well backed from 14–1 down to 9–1. It took her all her time to win though and Young Inca gave her a real race to the line. The latter was carrying a 6 lbs penalty for his Chepstow win and in allocating the weight for this we struck a balance between his rating today and the assessment from Race 2770 and set him in at 16. A small calculation puts the winner on its Race 2212 mark and we therefore feel we cannot be far out.

Race 2855	*1.45 Redcar*	*5 furlongs*	*Good–Firm*	*September 25th*	(10.0=52)					
2523	Mel's Choice	4	7	10	20	–	21	7–4		
2548	Rambling River	5	8	8	32	Neck	32	7–1		
2480 (2774)	Bri-Eden (+7)	8	10	2	54	3	47	15–2		
2094 (2494)	Dutch Girl	5	8	2	26	1	(19)	8–1		
2303 (2663)	Music Night	5	7	11	21	1	(13)	16–1		
2770	Bella Travaille (+12)	4	7	7	17	Head	(7)	33–1		

Analysis: Mel's Choice and Rambling River were both set to do no more than in their recent races and they had the race between them. Music Night and Hexgreave Star were also not without hope and Music Night did best of that pair.

The first two had done exactly what they should have done and we leave Rambling River at his 32 level and credit Mel's Choice with 1 lb for the neck win. Bri-Eden's penalty had put him on a higher figure than ever before and in the circumstances ran a good race. He was obviously not yet done with and in fact he proved a really good bet when winning Race 3041 at Ascot two weeks after this.

Race 2868	*4.30 Goodwood*	*5 furlongs*		*Soft*	*September 27th*			(4.9.12=50) (3.9.12=52)
2516	Avonmore Wind	3	9	5	45	–	47	5–1
2770	Brentex	4	8	1	25	Neck	26	4–1
2648	Little Starchy (+7)	4	8	6	30	3	28	6–1
2717	Harpers Bazaar	3	8	9	35	1½	32	8–1
(2748)	Singing Sailor	3	8	13	39	Short-head	36	8–1
2059 (2603)	Amorous	4	9	1	39	Head	35	14–1

Analysis: Things were getting difficult now with many horses out for the "hay and corn stakes" and it was becoming common to find four or five horses separated by only a couple of pounds in our pre-race assessments. At this time of the year betting opportunities are few and we could have no financial interest in this. Sufficient satisfaction was derived from finding that the eventual result bore some relation to our figures! Such was the case here and Avonmore Wind's figure of 44 from Race 1347B was only 1 lb below that he was asked to do here and Brentex was also within a pound or two of his most recent figure. We put Brentex on his recent 26 mark and rated from that taking note of the soft going allowances.

Race 2883	*3.15 Hamilton Park*	*6 furlongs*		*Heavy*	*September 28th*			(4.9.2=32) (3.9.2=36)
2663	Mary Maguire	5	8	3	19	–	22	15–2
2728 (2811)	Fairgreen	4	8	2	18	4	17	12–1
2728	Prionsaa	4	7	7	9	2½	6	8–1
2388 (2655)	Nice Value	8	8	2	18	¾	14	14–1
2734	Benfen	3	9	5	39	¾	34	9–1
(2745)	Rublink (+5)	3	8	4	24	1½	17	12–1

Analysis: Mary Maguire had twice recently returned a figure of 22 and rated at 19 for this eighteen runner event was being given an excellent chance to win her second race of the season. With A. Nesbitt on board, the same boy who had won on her before, Mary Maguire made no mistake and came through to win very easily by 4 lengths. Satisfied that our rating was correct we wrote her in at 22 and assess the rest after noting the going.

Race 2920	*3.30 Newmarket*	*6 furlongs*	*Good*	*September 29th*			(9.6=57)
2190	Purnima	3	7 10	33	–	36	8–1
2643	Off the Hook	3	9 3	54	3	52	6–1
2561 (2690)	Northorpe	3	8 5	42	2½	(35)	14–1
2690 (2749)	Hampton Bay	3	8 5	42	¾	(35)	11–1
1393 (2255)	Skyboot	3	7 11	34	Head	(27)	25–1
2404 (2737)	Welwyn	3	8 11	48	¾	(41)	14–1

Analysis: Another very difficult race but Purnima proved his running in Race 2190 to be quite wrong and did in fact run right up to his Nottingham figure of 34 in Race 1482.

Off the Hook was in tip-top form and we assess this race by using his current rating of 52 as the guide to the rest.

Race 2950	*2.0 Haydock Park*	*6 furlongs*	*Soft*	*October 2nd*			(4.9.2=47) (3.9.2=50)
2617	Kathred	4	8 4	35	–	37	16–1
2548	Cyril's Choice	3	9 11	59	1½	59	8–1
2920	Purnima (+9)	3	8 8	42	½	42	6–1
187 (2508)	Swinging Rhythm	4	8 0	31	1	30	14–1
2737	Polly's Brother	4	8 10	41	Neck	40	11–4
2737	Murillo	6	9 10	55	1	53	7–1

Analysis: It would have been nice to see the consistent Cyril's Choice get some recompense for his misfortune in Race 2548 but though the 3yo ran well again he was no match for the year older Kathred in receipt of 21 lbs and who had come down in the official ratings since mid-summer. Purnima had run surprisingly well with a 9 lbs penalty and was obviously right at his best. Polly's Brother had been −5 with us on his Ayr Gold Cup form but could not reproduce the figure and had perhaps gone over the top for the year. In soft going we cannot allow much for the distances involved and we share 4 lbs out as shown between the first six.

Race 2995	*4.30 Wolverhampton*	*5 furlongs*			*Soft*	*October 5th*	(4.9.4=32) (3.9.4=33)	
497 (1171)	Hazim	3	9	5	34	–	36	20–1
2338	Miss Trilli	3	8	13	28	½	29	16–1
2840	Morse Pip	3	8	13	28	1	28	8–1
2455	Dragunn	3	8	6	21	1½	19	16–1
2868	Brentex	4	8	11	25	Neck	23	9–2
2655	Quae Supra	5	7	8	8	Neck	6	12–1

Analysis: If the reader cares to refer to Races 153 and 497 he will find Hazim running to figures of 38 and 37 from an official handicap mark of 40. Apart from one outing over 1 mile in June, when he made no show, the colt had been eating the bread of idleness since then and even though he looked well in at −3 we could not seriously fancy him. He was brilliantly ridden by Paul Cook who took Hazim to the front in the last few strides to win very cleverly by ½ length. With little separating the first six we share 4 lbs as shown. Miss Trilli seems now to have found her right level after the dizzy heights of the spring when she was rated at 53.

Race 3018	*3.45 York*	*5 furlongs*			*Good–Soft*	*October 6th*	(8.7=19)	
2212 (2868)	Royal Diplomat	5	8	7	19	–	19	10–1
2883	Fairgreen	4	8	6	18	Short-head	17	12–1
2855	Mel's Choice (+7)	4	9	1	27	2	23	6–1
2855	Rambling River	5	9	6	32	1	27	7–2
2770 (2835)	Durandal	5	8	10	22	Short-head	17	12–1
2855	Music Night	5	8	8	20	¾	14	10–1

Analysis: That boy again! Steve Dawson rode a lovely race to win by a short-head on the faltering Royal Diplomat from Fairgreen, runner-up to Mary Maguire a few days earlier. In Race 2117 he had got a figure of 21 from us but had carried 12 lbs overweight. However, he had then gone on to win Race 2212 to record a figure of 14 and we were not really confident that we had his measure. The official handicapper had put him on the 19 mark for this race and was right on target since the form shown here against Fairgreen sets him firmly on that level. Working back from there puts most of the others about right, with the exception of Rambling River who had rather a lot to do from 2 furlongs out and was never able to really get near enough to challenge the leaders.

Race 3031	*4.0 Lingfield*	*6 furlongs*		*Heavy*		*October 7th*		(4.9.7=32) (3.9.7=35)
(2537)	Brough Scott	3	8	2	16	–	14	33–1
1623 (2717)	Princess Virginia	3	9	6	34	2½	29	25–1
2781	Preparation (+7)	3	9	3	31	1½	24	9–2
(2655)	Godstruth	3	8	10	24	½	17	12–1
(2715)	Mardi Gras	3	8	2	16	1	8	25–1
107 (2947)	Banbury Cross	4	8	1	12	½	4	25–1

Analysis: With twenty-five runners trooping down to the start of a sprint handicap to be run in heavy going, only those weak in the head would entertain thoughts of having a bet and it should have come as a surprise to no-one when a 33–1 chance won the race. Brough Scott had no form to speak of and we would have fancied the chances of his human namesake more even with 8.2 on his back! The best guide to assessing this race was Preparation who finished third. She was well established at 24 in recent races and we rated the others from her figure as shown. It was probably mere coincidence that Princess Virginia came out on the same figure as Race 1623.

Race 3041	*3.0 Ascot*	*5 furlongs*		*Heavy*		*October 9th*		(4.9.6=47) (3.9.6=48)
2855	Bri-Eden	8	9	6	47	–	49	13–2
2868	Singing Sailor	3	8	11	39	5	36	14–1
2950	Kathred (+7)	4	9	1	42	Neck	37	7–1
428 (2840)	Anstruther	3	9	8	50	Short-head	45	25–1
2868	Avonmore Wind (+7)	3	9	10	52	½	46	11–2
2596 (2939)	Ferryman (+7)	6	9	3	44	1½	36	5–2

Analysis: In Race 2868 we referred to the lack of betting opportunities at this time of the year but here in Bri-Eden we had one that could not be missed! Three of the eight runners were carrying 7 lbs penalties and, in consequence, all had "plus" assessments, whereas Bri-Eden, on his running in 2480, was in at −2.

The actual assessments were as follows:

Bri-Eden	−2
Singing Sailor	+3
Kathred	+5
Avonmore Wind	+5
Ferryman	+9
Anstruther	?

(In all honesty it must be pointed out that Fly Baby, set to carry 9.11 equivalent to a rating of 53, was therefore −4 with us on her running in Race 1930. On her record, however, we thought she had little chance of staying even 5 furlongs in heavy going, let alone on the very testing Ascot course. Anstruther also was well treated on running as far back as April but had done absolutely nothing in four races since.)

As we viewed the race Bri-Eden had 5 lengths in hand and he won by precisely that distance. Rating was easy. The winner is put in at his Race 2480 figure of 49 and the rest just drop into place.

A very satisfying race marred only by the 10p in the £ deduction following the late withdrawal of Balatina. Incidentally, the dual forecast paid £103.70 to a £1 stake.

Race 3054	*3.15 Pontefract*	*5 furlongs*			*Good–Soft*	*October 11th*	(4.9.0=28) (3.9.0=29)	
1159 (2590)	Courageous Buzby (+3)	6	8	5	19	–	18	12–1
2770	Lord Scrap	3	8	7	22	1	20	14–1
2840	Pusey Street (+10)	5	9	7	35	1½	31	11–2
2166 (2883)	Magnamala	3	8	0	15	½	10	20–1
1028 (2805)	Central Carpets	3	7	13	14	¾	8	50–1
1030 (2920)	Spanish Point	3	8	9	24	1	17	20–1

Analysis: Pusey Street had Lester Piggott on her back this time instead of the successful apprentice M. Hills in Race 2840 and, with a 10lbs penalty putting her on a rating of 35, she had an enormous task, being asked to do more than she had ever done before. She was not up to it but ran a good race to finish third beaten only 2½ lengths by the winner. We considered that we had Lord Scrap accurately assessed at 20 – see his last two races – and we took that figure as the key to this race.

Race 3068	*3.30 Warwick*	*5 furlongs*		*Soft*		*October 12th*		(4.9.7=32) (3.9.7=33)
1803 (2811)	Pokerfayes	3	7 8	6	–		7	14–1
2995	Brentex	4	9 1	26	Short-head		26	10–3
(2995)	Fairdale	4	7 11	8	$1\frac{1}{2}$		7	33–1
(2166)	Gerardina's Boy	3	7 12	10	$1\frac{1}{2}$		7	33–1
2136 (3025)	Sparkling Form (+10)	3	8 6	18	2		13	3–1
(2781)	Vee Bee	3	7 7	5	Head		0	33–1

Analysis: Pokerfayes had received an assessment of 19 in Race 1364 back in June but how much could we rely on that? The best he had done since then was to run third in an all-aged selling race at Beverley on September 23rd although in fact that was not such a bad effort. He had Fairgreen, rated about 17 with us, about a length behind when Pokerfayes was in receipt of 12 lbs, so the chances were that Pokerfayes was well up to his lowly rating of 6 for this race. He only just won by a head from Brentex and we take the latter to have run to his best figure of 26 for clarification of the race.

Race 3077	*4.15 Folkestone*	*6 furlongs*		*Heavy*		*October 12th*		(5.9.8=32) (3.9.8=35)
1411 (2890)	Hawks Nest	3	7 12	11	–		15	9–1
2655	Bernard Sunley	3	9 6	33	4		33	5–1
1317 (3031)	Scottish Agent	6	7 8	4	6		0	8–1
2995	Quae Supra	5	7 12	8	Head		0	4–1
134 (3031)	Heathen Prince (+7)	4	8 4	14	$\frac{1}{2}$		4	16–1
1846 (1911)	Bokara in Shallah	5	8 2	12	Head		0	7–1

Analysis: Since her last appearance with us in Race 1411, Hawks Nest had taken a sharp drop in the official rating list and from a rating of 27 she had nose-dived to her current figure of 11. Not that her form deserved better as she had done practically nothing of note all the season. In this apprentice handicap she found some form again and won by an easy 4 lengths. The race was a poor one, although Bernard Sunley is not a bad sort and, since he runs best on soft going, we take his rating of 33 to be the right one and use that as the guide for the others, three of whom get zero ratings.

Race 3084	*4.45 Redcar*	*6 furlongs*	*Soft*	*October 12th*				(4.9.11=38) (3.9.11=41)
2041 (2728)	Blessed Silence	4	7	10	9	–	10	16–1
2333	Legal Sound (+1)	3	7	13	15	¾	15	16–1
3018	Music Night	5	8	7	20	1½	18	10–1
1878 (3025)	Biddable	3	7	8	10	1½	6	13–2
2883	Mary Maguire (+10)	5	9	3	30	½	25	7–2
2484 (2883)	High Port	3	8	8	24	1	18	33–1

Analysis: In Race 2041 we had established Blessed Silence on the 12 mark after having doubts about the figure from Race 1724 where he had carried 8 lbs overweight. The colt had not run to that figure in two races since but had run quite well on both occasions, finishing seventh of seventeen to Off the Hook in Race 2590 and eighth of eleven behind Kaimlaw in Race 2728.

He was favoured by the draw here and made all the running to just hold off the strong challenge of Legal Sound. The latter had run a good race and the handicapper was unlikely to be far out. Using Legal Sound's figure as the anchor we share 7 lbs among the first six to compensate for the distance involved.

Race 3093	*3.0 Haydock Park*	*6 furlongs*	*Soft*	*October 13th*				(4.9.3=42) (3.9.3=45)
2415 (2625)	Azaam (+1)	4	8	1	26	–	27	10–1
3041	Kathred (+7)	4	9	3	42	3	40	5–1
2781	Kash-In	3	8	6	34	¾	31	8–1
1595 (2603)	Havon Cool	6	8	12	37	Head	33	14–1
3054	Courageous Buzby (+8)	6	7	13	24	1½	18	5–1
3018	Fairgreen (+1)	4	7	8	19	3	12	5–1

Analysis: Havon Cool (−5) and Azaam (−2) were best-in for this race but of the two Azaam looked a better prospect. His second to Silojoka in Race 2117 for a form figure of 28 had later been followed by a very respectable sixth of fourteen to Camisite in Race 2415. With quite acceptable form over sprint distances, it was, therefore, surprising to see him run in a ladies' race over 1 mile at Doncaster on St. Leger day where he ran fifth to Shaady after a slow start.

Havon Cool, on the other hand, since Race 1595, had been placed once in five races over distances from 7 furlongs to 9 furlongs.

Azaam had won the Victor Ludorum Hurdle on this course in March and showed his versatility by being with the leaders throughout to come away in the last furlong and win by a very comfortable 3 lengths. Kathred had done well with a 7 lbs penalty and to rate this we set her at 40, being a point between her 37 in Race 2950 and her current rating of 42 which included the penalty. Adjusting the rest in line with that put Courageous Buzby on the same mark as his recent win, thus acting as some slight confirmation. Fairgreen's below form performance was put down to an inability to get the trip by *Raceform Notebook* despite his second to Mary Maguire over the very testing 6 furlong course at Hamilton in heavy going (Race 2883).

Nevertheless he has never won a race beyond the minimum distance over which he won later at Catterick in Race 3135.

Race 3112	*2.30 Newmarket*	*6 furlongs*			*Good*	*October 15th*	(6.9.1=53) (3.9.1=56)	
2617 (2737)	Vorvados (+1)	5	8	6	44	–	46	7–1
2920	Off the Hook	3	9	0	55	1	54	10–1
775	Davenport Boy	6	8	9	47	Short-head	46	16–1
1525 (2920)	Master Cawston	3	8	0	41	Neck	39	16–1
3018	Rambling River (+1)	6	8	0	38	Dead-heat	36	11–1
2737	Camisite	4	9	7	59	1½	54	13–2

Analysis: Master Cawston disappointed us here! On his earlier form he had run to a figure of around 48/49 and, following unplaced efforts in the Goodwood Stewards Cup on a rating of 49 and in Race 2920 when rated at 46, he was now down to a very tempting level of 41. In addition he had shown his best form in September in the previous season and we took him to be the sort to shine in the autumn. So much for the logic of it all! Well, he did not win but ran a really cracking race to dead-heat for fourth place after looking the likely winner till he was swallowed up close home.

Rating was clear enough and 4 lbs was shared between the first five horses. This put Vorvados on the highest figure he had recorded but he had put up a good performance to win this. Master Cawston continued to let his supporters down in two more races before the end of the season and was not the horse he had been in mid-summer.

Race 3135	*4.50 Catterick*	*5 furlongs*		*Good–Soft*		*October 16th*	(4.9.0=28) (3.9.0=28)	
3093	Fairgreen	4	8	5	19	–	22	6–1
3054	Central Carpets	3	8	0	14	2	14	20–1
2995	Miss Trilli	3	9	0	28	½	27	5–1
2663 (3054)	Miss Nelski	5	7	11	11	1	9	20–1
(3094)	Flying Tyke (+1)	7	8	3	17	Neck	15	25–1
2883	Prionsaa	4	7	12	12	¾	9	14–1

Analysis: Twenty-one runners over the sharp 5 furlong course at Catterick with its left handed swing into the straight after 2 furlongs is not exactly what could be called an ideal betting medium and to attempt to make a choice out of half a dozen horses within a pound or two of each other is asking for trouble.

Fairgreen appreciated the return to 5 furlongs and won his first race of the present season in good style.

On good–soft going we share 6 lbs between the first six as shown above.

Race 3159	*3.45 Leicester*	*6 furlongs*		*Good–Soft*		*October 18th*	(8.8=28)	
3084	Legal Sound	3	7	8	14	–	16	14–1
3077	Hawks Nest (+2)	3	7	7	13	Short-head	14	13–2
2484 (2717)	Gentle Star (+1)	3	7	7	13	2½	9	25–1
3077	Bernard Sunley	3	8	13	33	½	28	16–1
3031	Godstruth	3	8	4	24	½	18	20–1
2734 (3031)	Open the Box	3	7	12	18	2	11	33–1

Analysis: With so little of the season remaining many horses were being brought out again quickly on recovery missions and winner finding was by now well-nigh impossible. Assessing the races is done for completion but, of course, means very little for the future.

Hawks Nest confirmed her return to form with a fine run and almost caught the winner on the line. Her rating could not be far out and we put her in at 14 being mid-way between its present handicap mark and our rating of 15 in Race 3077. We rate the others in line with that and note that the difference between Hawks Nest and Bernard Sunley is now 14 lbs as against the 18 lbs in Race 3077.

Race 3185	*3.20 Sandown Park*	*5 furlongs*	*Soft*	*October 20th*				(9.13=48)
3041	Ferryman	6	9	2	37	–	39	7–2
3041	Singing Sailor	3	9	3	38	$1\frac{1}{2}$	38	9–2
3041	Avonmore Wind	3	10	0	49	2	48	9–2
1195 (3112)	Gamblers Dream	5	9	3	38	Short-head	36	15–2
2516 (3112)	Lindsey	3	9	13	48	1	45	11–1
3112	Master Cawston	3	9	6	41	4	(34)	10–3

Analysis: Three of the runners here had taken part in Race 3041 and on our assessments there was little to choose between them. They duly finished in the first three places. Sharing 4 lbs between the first four put Singing Sailor on the same figure as his current rating. Master Cawston was favourite but let his backers down once more.

Race 3190	*3.15 Redcar*	*6 furlongs*	*Good–Soft*	*October 21st*				(4.10.0=42) (3.10.0=44)
3084	Music Night	5	8	5	19	–	21	7–2
(3018)	Batoni	3	9	4	34	Head	35	10–1
3084	High Port	3	8	6	22	1	22	14–1
2353 (3045)	Ben Jarrow	3	9	8	38	$\frac{3}{4}$	36	14–1
3084	Blessed Silence (+7)	4	8	2	16	1	13	20–1
3093	Azaam (+10)	4	9	7	35	Short-head	31	9–2

Analysis: Apart from Batoni the first horses past the post were those with the best recent form of which Music Night looked the best-in at +1 from Race 3084. Between the first four 4 lbs were split whilst Blessed Silence and Azaam "lose" 3 lbs and 4 lbs respectively.

Race 3201	*1.30 Doncaster*	*6 furlongs*	*Good*	*October 23rd*				(4.8.7=45) (3.8.7=47)
2328 (3112)	Dawns Delight	4	7	7	31	–	34	50–1
1145 (2845)	Sparkling Boy	5	8	5	43	$\frac{1}{2}$	44	20–1
3112	Camisite	4	9	7	59	$2\frac{1}{2}$	55	10–1
3041	Anstruther	3	8	6	46	$\frac{1}{2}$	43	11–1
2950	Murillo	6	9	1	53	$\frac{1}{2}$	49	9–1
2950	Cyril's Choice	3	9	6	60	Head	56	9–1

Analysis: A look back at Race 2328, won by the brilliant Soba, will show Dawns Delight on the 34 mark. It was not at all a bad performance either, with some very useful sprinters further behind Soba than he was. For this race, therefore, we had a horse with a form assessment of −3, a soft going specialist, drawn best of all, ridden by a 7 lbs claiming boy and on offer at 50–1! Our enthusiasm, however, was somewhat tempered by the fact that he had run unplaced in four races since then but they had all been competitive sprint handicaps and Dawns Delight had shown up quite well in most of them.

The result – a 50–1 winner – serves to bring home the moral that, if a horse has a good figure not too far distant and has clearly not lost its form completely, then it must always be worth consideration.

Of course, Dawns Delight was not the only horse with a chance on our figures and Sparkling Boy was actually −9 taken from Race 1145 way back in June. He had since run deplorably in seven races but now he combined with Dawns Delight for a dual forecast of just over £209. The computer straight forecast paid a magnificent £719 but it was not really as impossible as that seems to indicate. One must, therefore, always bear in mind one of racing's truisms – what a horse has done once it can always do again – the trouble lies in knowing exactly when!

In order not to make the figures too far removed from previous assessments of well established horses we split a maximum of 7 lbs between the first six as above.

Race 3218	*3.0 Chepstow*	*6 furlongs*			*Soft*	*October 25th*		(4.9.8=33) (3.9.8=35)
3054	Pusey Street	5	9	6	31	–	37	7–1
2655 (3026)	In Rhythm	5	8	13	24	5	25	12–1
3018	Royal Diplomat	5	8	12	23	1	23	9–1
(2050)	Minica (+1)	5	7	7	4	Short-head	4	50–1
3031	Preparation	3	8	11	24	2	22	15–2
2717	Sound of the Sea	3	8	10	23	Neck	21	12–1

Analysis: As the oft quoted expression goes, Pusey Street certainly "goes for a boy". On two occasions in thirteen outings to date she had been ridden by an apprentice and won both times. She had been re-handicapped after her win in Race 2840, where she had been on the 27 mark and was now on an official level of 31. On our figures she had run to this when third to Courageous Buzby in Race 3054 so did not have to do any better than that to show up well here. She had won over 6 furlongs as a 4yo but had not essayed that trip in any of her outings this season. The sixth furlong might have been a problem in soft going but it really made no difference and she won very easily by 5 lengths.

For handicapping purposes we have to treat this race in the same fashion as Race 2590 where an easy winner had a group of horses lumped together some 4 lengths behind. We therefore shared 3 lbs between the group as demonstrated and gave the winner full value for the easy win.

Doing this puts three of the four beaten horses on figures within a pound or two of their existing ratings, the only discrepancy being Royal Diplomat who appears to have run some 4 lbs above his figure in Race 3018 where he had beaten Fairgreen a short head. However, this made some sense in the light of Fairgreen's subsequent performance in Race 3135 where he had also improved upon his Race 3018 figure by about 5 lbs. In view of that we were satisfied that our latest ratings were correct.

Race 3226	*3.45 Edinburgh*	*5 furlongs*		*Good*	*October 25th*			(9.2=30)
(2890)	Nanushka (+2)	3	7	7	7	–	12	20–1
1821 (3084)	Blochairn Skolar (+3)	4	7	7	7	½	10	16–1
3135	Miss Nelski	5	7	11	11	2	9	6–1
3054	Spanish Point	3	8	9	23	¾	19	10–1
2995 (3135)	Dragunn	3	8	6	20	1½	15	14–1
2855 (3135)	Bella Travaille	4	7	8	8	¾	2	14–1

Analysis: Nanushka had run in five races including sellers prior to this without setting the Thames on fire and was on the minimum mark here. Ridden by a 7 lbs claimer she left her previous form well behind and held on well to win by ½ length from the front-running Blochairn Skolar. They were a poor lot and we used Miss Nelski's figure of 9 from Race 3135 as the key without any great confidence.

Race 3231	*2.15 Nottingham*	*6 furlongs*		*Soft*	*October 25th*			(4.9.10=37) (3.9.10=39)
2190 (3159)	Cheri Berry	3	8	10	25	–	28	33–1
3190	Azaam (+10)	4	9	8	35	3	35	15–2
3068	Brentex	4	9	0	27	1½	25	7–2
711 (1926)	Piencourt	4	9	7	34	Neck	32	25–1
3185	Master Cawston	3	9	12	41	2½	37	16–1
2920	Northorpe	3	9	12	41	2	35	16–1

Analysis: Big priced winners were as thick on the ground as the leaves and here was another to bring a smile to the bookmakers' faces. Yet Cheri Berry was not without a chance to the form student. In Race 2190 she had earned a form assessment of 30 when second to Lindsey and as recently as Race 3159 she had been prominent all the way when eventually finishing seventh of twenty-two runners behind Open the Box. On that reckoning she was not a 33–1 chance.

Azaam was getting the taste for flat-racing, having his third race within the space of twelve days and again ran a good race.

To rate these we shared 5 lbs between the first four with adjustments for the fifth and sixth as shown.

Race 3266	*1.45 Leicester*	*6 furlongs*	*Soft*	*November 1st*				(8.10=22)
2995	Morse Pip	3	9	2	28	–	28	8–1
1601 (3235)	Transflash	3	7	13	11	1	10	10–1
3159	Legal Sound (+7)	3	8	10	22	1½	19	11–1
(3147)	Trade High	3	7	8	6	3	0	10–1
2291 (3218)	Blue Cloud	3	8	4	16	1	9	40–1
3159	Bernard Sunley	3	9	4	30	Neck	(23)	16–1

Analysis: As Legal Sound is beaten here on a rating of 22 which included a 7 lbs penalty it looked unlikely that she had run to that figure. We decided to take a point mid-way between her Race 3159 figure of 16 and her present "rating" of 22, write her in at 19, work the rest out from that starting point and see how it looked.

Well, Morse Pip came out the same as in Race 2995, Transflash some way behind its somewhat doubtful figure of Race 1411, Blue Cloud below another unreliable figure from Race 2291 and Bernard Sunley some 5 lbs below recent form. The latter was not thought to have been too keen at the finish however and it looked possible that he had indeed run below form. Consequently, the assessments were completed as above. This was a little hit-and-miss but it was unlikely that we would be taking these figures as Holy Writ come next March!

As a matter of interest, the final rating list of the flat racing season had Morse Pip in the 29–25 bracket, Legal Sound in the 19–15 group and Bernard Sunley in the 34–30's. The handicapper has obviously not taken too much notice of Bernard Sunley's defeat here otherwise he would have included that animal in the 24–20 group.

Race 3305	*3.45 Doncaster*	*5 furlongs*		*Soft*	*November 5th*		(8.3=34)
2338 (2717)	Will George (+5)	3	7 7	24	–	27	33–1
2868	Little Starchy	4	7 13	30	2	30	20–1
2219 (3236)	Karen's Star (+9) Disq. Placed 4th	5	7 11	28	Head	27	33–1
2494 (3201)	Friendly Fun Placed 3rd	7	7 12	29	½	27	20–1
2840 (3231)	Sailor's Prayer	4	7 12	29	½	26	20–1
3231	Piencourt (+2)	4	8 5	36	Neck	33	16–1

Analysis: Will George had earned an assessment of 30? when he won Race 2338 so was well in here on an official mark of 24. He had run once since then when out of the first nine behind Sound of the Sea in Race 2717 when he was racing on his new official level of 24.

In winning this Will George set up an estimated figure of 27 so both we and the official handicapper were 3 lbs out.

There is little point in discussing this race for the future and the assessments were made by sharing 6 lbs for the distances between the first six.

CONCLUSION

In the preceding pages we have tried to show the reader a logical and practical way of establishing reasonably accurate form assessments for every horse capable of finishing in the first six in 5 and 6 furlong handicaps. We should, however, emphasise that the serious form student need not necessarily confine his or her interest solely to races run over sprint distances; for, once the general principles of handicapping are understood, there is no reason why one cannot concentrate upon a group of horses running over longer distances. The problems are much the same except that the same weight-for-age allowances cannot be used for such races.

To compensate for a length 3 lbs may well be sufficient over 5 furlongs but would be far too much to allow for a similar margin over, say, 1½ miles. In such a case it would be normal to allow approximately 1 lb per length but only experience will show the correct way to proceed in similar circumstances or over varying distances.

We have a preference for sprint handicaps for reasons which are stated elsewhere and because they lend themselves very well to our methods which we hope to have demonstrated in some detail.

It will, nevertheless, be clear that it is not possible to lay down hard and fast rules when dealing with such a subject and that is probably the reason why there is such a marked lack of literature on this particular aspect of horse-racing. Subjective analysis is by its very nature dependent upon individual judgments. No two people will come to exactly the same conclusions or, in our case, the same form assessments in any particular race even though they are using identical data – purely factual information consisting only of the actual result, the weights carried and the distances involved.

The reason for such divergence of opinion is quite simple if one considers the differing views that can be taken of, say, a short-head win.

Firstly, was the winner all out or was it a "clever" win as a result of superlative judgment on the part of the jockey? Or was it lucky to win in that the second horse encountered all the trouble that was going? Even, perhaps, could it have won by a greater margin had it been ridden to better advantage?

Then again, consider the question of placed horses.

When a horse finishes second, beaten, say, ½ length, did it give the winner a hard race or was it merely "coasting" into second place with no other horse near enough to challenge it for the runner-up prize? Or was it given a desperately hard fight to hold on to its second place spot, thus making its distance behind the winner more meaningful?

One could also consider the animals that finish fourth, fifth and sixth in that it is often well nigh impossible to decide whether they could have finished closer to the winner had they been ridden out in accordance with the rules of racing!

All these and other imponderables combine to make every race an individual affair with multitudinous permutations creating a truly fascinating exercise in logical thought.

For these reasons the reader is cautioned against regarding ones figures as infallible, based as they are on judgments and on decisions which may well be faulty. Accept disappointments and times when the figures appear to be wildly amiss as all part of the game, but always persevere in the knowledge that one is at least pursuing the never ending quest for winners in a sane and sensible way.

On an earlier page we suggested that the real art in calculating form assessments following a race lay in deciding which of the horses had run to their rating. In other words to be able to study the actual result and make a decision as to which of the horses concerned had "run to form", i.e., within a pound or two of their previous form assessments.

It is, of course, essential to have as much information as possible concerning the actual running of a race and newspaper reports should be studied in order to get a clear picture of all the circumstances that may have affected the result. *Raceform Notebook* is particularly useful in this respect and often gives valuable information which is very helpful for guidance in such matters.

The answer to the question as to which of the animals concerned have run to their figure can often be found by reference to the pre-race assessments which we have calculated in advance and perhaps at this stage we should look at this a little more closely.

These assessments are, of course, based on our previously calculated figures and show which of the horses involved have the best chances at the weights.

Students should work in a methodical way and keep an alphabetical list of horses in an exercise book with their individual ratings in order that one can readily establish a figure for every listed horse.

Calculating the pre-race assessments should be done in the following manner.

It will be recalled that we will have established a weight equation for every race that we have taken from the *Racing Calendar* and that above each race will be a set of figures such as (9.0=36). This, of course, tells us that a horse carrying 9.0 has an *official* rating of 36, a horse carrying 8.11 is *officially* rated at 33 and so on.

On the day of the race therefore, we use the appropriate equation to write the *official* rating alongside each horse. Then we look up our alphabetical list and make a further note of the *best* figure we have for each horse. The final step will be to compare our figure with the *official* rating and this will tell us if the horse is carrying more or less weight than our figure. What we are looking for is a horse set to carry *less* than our best figure in which case he will be a "PLUS" with us. Let us look at a hypothetical case.

(9.7=40)

Speedy Handicap *Sandown Park* *5 furlongs* *May 24th*

Horse and weight			*Official rating*	*Our figure*	*Form assessment*
Alfresco	9	7	40	36	+4
Breadbin	9	2	35	34	+1
Claudius	8	12	31	31	–
Dogsbody	8	6	25	27	−2
Everglades	7	13	18	12	+6
Fancy That	7	7	12	8	+4

Dogsbody is therefore "best-in" at −2, followed by Claudius at – and Breadbin at +1. As far as the actual assessments are concerned the race is between those three.

We mentioned earlier that we take the *best* figure for each horse and here we must repeat what we have said before. What a horse has done before he can always do again but one has to temper this with a little common sense. As a general rule it is prudent to take any previous form into consideration unless the horse in question has run below that figure in several races since and you are therefore satisfied that it is unlikely to reproduce the form. Be quite sure, however, that no adequate reasons exist for its defeats. If a horse sets up a figure on firm going but fails to perform to that level on soft going, one must always be prepared for a return to the original figure should it once again encounter firm going. But undoubtedly the best form is recent form and a figure set up within the past two or three weeks is usually the most reliable. It will be found that most winners have had an outing during this period.

In the analytical notes following each race we tried to indicate the factors that could influence one's judgment in making a selection and readers will recall that in many cases we pointed out the significance of the apprentice allowance. Of the 277 races under review a total of 24 were confined to apprentices or amateurs and, of the remaining 253 races, just 50 were won by horses ridden by an apprentice, or about one in five. At first sight this may not seem a particularly impressive average but it must be borne in mind that apprentices ride relatively few of the horses involved and in reality the number of winners is really quite good. The allowance may well make all the difference for jockeyship is not so much at a premium in all-the-way sprints, unlike distance races where judgment of pace and tactics are all-important. We repeat here that the apprentice allowance is ignored when entering races in our records book, which must always show the weight that the horse was set to carry prior to any deduction.

A word here about a rise in weights. One often finds that, consequent upon the withdrawal of top weights, the weights for the rest of the entries are raised, sometimes quite considerably. Not all papers give this information and it is important that a quick check is made with the *Racing Calendar* to find out whether or not the weights have been raised.

Let us take a case where the weights have been raised say, 10 lbs and our weight equation states 9.2=56. Due to the rise in weights any horse set to carry 9.2 will now have to carry 9.12 but we must bear in mind that the horse was a "56" with us and must still be that figure regardless of any rise affecting the actual weight that it carries.

One way to clarify the situation is to amend the equation to read 9.12=56, that is to say, to *add* the 10 lbs to the first part of the equation. On the other hand if the rise is something like 21 lbs then to alter the equation to read 10.9=56 gives a somewhat unwieldy figure from which to work. In such a case it is probably easier to *deduct* the 21 lbs from the *second* figure so as to read 9.2=35.

The end result is the same but it makes for easier working.

Making the Selection

In making a selection one has to weigh up all the various factors but one piece of advice we would give is – do not be put off by the price. Horses with good form are often a bigger price than they ought to be simply because punters tend to forget, whereas your record book will tell you all you need to know about any particular horse in the race in question; and remember that you will be in possession of real information – the sort that springs from first-hand knowledge and not what the milkman has heard from his brother who knows a friend of the blacksmith!

Few horses win from a substantial "plus" figure and if your figures show that a horse is set to carry 5 lbs or 6 lbs more than its best form figure then – forget it! The only exceptions to this rule are horses carrying a substantial penalty who are, nevertheless, at the very top of their form and those whose previous low figure was obtained on their first outing of the year when some improvement can be expected.

Ironically, one should also be very wary of a large "minus" figure, indicating that the horse is carrying a lot less than its best form figure, if the figure was obtained in the distant past and the horse has failed to run to that figure in several races since. The "minus" figure is solely because the handicapper has dropped the animal in the official ratings and a substantial drop of this kind is never a good sign. It is, of course, entirely possible that any horse will suddenly produce its old figure and one must examine its recent form carefully for any suggestion that it may be returning to form. The evidence that it may no longer be capable of its previous best figure is often very strong however and a few moments spent in investigation will be well worth while.

The ideal situation for our purposes is where we have a good reliable figure for every horse but often one can compromise by being satisfied with a figure for every horse in the betting forecast. It is, of course, necessary to calculate a figure for all of our listed horses so as not to be caught by surprise.

We will obviously take notice of such pointers as previous course winners, liking for the going, time of the year, class of the race and riding arrangements but the most important single factor is the form assessment. Horses win when they are well-handicapped and we are in a better position than most to be able to know when this is so.

Let us now return to the question of re-assessing the figures after the race is over.

It follows that, if the actual result corresponds closely to our pre-race assessments then we need only consider minimal amendments. If, for example, we had been on the mark with our example race and Dogsbody had beaten Claudius by ½ length with Breadbin a neck away third then we can feel very satisfied that they have run to form and that we can use them to calculate the rest of the horses. We will not always be as fortunate as this however but it would be sufficient confirmation of our figures if just two finished as they should. If, for example, Dogsbody won the race beating Breadbin a length with Claudius back in fifth place we could safely assume that the first two had run to their figure, rate the rest from there and then perhaps look for a reason why Claudius had run below form. He may have been badly away, unlucky in running, or simply had an off-day but, whatever the reason, we give him a form figure in line with the actual performance.

The many races we have analysed will have shown a multitude of differing circumstances and we hope that we have shown how the "key" horse has been arrived at in the vast majority of cases.

Horses that seem always to run to within a pound or two of the rating are enormously valuable to us and such paragons of virtue can often be used as the guide to the rest of the horses.

There are many pointers that can be used to decide the "key" horse and readers should try to develop their judgment in this because it is absolutely vital. Look especially for horses that have run to practically the same figure on its last couple of outings, is well backed and runs a really good race to be close up to the winner. Such horses are ideal candidates to use as the "standard", especially if their form assessment is within a pound or two of its *official* rating. In such cases it is often wisest to use the official rating as the benchmark for you are then using expert opinion to consolidate ones own figures.

To recapitulate, therefore, we are looking for a horse that is in form, has run well and appears to be running to its official rating backed by our pre-race assessments.

Perseverance will give one the experience to be able to do this but, at all times, be logical in ones approach. The selection of the "key" horse is most important for calculation of the form assessments and it is essential to back its selection with as much confirmation as possible. This may of course, only come later, which brings us to another important point.

For the purposes of this book we have made no attempt to amend previous figures from the original assessments calculated after each race even when subsequent events have shown them to be wrong. In general, however, ones own endeavours should take such things into account and there is no reason why assessments should not be amended in the light of further evidence.

Be wary, however, of uprating or downgrading the entire figures in one race solely on the subsequent performance of one horse, especially if by so doing the resultant assessments are wildly at variance with previous figures. Treat each horse as an individual and amend its figure in keeping with its own performances.

It is, in fact, a common error to make the assumption that, if two horses finish exactly together and one goes on to set an improved figure, the other would automatically go on to do the same. It may well do so but, equally, it might not and the form student is well advised to treat collateral form of this kind as a pointer and no more than that. Always look for confirmatory evidence before indulging in any drastic alteration of existing figures as a result of a prominent showing by just one horse who may well have improved beyond all expectations. Imagine the chaos if one upgraded those horses beaten by Soba in the light of that filly's subsequent form!

Have confidence that the comparatively small amount of homework required will pay dividends; and take some consolation in the fact that you will be a specialist with real expertise in a little understood but all-important aspect of horse-racing.

Finally, it is my earnest wish that the purchase of this book will turn out to be one of the better investments of your racing life.

Index

Numbers after entries refer to the horse's *last* appearance in this book, by Race Number. They do not refer to page numbers.